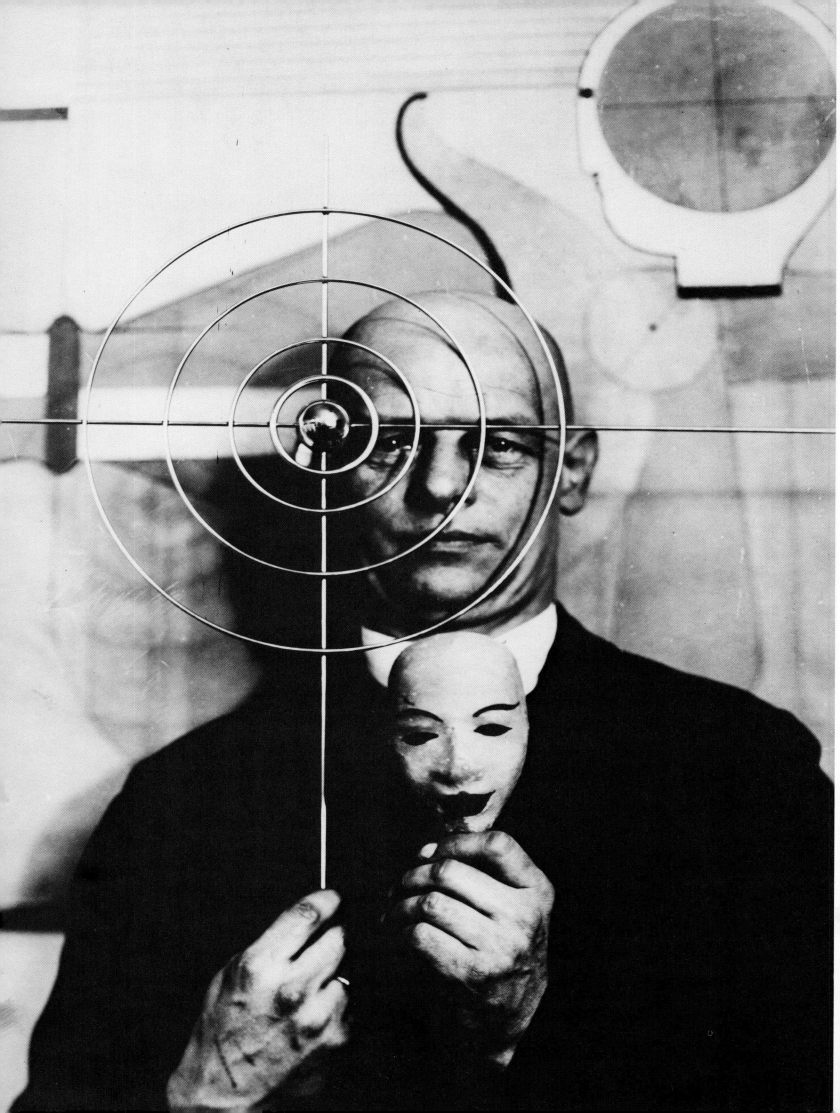

OSKAR SCHLEMMER

Arnold L. Lehman and Brenda Richardson, Editors

with texts by

Vernon L. Lidtke
Karin von Maur
Nancy J. Troy
Debra McCall

THE BALTIMORE MUSEUM OF ART

DATES OF THE EXHIBITION

The Baltimore Museum of Art
February 9–April 6, 1986

IBM Gallery of Science and Art, New York
May 13–July 5, 1986

San Francisco Museum of Modern Art
August 7–October 5, 1986

Walker Art Center, Minneapolis
November 9, 1986–January 4, 1987

SPONSORS

USF&G Corporation
Federal Republic of Germany
National Endowment for the Arts
National Endowment for the Humanities
The J. Paul Getty Trust
Lufthansa German Airlines

LENDERS TO THE EXHIBITION

The Baltimore Museum of Art
Kunstmuseum Basel, Öffentliche Kunstsammlung
Bauhaus-Archiv, Berlin
Staatliche Museen Preussischer Kulturbesitz, Nationalgalerie Berlin, Galerie des 20. Jahrhunderts
Galerie Beyeler, Basel
Daimler-Benz A.G., Stuttgart
Kunstmuseum Düsseldorf Graph. Sammlung
Museum Folkwang Essen
The Heirs of Emil Frey
Hamburger Kunsthalle
Harvard University Art Museums (Busch-Reisinger Museum)
Sammlung und Archiv für Künstler der Breslauer Akademie, Kassel
Staatliche Kunstsammlungen Kassel
Leonard and Evelyn Lauder, New York
Wilhelm-Lehmbruck-Museum der Stadt Duisburg
Städtische Kunsthalle Mannheim
The Museum of Modern Art, New York
Private Collections (Frankfurt, New York, and Stuttgart)
The Saint Louis Art Museum
C. Raman Schlemmer
Karin and U. Jaïna Schlemmer Collection
U. Jaïna Schlemmer
Family Estate of Oskar Schlemmer
Oskar Schlemmer Theater Estate, Collection UJS
Galerie der Stadt Stuttgart
Staatsgalerie Stuttgart
Ulmer Museum
Museum moderner Kunst, Vienna

Ascending the Stairs. (1923). Oil. 39 × 34⅝ in. Collection of
Leonard and Evelyn Lauder, New York. [Cat. no. 36].

Oskar Schlemmer was a protean figure of early twentieth-century modernism. His achievement is prodigious in the visual arts, in theater design and production, in pedagogy. Despite Schlemmer's seminal role in what is now seen as the revolution of German art between the wars, his work has remained little known outside Germany, especially in comparison to the international reputations of many of his colleagues from the Bauhaus era. For an American audience, this retrospective exhibition and its accompanying publication represent the first major opportunity to examine the paintings, sculpture, drawings, prints, graphic design, and theater conceptions that comprise Schlemmer's prolific oeuvre.

To the general public the name Schlemmer, unlike those of Gropius, Kandinsky, or Klee, may be totally unfamiliar. To specialists the name Schlemmer evokes immediate recognition but equally frank acknowledgment of only limited awareness of the artist's virtuosity and influence. To many, the name Schlemmer is synonymous with a single painting, the *Bauhaus Stairway*, which is virtually an architectural fixture of The Museum of Modern Art in New York, where for decades it has hung at the landing of the museum's stairwell, figuratively and literally linking two floors of modernist art history. This painting—which Schlemmer himself conceived to be a symbolic representation of Bauhaus enlightenment, of youth in transition from one generation to another, of the potential for transformation in art and life from the rigid sociopolitical strictures of the past to the utopian freedoms of the future, and, most suggestively, of the role of art and artists in leading that revolution—is indeed a worthy and appropriate exemplar of Oskar Schlemmer's artistic ambitions. At the same time, however, a singular focus on the *Bauhaus Stairway* would too narrowly define Schlemmer as an easel painter with a somewhat mystical approach to

figuration and color. In fact, his thirty-year career is dazzling for its range, depth, and idiosyncrasy. Despite his attachment to the Bauhaus, Schlemmer adopted no single medium or style so consistently as to be identified with any movement. His draftsmanship is marked by lyric fluidity at one moment and doctrinal rigor the next; his color ranges from glowing romantic pastel hues in one work to somber, shadowed earth tones in another; his imagery encompasses the representational and the abstract; his figures alternately inhabit ambiguous architectural spaces and imaginatively constructed transcendental spaces. Like many of his Bauhaus colleagues, Schlemmer earned a reputation as teacher and theoretician as well as painter and sculptor. And his work in the theater and architecture, his ambition to subsume all of the arts in a new life form, set him apart as uniquely gifted, mercurial, and unclassifiable.

The present exhibition had its inception a decade ago, when I first became convinced that a major Schlemmer show was overdue in America. When I came to The Baltimore Museum of Art in 1979, I discovered that Brenda Richardson, Assistant Director for Art and Curator of Painting and Sculpture, shared my conviction, and we joined forces to bring such a project to reality. We traveled to Stuttgart on numerous occasions to meet with Frau Tut Schlemmer, the artist's widow, with Frau U. Jaïna Schlemmer, the artist's daughter, and with C. Raman Schlemmer, the artist's grandson who serves as official representative of the Schlemmer Family Estate. At the same time we met with Professor Dr. Peter Beye, Director of the Staatsgalerie Stuttgart; with Dr. Karin Frank von Maur, Staatsgalerie curator and director of the Oskar Schlemmer Archiv at that museum; and with Dr. Ulrike Gauss, curator of graphic arts at the Staatsgalerie. Since much of Schlemmer's work is housed at the Staatsgalerie Stuttgart, either

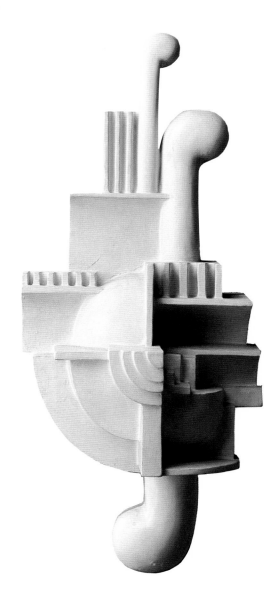

Ornamental Sculpture. (1919). Plaster. 18⅞ × 8¼ × 3½ in. Stadtische Kunsthalle Mannheim: Schlemmer Family Estate Deposit. [Cat. no. 52].

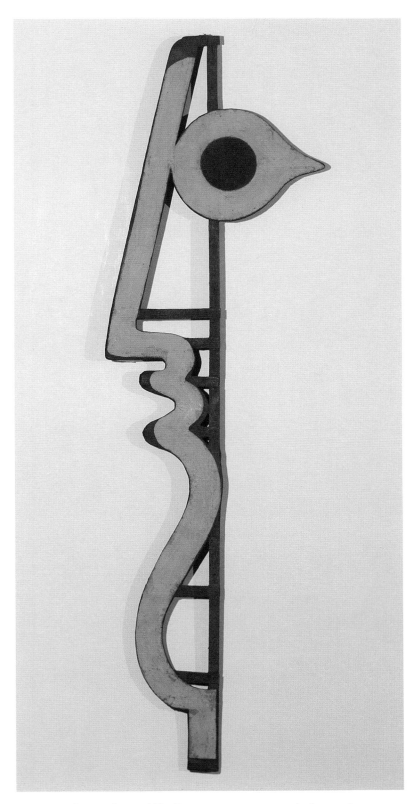

Profile in Yellow. (1922). Tempera on canvas, stretched over wire and wood framework. 58¾ × 16½ in. Staatsgalerie Stuttgart: Oskar Schlemmer Theater Estate, Collection UJS Deposit. [Cat. no. 68].

Dancer (The Gesture). (ca. 1922). Ink and watercolor. 5⅞ × 4⅜ in. Staatsgalerie Stuttgart: Schlemmer Family Estate Deposit. [Cat. no. 110].

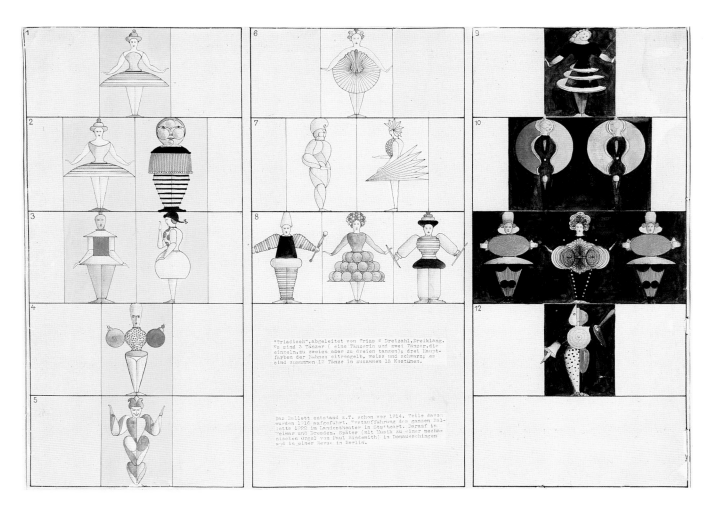

Figurine Plan for The Triadic Ballet I. (1924–1926). Ink, watercolor, poster paint. 15 × 21 in. Harvard University Art Museums (Busch-Reisinger Museum), Museum Purchase. [Cat. no. 92].

as part of the museum's collection or as part of the Family Deposit, it was essential to obtain the museum's support for the Baltimore project. Both the Family and the Staatsgalerie were uniquely supportive and enthusiastic about our exhibition proposal and have continued, to the present, as integral components in this ambitious international collaboration. In particular, Raman Schlemmer devoted himself with admirable dedication and commitment to assure that this first American retrospective exhibition could be the optimum representation of his grandfather's work. Whatever his other professional obligations, Raman Schlemmer responded fully to Baltimore's needs, whether logistic, diplomatic, or documentary. He readily made available all of the resources of the Family Estate, and participated actively in each phase of the exhibition and publication organization. Jaïna Schlemmer, custodian of all Schlemmer theater materials, assumed

full responsibility for coordinating the restoration and reconstruction of the figurines from Schlemmer's *Triadic Ballet* that form such an essential and dramatic component of the Baltimore exhibition. She too became virtually a full-time associate during the final year of the exhibition's production.

At the Staatsgalerie we found colleagues of rare professionalism and dedication. Their commitment to Schlemmer's work and to the significance of the American exhibition forged a collegial relationship between Stuttgart and Baltimore which has proven to be one of profound empathy and friendship. Even in the midst of the Staatsgalerie's major expansion program, Dr. Beye committed his institution and his staff to the remarkable level of cooperation necessary to make the exhibition a reality. Dr. von Maur and Dr. Gauss have offered curatorial leadership and practical cooperation to an unprecedented

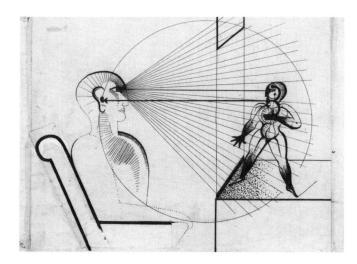

Man the Dancer (Human Emotions) I: Performer and Spectator II.
(ca. 1924). Ink, with collage. 8⅝ × 11⅜ in. Bauhaus-Archiv,
Berlin. [Cat. no. 135].

degree over an extended period of time, ranging from research to conservation to photography to framing to shipping. Dr. von Maur, whose career has been devoted to the work of Oskar Schlemmer, proved to be of invaluable assistance in all of our preliminary deliberations about the exhibition contents. Without the benefit of the exhaustive documentation in Dr. von Maur's two-volume catalogue raisonné (published 1979) of Schlemmer's work, our task would have been immeasurably more difficult, perhaps impossible.

From the earliest discussions with the Schlemmer Family, one of the most pressing concerns was the specific American circulation of the proposed Schlemmer exhibition. Because the work was little known through firsthand viewing in this country, geographic distribution was deemed to be essential. We were extremely gratified by the enthusiastic interest expressed by colleagues throughout the country when announcement of the forthcoming Schlemmer exhibition was made. Almost immediately, commitments were made by the IBM Gallery of Science and Art, New York; the San Francisco Museum of Modern Art; and the Walker Art Center. I am extremely grateful to my colleagues David Hupert and Robert Murdock (New York), Henry Hopkins (San Francisco), and Martin Friedman (Minneapolis), as well as to their support staffs, for their generous and professional involvement in the Schlemmer exhibition. By the close of the tour, which begins in Baltimore in February 1986 and ends in Minneapolis in January 1987, as many as half a million visitors will have had their first direct experience of the art of Oskar Schlemmer.

From the outset, too, we understood that this was an exhibition and publication project of international scope that would require the endorsement and financial support of both public and private resources. The initial commitment of the Federal Republic of Germany was gratifying in its unusually generous subsidy toward the costs of the exhibition and publication. It is a pleasure to acknowledge the warm cooperation of His Excellency Dr. Peter Hermes, former Ambassador of the Federal Republic of Germany, of His Excellency Gunther van Well, present Ambassador, of former Cultural Counselor Dr. Haide Russell, and of present Cultural Counselor Mrs. Eleonore Linsmayer, in assigning the highest priority and support of the Embassy to the Schlemmer project. The United States Government, through the auspices of the National Endowment for the Arts and the National Endowment for the Humanities, also supported the exhibition and publication through generous grants. NEA funds were granted in sponsorship of the exhibition, and NEH funds were awarded to the catalogue. This Museum's partnership with business in support of the arts found continued expression in the enthusiastic involvement of USF&G Corporation as national sponsor of the exhibition. The enlightened corporate leadership of USF&G Chairman Jack Moseley assured a level of support comparable to the significance of the project. As with USF&G's earlier sponsorship of the Baltimore-Stuttgart collaboration on the exhibition of Mondrian's drawings, the company assigned to the Schlemmer exhibition a high profile in its corporate commitments and underwrote substantial exhibition expenses as well as related activities. Additional funds were awarded by The J. Paul Getty Trust to assure publication of the exhibition catalogue in fully-illustrated, scholarly scope. In addition, Lufthansa German Airlines contributed transport services for the extensive trans-Atlantic shipment of works of art. It is only due to this network of public and private support that the exhibition and its ambitious monographic catalogue could be realized fully.

Because the Museum proposed to publish the first substantive work in English on the subject of Oskar Schlemmer and his work, we turned to several scholars and specialists who could best articulate this work to a new audience. Dr. von Maur, indisputably the foremost authority on the art of Schlemmer, agreed to write the book's central text on Schlemmer's painting, sculpture, and graphics. As the author of several definitive German works on Schlemmer, Dr. von Maur brought to this assignment an unparalleled level of information about and sensitivity to the artist's career. Dr. Vernon L. Lidtke, Professor of History at The Johns Hopkins University and noted authority on the sociopolitics of Germany between the wars, contributed an introductory text to set the scene of Schlemmer's achievement. Dr. Nancy J. Troy, Associate Professor of Art History at Northwestern University, specialist in De Stijl and, in particular, scholar of those art forms that merge theater and architecture, addressed Schlemmer's activity in those arenas. And Debra McCall, choreographer and dance historian, noted for her reconstruction of several of Schlemmer's ''Bauhaus Dances'' for contemporary performance, offered a personal reminiscence revelatory of the practical and theoretical bases of Schlemmer's approach to dance. To each of our authors, we owe a very special debt of gratitude for the remarkable eloquence and intelligence with which they approached their subjects.

For the staff of The Baltimore Museum of Art, the Schlemmer project has been both absorbing and demanding for almost five years. Brenda Richardson has worked with me from the beginning: together we selected the works to be included in the exhibition, determined the scope and

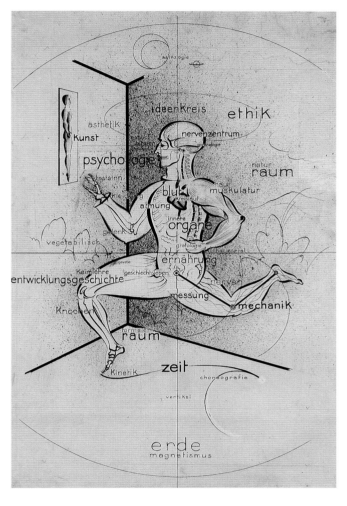

Man in the Sphere of Ideas. (ca. 1928). Ink, paint, and pencil. 29⅜ × 19¼ in. Family Estate of Oskar Schlemmer. [Cat. no. 167].

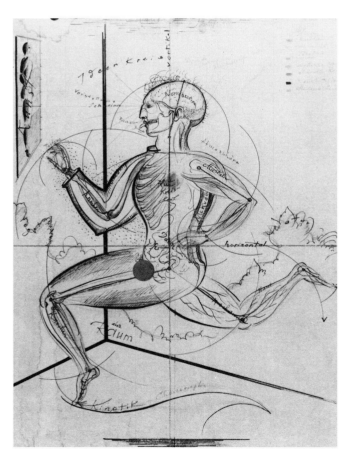

Man in the Sphere of Ideas. (ca. 1928). Ink and pencil. 20⅞ × 16⅛ in. Bauhaus-Archiv, Berlin: Schlemmer Family Estate Deposit. [Cat. no. 166].

contents of the book, arranged the exhibition's circulation, conducted negotiations with public and private lenders, and charted the course of the project from its inception. She assumed administrative management of every detail of the exhibition and its publication, including cataloguing of the works and editing of manuscripts. Without her extraordinary professional collaboration, this project could not have been realized.

Over many months we had the delightful collaboration of Dr. Krishna Winston of Wesleyan University, whose earlier sensitive translation of the *Letters and Diaries* of Oskar Schlemmer led us to her for all of our own translation needs. Dr. Winston consulted on every translating issue (from titles to mediums of works of art) and, most significantly, translated from the German the von Maur text for the present publication. Trish Waters, the Museum's Curatorial Associate and assistant to Brenda Richardson, assumed daily responsibility for the coordination of the myriad technical details of a project of this scope, and contributed invaluably to the clarity and efficiency of the organizational effort. Faith M. Holland served as co-editor with Brenda Richardson for all of the texts in the Schlemmer book and worked especially closely with Dr. Winston on the von Maur translation. Audrey Frantz, Director of Publications, managed the book's production with impeccable grace and skill. The book's quality is thus due to the dedication and unqualified standards of, in equal measure, Richardson, Frantz, Waters, and Holland. The eloquence and refinement of the book's design are a product of the taste and judgment of Alex and Caroline Castro, Hollowpress, and its extraordinary printing quality reflects the characteristic dedication of Schneidereith & Sons, Baltimore.

Coordination of the exhibition's contents (insurance, packing, and shipping arrangements) fell to the supervision of Registrar Melanie Harwood, whose concern and efficiency guaranteed the safety of the works of art assigned to our care. The Museum's Development Office, under the direction of Martha Parkhurst and with the assistance of Joy M. Peterson, prepared the thorough presentations that successfully resulted in needed financial support from multiple sources. Faith Holland coordinated international publicity efforts, and Terry Bachmann managed an impressive program of social and educational activities in conjunction with the Baltimore showing. Karen E. Nielsen, Installation Coordinator, supervised the design and production of the Schlemmer installation, including a very special setting for the *Triadic Ballet* figurines. In the end, of course, and as it should be, there is no member of the Museum's staff who is not involved in some aspect of the exhibition's presentation to the public. To each and every one of them, we extend our gratitude for the constancy of their service.

Schlemmer loans came from around the world. German museums were our primary and most critical point of contact, since virtually all of Schlemmer's most important paintings and sculpture have found their way into public collections in the artist's native land. In addition to the Staatsgalerie Stuttgart, without whose cooperation no Schlemmer project of any magnitude would be possible, we found exceptional cooperation among our colleagues at the Bauhaus-Archiv, Berlin. Museums in Basel, Berlin, Duisburg, Düsseldorf, Essen, Hamburg, Kassel, Mannheim, Ulm, and Vienna also extended their support by making significant loans available for the exhibition. In this country major loans were readily granted by The Museum of Modern Art, New York; by the Busch-Reisinger Museum of the Harvard University Museums, Cambridge, Massachusetts; and by The Saint Louis Art Museum. Baltimore's collection is also represented in the exhibition, with its *Abstract Figure* from the Wurtzburger Collection. Private owners were equally supportive, despite their intimate relationship to these often rare and fragile works by Oskar Schlemmer. Individuals in both Germany and the United States generously agreed to part with their works for the extended period of the exhibition tour, and we are exceedingly grateful for their cooperation.

Finally, I wish to extend my sincerest personal gratitude to the Board of Trustees of The Baltimore Museum of Art, and in particular to current President Margot W. Milch and past Presidents Robert M. Thomas and Calman J. Zamoiski, Jr., for their support and encouragement of this, the single most ambitious exhibition project undertaken by the Museum. Their confidence in the administrative and curatorial judgments of the staff is unwavering, even in the face of unprecedented financial obligation and, always, with regard only for the integrity of the project as a reflection of the Museum's responsibility to scholarship in the history of art. For their dedication and loyalty, I am deeply grateful.

ARNOLD L. LEHMAN
Director

Dark Figure with White Sheet of Paper. (1931). Watercolor. 10⅞ × 8⅝ in. Staatsgalerie Stuttgart. [Cat. no. 184].

Nude, Woman, and Approaching Figure. 1925. Oil. 50⅜ × 25¼ in.
Staatliche Museen Preussischer Kulturbesitz, Nationalgalerie Berlin,
Galerie des 20. Jahrhunderts. [Cat. no. 20].

Twentieth-Century Germany: The Cultural, Social, and Political Context of the Work of Oskar Schlemmer

Oskar Schlemmer's lifetime spanned years of radical change in German politics, society, and culture. Born in 1888, the same year that William II took the throne of the German Empire, Schlemmer lived to witness not only its demise in 1918, but also the collapse of its successor, the Weimar Republic (1919–1933), and the seizure of power by Adolf Hitler and the National Socialists in 1933. For a decade he endured Nazi defamation and persecution, until he died in 1943. Had Schlemmer lived but two years longer, he would also have witnessed the collapse of the brutal, racist, and destructive rule of National Socialism, the regime that had stripped him of his professional positions and condemned his art, along with that of many others, as "degenerate." Schlemmer died an exile within his own country, unable after 1933, except on two occasions, to display his work publicly and scarcely able to earn a living. His life had paralleled the panorama of some of the heights and the miseries of Germany in the late nineteenth and twentieth centuries.

The Setting: Imperial Germany

At the time of Schlemmer's birth Germany was a thriving, energetic, and even creative society. But it was also characterized by harsh social realities and sharply conflicting cultural currents. The formal unification that had been achieved in 1871 was cast in a political structure that gave the Prussian state an overwhelming position of power within the new system, reserved large areas of decision making to the Emperor (also the King of Prussia), and minimized the strength of representative bodies, notably the Reichstag, the national parliament. Prussia's political dominance, the result in part of the success of its army in the wars of unification (1864–1871), meant also that the professional military structure and its values would be officially promoted and honored in the new German state. One German historian, not himself hostile to the Prussian spirit, has nonetheless written of the "militarization" of the German middle classes in the late nineteenth century, and another has described the Prussian army as a "state within the state."[1]

A martial spirit thus influenced a substantial portion of the German population. When the Imperial government launched a large naval program in 1898, the navy too enjoyed the enthusiastic support of important segments of the middle classes, as reflected in the popularity of the Naval League. This celebration of the military spirit among certain segments of the population went hand in hand with the mobilization of nationalist sentiment through a number of other voluntary patriotic associations. Germany's active policy of colonial expansion, launched in the middle 1880's, was eagerly and sometimes irresponsibly promoted by the Colonial League and the Pan-German League.[2] Other associations also reveled in the expansion of German power in Europe and throughout the world, but not all Germans shared these militarist and imperialist values.

The most articulate critics of German militarism and imperialism were in the Social Democratic party, which directed its appeal to working people and adopted a Marxist program in 1891. Already in 1890 it had received more votes than any other party in the Reichstag, and by 1912 it also had the largest number of deputies (110 out of a total of 397). The vitality and constant growth of the Social Democratic labor movement were the most striking manifestations of deep social cleavages in German society.

Social tensions also grew out of religious differences. During the 1870's the anti-Catholic policies of the Prussian state, in the so-called *Kulturkampf* (Struggle for Civilization), deepened the long-standing fissure between Protestants and Catholics in Germany. Although the Prussian state ameliorated its harsh anti-Catholicism in the 1880's, the wounds did not heal quickly. Catholics constituted more than one-third of the German population at the end of the nineteenth century, but in Prussia and other Protestant-dominated states they continued to experience discrimination. In regions where they were in the majority, especially in Bavaria, they embraced local patriotisms and looked upon the German Empire with considerable reservation.

Along with religious affiliation, local and regional identities continued to play a strong role in the social and political consciousness of most Germans—and do so even today. The formation of the national state did not erode regional loyalties. As a Swabian, for example, Oskar Schlemmer retained a deep attachment to his native region and to Stuttgart, although he also adapted well to life in other cities, notably Weimar, Dessau, Breslau, and Berlin.

Economic Growth, Industry, and Technology

The vitality and the conflicts of German society were produced in large part by an economy that was growing rapidly and steadily and bringing with it the social disruptions common to countries in periods of industrialization and urbanization. By the beginning of the twentieth century, when Oskar Schlemmer was attending the Oberrealschule (Advanced High School of Science and Arts) in Göppingen, Germany had the most powerful industrializing economy of any European country, including Great Britain. Modern industry and technology had become commonplaces in the lives of the majority of Germans, even when many of them were reluctant to accept that reality. The distribution of political power, however, lagged behind these economic developments. The Prussian aristocracy continued to hold many of the leading positions in the state.

Germany was modernizing at an exceptionally rapid pace. Before the First World War it surpassed Great Britain in the production of coal and iron. In certain industries, chemicals for example, German entrepreneurs, like Friedrich Bayer in Elberfeld, demonstrated a special eagerness to make advances through the employment of highly trained technicians, many of them educated at the numerous technical colleges that had been founded since the 1870's. The German electrical industry, identified especially with the firms founded in the late nineteenth century by Werner von Siemens and Emil Rathenau laid the foundation for the widespread electrification of the lighting and transportation systems in German cities that began in the late 1880's.[3] By 1913 Germany was the world's largest producer of electrical products.

Similar advances were made in metallurgy and machine building, and especially in the development of the internal combustion engine that led to the great expansion of the automobile industry. In 1882 Gottlieb Daimler, a talented machine builder, set up his automobile motor works in Cannstatt, a small town that Stuttgart incorporated in 1904. The environment in which Schlemmer grew up combined the natural beauties of the Neckar valley region with the industrial and technological innovations of the modern urban world.

Arts and Crafts

The work of Oskar Schlemmer is rightfully thought of in connection with the exciting years of the Weimar Republic and institutions like the Bauhaus, but it is important to emphasize that much of his artistic orientation had been shaped in an earlier era. At about fifteen or sixteen, in 1904, he left school in Göppingen and apprenticed in a wood-inlay shop, after which he attended a Fortbildungsschule (Continuation School) for a short time and then enrolled for one semester in the Stuttgart Kunstgewerbeschule (School of Arts and Crafts). In the fall of 1906 he entered the Akademie der bildenden Künste (Stuttgart Academy of Fine Arts), where, with some long interruptions, he remained a student until 1919.[4] Before entering the Akademie, however, much of his early training had all the marks of the handicraft tradition that had remained strong in the numerous schools of arts and crafts scattered throughout Germany.

It is noteworthy that about the time that Schlemmer was completing his apprenticeship an organization was taking shape in Germany that was designed to integrate the spirit of the arts and crafts with modes of modern industrial production. The objective was to raise the aesthetic quality of mass-produced goods. This organization, the German *Werkbund*, officially founded in 1907, took much of its inspiration from the Arts and Crafts movement of William Morris in England, but had many sources of encouragement from within Germany itself.

Miracle of the White Nun. (1914). Mural decoration for the *Werkbund* pavilion, Cologne. 98⅜ × 147⁹⁄₁₆ in. No longer extant.

The *Werkbund* became a potent force for improved industrial design in Germany, and many of the outstanding figures in crafts, the decorative arts, and architecture were, even before the First World War, in one way or another associated with it. These included Peter Behrens, Walter Gropius, Hans Poelzig, Bruno Taut, and Henry van de Velde. Even the young Schlemmer had direct contact with the *Werkbund* when his teacher, Adolf Hölzel, chose Schlemmer and several other students to execute a wall painting commission for one of the buildings in the great *Werkbund* exhibition of 1914 in Cologne.[5]

Although still a student at the Akademie when he did the wall paintings in Cologne, Schlemmer had absorbed much of the spirit of modernism and was developing an appropriate style of his own. The modernist inspiration came as much from the world around him as from the Akademie. The Akademie in Stuttgart was not as presti-

Adolf Hölzel and his Students (Oskar Schlemmer second from right), ca. 1914.

gious within Germany as those in Düsseldorf, Dresden, Berlin, and Munich, but its great virtue for Schlemmer was the inspiration and progressiveness of his most important teacher, Adolf Hölzel. No academy of art in Germany was open to all of the new currents in the arts in Europe, and in this respect Stuttgart was no more conservative than the others.

Modernism

Schlemmer's formative years at the Akademie before 1914 coincided with enormously important and innovative developments in nearly all aspects of European and German cultural life. Many of the movements, ideas, and styles later associated with Weimar Culture originated and, in some cases, flourished in the decade prior to the First World War. As a young art student at the Akademie, Schlemmer was aware of much that was going on around him technologically and artistically.

Throughout the German-speaking areas of Europe proponents of modernism, however they understood that concept, had been especially prominent since the 1880's. In most of the arts there were manifestations of sharp breaks with the past and of a self-consciousness among many creative people that they were articulating something "modern." Although the concept was broad and difficult to define precisely, it nonetheless denoted a rejection of forms and orientations of the past, and proclaimed the view that the arts belonged to the contemporary world and had to draw from it and speak to it if they were to continue to play a significant role in German life.

In literature and drama, the young Naturalists of the 1880's and 1890's not only broke with the prevailing Realist and Romantic styles, but were especially shocking because most of them believed that the mission of modern literature was to describe and analyze the brutal social realities and psychological anxieties of contemporary society. The idea that literature should deal with hopeless misery and social degradation repelled many educated Germans, and the fact that two foreign writers, Emile Zola and Henrik Ibsen, exercised considerable influence on many young German Naturalists persuaded other traditionalists that the new movement was fundamentally non-German.

At the end of the 1880's, a group of Naturalists founded their own theater society for the performance of modern drama, the *Freie Bühne* (Free Stage), and it was not long before other sympathizers founded still another theater society, the *Freie Volksbühne* (Free People's Stage), the latter in close association with leading members of the Social Democratic party in Berlin. The link between Naturalism and Social Democracy did not endure for long—the two groups had more disagreements than commonalities—but traditional-minded Germans were easily persuaded that Naturalism was not only modern but also politically subversive. By the beginning of the twentieth century Naturalism appeared to have run its course, but the success of Gerhart Hauptmann's Naturalist plays in the 1890's, especially of *The Weavers*, left no doubt that some of Germany's most talented writers belonged to a movement that self-consciously thought of itself as "modern."

Subsequent trends in German literature prior to the First World War reflected diverse tendencies, from the refined aestheticism of writers like Stefan George, Hugo von Hofmannsthal, and Rainer Maria Rilke, to the scathing social drama of Frank Wedekind—author of the *Lulu* plays, later used by Alban Berg as the text for an atonal opera—and the biting satire in Heinrich Mann's novels, *Professor Unrat* (1905) and *The Subject* (completed in 1914, published 1918). In both novels Heinrich Mann skillfully exposed cultural and political weaknesses in German society. Less critical of the social system and more talented as a writer, Heinrich's younger brother, Thomas Mann, established his literary reputation with *Buddenbrooks* (1901) and several novellas, notably *Tonio Krüger* (1903) and *Death in Venice* (1913).

Despite the preeminent literary position achieved by Thomas Mann, the emergence of Expressionism had even greater significance for subsequent German cultural history. For Expressionism was a movement and style not only in literature, but in essentially all of the fine arts, as well as in architecture. Its impact in literature was felt only to a limited degree before 1914, but its explosive character made itself apparent from the beginning. One of the first Expressionist plays was by the young Viennese painter, Oskar Kokoschka, whose raw dramatic treatment of the conflict between man and woman, *Murderer, Hope of Women*, had its premiere performance in 1908. It was a piece that Schlemmer later came to know well and for which he produced the stage sets in 1922. Kokoschka's career as a writer was limited, but others of the early Expressionist movement matured into renowned authors, including Gottfried Benn, Franz Kafka, Georg Kaiser, and Franz Werfel. Literary Expressionism reached its apogee at the end of the war and, along with its counterparts in the other arts, gave one predominant definition of what was to be understood as cultural modernism.

The growing strength of modernism was amply evident in painting in Germany, especially in the group of young

Oskar Kokoschka (Austrian, 1886–1980). *Herwarth Walden*. 1910. Oil. 29½ × 26¾ in. Staatsgalerie Stuttgart. [Not in exhibition].

painters in Dresden known as *Die Brücke* (The Bridge). Ernst Ludwig Kirchner, Erich Heckel, Otto Müller, and Karl Schmidt-Rottluff, to name the most prominent, were already producing their forms of Expressionism before the performance of Kokoschka's notorious play. Almost simultaneously in Munich *Der Blaue Reiter* (Blue Rider) was forming, but it had its most profound impact only around 1912. The stunning array of talented painters in the *Blaue Reiter* group—for example, Franz Marc, Wassily Kandinsky, August Macke, and Gabriele Münter—increased dramatically the public visibility of German Expressionism.

Since before the turn of the century, the modernist influences in the visual arts in Germany were promoted in several cities through the formation of independent associations of artists, generally known as secessions. Although they shared a common dissatisfaction with the dominant organizations for the exhibition of art at the time, secessionist organizations did not have a unified artistic style. Within each organization several styles were often represented. In the German-speaking world the first of these secessionist organizations appeared in 1892 in Munich. Its members included representatives of Realism, Impressionism, and *Jugendstil*. A few years later, in 1898, the Berlin Secession was formed under the leadership of the German Impressionist painter, Max Liebermann. And in Austria a year earlier the Vienna Secession began a short but brilliant career with such talented members as the painter Gustav Klimt and the architect Otto Wagner. In all instances the secessionist organizations were significant not only as associations through which their own members could exhibit, but also, and in many ways more importantly, for their interest in exhibiting the works of innovative foreign painters.[6]

On the eve of the First World War the most vigorous advocates of modernism in the visual arts were men like Herwarth Walden and Franz Pfemfert. Both devoted themselves for several years to the promotion of the most recent artistic trends—particularly Expressionism, Cubism, and Futurism—Walden through *Der Sturm* (founded in 1910) and Pfemfert in *Die Aktion* (founded in 1911). Walden's gallery in Berlin, also called Der Sturm, became a central meeting place for avant-garde artists, and Walden exercised considerable influence through his widespread contacts and his total commitment to the cause of modernism. Oskar Schlemmer too was drawn to the circle of creative people around Walden, but the young artist from Stuttgart found the irrationalist and ecstatic impulses in Expressionism disagreeable. Instead, he articulated a view of artistic modernism that embodied rational order and discipline.

Modernity, whether in the form of new technology and growing cities or in cultural innovation, could also be threatening. In their search for the social and intellectual origins of National Socialism, historians of Germany have often placed special emphasis on currents of antimodernism, cultural pessimism, and neoconservatism in the decades prior to the First World War.[7] There is much to be said for this view, for it is true that many Germans found it difficult to accept and adapt to the changing realities of the modern world. Some took refuge in memories or fantasies about what the society had been in centuries before, while others denounced modernity, blamed it for their discontents, and looked for its evil progenitors in people they did not happen to like, such as liberals, foreigners, revolutionaries, Marxists, and Jews, or anyone who disagreed with their conception of the "true" values of German society. Some opponents of the modern world were indeed extremists, prepared to endorse crackpot remedies and xenophobic policies, but others were rea-sonable and balanced conservatives, people who cherished traditional customs, styles, and values. Their distrust of modernity rested in good part on their belief that it was superficial and transitory.

Cultural and Personal Impact of the War

The First World War disrupted every European society and transformed many of them in ways that few people could have anticipated before its outbreak. Europeans had for years feared that a war would break out, but no one had envisioned the kind of warfare that actually took place. Although very little of the fighting occurred on German territory, in every other respect Germany felt the full impact of the war and its consequences. At the outset, in August of 1914, a mood of fervent patriotism and exuberant optimism swept over almost every segment of the nation. Young men throughout Germany rushed to serve their country, and these included Oskar Schlemmer, who enlisted and, as a soldier in the Queen Olga Grenadier Regiment of the Württemberg army, was sent to the western front no later than September 24, 1914.

What began with a surge of enthusiasm for the German fatherland, ended in military defeat, political collapse, social upheaval, cultural reorientation, and, for many, profound personal and psychological distress. The initial expectations, along with the ensuing tensions, exaggerated nearly every kind of response. Even the most learned and the most artistically talented Germans were swept away by a swirl of emotional claims and counterclaims. Scores of scholars, scientists, pastors, teachers, and other professional groups publicly demanded that Germany should not cease fighting until it had annexed important territories. Germany was heralded as a land of deep and profound culture (*Kultur*) in sharp contrast to the shallow "civilization" of western nations like France and England. Thomas Mann spent more than three years elaborating on this thesis in *Reflections of a Nonpolitical Man* (published 1918), a strange and troubled work that seems to stand in contradiction to the noble aestheticism of his novels and short stories.

Other young intellectuals and artists underwent deep psychological and intellectual changes as a consequence of their encounters with the horrors of trench warfare, and it was Schlemmer's generation, broadly defined, which was most directly affected. While some educated Germans clung even more tenaciously to traditional values of patriotism, social hierarchy, and authoritarianism, others were distraught, disenchanted, and rebellious. Many were psychologically crippled, and others were transformed into fierce critics of existing political systems. Ernst Ludwig Kirchner suffered a nervous breakdown within six months after the beginning of the war; Otto Dix volunteered immediately but the experience soon changed him into one of the most powerful critics of the whole system; Max Beckmann, already a moderately successful painter, also volunteered and suffered a nervous breakdown by 1915; and Georg Grosz's critical view of the bourgeois social world was made even more biting as a result of his war experiences. Many young writers were affected in similar ways. Bertolt Brecht, already a social critic, moved to an even more radical posture during the war. Ernst Toller, who enlisted as a loyal German, emerged a fiery revolutionary. In one respect or another, the war changed everyone. Even Schlemmer, who endured his war experiences with apparently little bitterness and much less emotional turmoil than many of his fellow artists, returned to civilian life ready to promote modernist views much more vigorously than before the war.

In sharp contrast, others reveled in their war experiences. Ernst Jünger earned his literary fame in novels that aestheticized the killing and death in the trenches. "War," he wrote, "the father of all things, is also our father. It has hammered us, chiseled us and hardened us into what we are."[8] Many veterans shared these sentiments and after the war found a temporary militarist home in the Free Corps, fighting revolutionary forces on the left. One Free Corps volunteer later wrote of his longing for war, how it had become a way of life: "People told us that the war was over. That made us laugh. We ourselves are the war. Its flame burns strongly in us. It envelops our whole being and fascinates us with the enticing urge to destroy."[9]

Revolution: Political and Cultural

The wide-ranging impact of the war only became fully evident once it ended, in considerable part because military control of the civilian population, economic regimentation, and censorship had silenced, on the surface, most of the tumultuous forces that were at work and which only burst forth in their full power in the autumn of 1918. At the outset, the overwhelming majority of socialists supported the government's war effort, but increasingly, during the final two years, a substantial number of socialists and workers became disenchanted and many of them pushed for revolution within the Independent Social Democratic Party (founded 1917) or its most radical wing, the Spartacists. Military failure and the collapse of the Hohenzollern monarchy meant that many of the old barriers to open expression had fallen. Although Germany did not undergo the kind of radical Bolshevik revolution that was even then taking place in Russia, the constitution of the Weimar Republic guaranteed Germans the political and civil rights that were enjoyed in other democracies. If German society was not revolutionized from top to bottom, and it was not, it is nonetheless true that there were fundamental changes in the political system. For a while, the conservative and reactionary groups in Germany were on the defensive or they remained passive as the momentum of revolution and change went forward. Despite the loss of the war, the personal hardships imposed by the continuation of the allied blockade, and the terms of the Treaty of Versailles that were repugnant to most Germans, many socialists, moderates as well as radicals, believed confidently that their movement could bring a new era of progress and humanitarianism to German society.

The political upheaval of the years 1918–1919 was accompanied by the most varied and singular cultural currents. On the one hand, a prevalent mood of cultural despair was reinforced and encouraged by the appearance in 1918 of such books as Oswald Spengler's *Decline of the West* and Thomas Mann's *Reflections of a Nonpolitical Man*. Spengler had commenced his book well before the outbreak of the war, but its fortuitous publication in 1918 suited the pessimistic sentiments of many Germans, and they purchased it by the thousands. Failure in war and the ensuing political upheaval left the German establishment distraught and disoriented, but not in total disarray.

On the other side of the cultural and political spectrum, movements appeared that challenged the relevance of all inherited political philosophies, social systems, and aesthetic assumptions. The most notable of these was the Dada movement, which had originated in Zurich about 1916, and became especially strong in Berlin and several other German cities in the immediate postwar years. It challenged all of the rationalist assumptions of previous generations, ridiculed the belief that the arts could be meaningful, and engaged in outrageous behavior designed to insult those who believed in the norms of civil society. Its intrinsic nihilism meant that Dada could not build the foundations for a new, positive culture, but in its short life it made the case dramatically for the timeliness of affirming nonsense and embracing the absurd. Hans Richter, himself a Dadaist, has correctly maintained that because of the special conditions in Germany, Dada in Berlin was particularly outrageous and negative.[10] But even the most convinced Dadaists, such as Johannes

Baader, Hugo Ball, Raoul Hausmann, Richard Hülsenbeck, and the Herzfelde brothers, Wieland and Helmut—the latter changed his name to John Heartfield—could not sustain a consistent negativism.

The confidence that the arts could contribute to the building of a new culture and society in Germany was reflected in numerous currents. In Berlin and many other cities, for example, organizations of visual artists sprang up, most of them with both a left-wing orientation and an assumption that their efforts would help in some way to improve society. The most prominent of these were the *Berliner Novembergruppe* and the *Arbeitsrat für Kunst* (Works Council for Art), both based in Berlin. The appearance of new organizations of artists in other cities is also notable, for example, *Das Junge Rheinland* in Düsseldorf, the *Dachverband progressiver Maler, Bildhauer, Architekten und Komponisten* (Group of Progressive Artists) in Cologne, the *Gruppe RIH* in Karlsruhe, and the *Gruppe 1919* in Dresden. Visual artists everywhere, especially the younger ones, seemed willing to engage in social and political movements to a degree never before known. Even Schlemmer, who had no taste for political involvement or a public activist role, late in 1918 represented a group of protesting art students on the newly founded *Rat geistiger Arbeiter* (Council of Intellectual Workers) in Stuttgart. Out of that experience emerged the Uecht Group, devoted to the promotion of modernism in art. Moreover, Schlemmer's wife, Helena Tutein, had close ties to the Spartacists and because of her political activities Schlemmer himself spent a few hours under arrest.[11] The events in Stuttgart were moderate by comparison with what happened in cities like Cologne, Munich, and Berlin.

There were similar stirrings in the other arts in the revolutionary period. It is also striking, however, that modernists were now moving into a position of control in established institutions. Expressionists and other members of the avant-garde were appointed to offices of leadership and authority in publicly-supported cultural institutions, a development that would have been impossible only two years earlier. Leopold Jessner, a socialist, became director of the Prussian State Theater (formerly the Court Theater) in Berlin and immediately staged Expressionist productions of both classical and modern drama. In Thuringia, the Socialist coalition government merged the former academy of art and the school of applied arts and, following the 1915 recommendation of Henry van de Velde, appointed Walter Gropius to head the new Staatliche Bauhaus in the classical town of Weimar. Gropius too favored socialism and was a leading member of several of the new radical organizations of visual artists. In every realm of the arts, old forms were

on the defensive as the advocates of innovation, reform, modernism, and cultural renewal moved with optimism.

The Weimar Republic: Politics and Economics

Political and economic realities directly or indirectly affected nearly every aspect of cultural life during the fourteen years of the Weimar Republic. Traditionalists, who earlier had taken pride in the uncritical idea that the best of German *Kultur* had been quintessentially unpolitical, now lived in an environment in which politics seemed unavoidably intertwined with everything. The change may not have been as drastic as it seemed on the surface because the influence of politics had always been a fact of cultural life, although often hidden from public view. In Weimar it was open and pervasive.

The existence of the Republic was itself a cause for the heightened awareness of political issues. The Republic, created out of Germany's defeat and compelled to accept the terms of the Treaty of Versailles, never won the allegiance of all segments of the German public, especially military men and political conservatives. They heaped abuse on the Republic and fostered the myth that the army had not lost the war, but that a "stab in the back," perpetrated by Socialists, Democrats, Jews, and the advocates of a negotiated peace brought about Germany's defeat. The fact that the Republic rested initially on the support of the Social Democratic, Catholic Center, and Democratic parties only reinforced the conviction of its right-wing opponents that it could not represent what they believed to be Germany's true interests. Many of them longed to destroy the Republic and to replace it with a military dictatorship, as revealed in the Kapp Putsch of March 1920, or with a regime of militarism and populist racism, evident in the Hitler Putsch of November 1923. Among conservatives and right-wingers, contempt for the democratic political system went hand in hand with hatred of the modernity and innovation that we now associate with the concept of "Weimar Culture." They denounced modern currents of thought and art as "cultural Bolshevism," often with no regard whatsoever to the actual substance or to the political convictions of the people they accused.

The Weimar Republic had no friends on the far left either. After the Spartacist group made a tragically abortive uprising to overthrow the provisional government in January 1919—when Rosa Luxemburg and Karl Liebknecht were killed by members of the Free Corps—its successor, the German Communist party, made several

Figurine Facing Right with Geometric Forms. 1923. Gouache. 22⅛ × 16⅛ in. Private Collection, Frankfurt. [Cat. no. 124].

Divided Figure Facing Left and Profile Head. 1923. Gouache. 23⅛ × 12⅝ in. Staatsgalerie Stuttgart: Schlemmer Family Estate Deposit. [Cat. no. 122].

attempts, especially in 1921–1923, to bring down the Republic. That these insurrections failed did not quiet the fears of many citizens that a Bolshevik revolution might still take place in Germany. The fact that by 1925, under the leadership of Ernst Thälmann, the Communist party faithfully followed the guidelines set down in Moscow undermined its credibility with many intellectuals on the left as well as with moderate Germans.

Economic disruption and an increasingly rampant inflation between 1918 and the end of 1923 contributed to the political instability and added to the Republic's failure to gain the respect of many Germans. Inflation created widespread hardship and a deep sense of despair. By late 1922 the German mark was inflating at such a rapid pace that average Germans felt compelled to spend their pay immediately, before its meager purchasing power would

be further devalued. The exchange rate between American dollars and German marks tells part of the story: in 1919 one dollar was worth 8.9 marks; in July 1920, 39.5 marks; in July 1921, 76.7 marks; in July 1922, 493.2 marks; in July 1923, 353,412 marks; and on November 15, the exchange rate stood at 4,200,000,000,000 marks to one dollar! ''How can you measure prices which change practically every hour—as they did during the last months of the inflation?'' one contemporary asked, and added, ''At the end of 1923, businesses paid wages and salaries not only twice a week, but every day. . . . As soon as I received my salary I rushed out to buy the daily necessities.''[12]

In view of this economic disaster, the surprising fact is that the Republic survived at all, not that it failed to gain prestige. But the restoration of currency stability in 1924 and a comparatively prosperous economy between 1924 and 1930 meant improved possibilities for the democratic system. Gradually, some of the early conservative opponents made their peace with the Republic, a trend that was assisted by the election in 1925 of the old military hero, Field Marshal Paul von Hindenberg. His election to the presidency in that year also symbolized the conservative shift which had been going on for some time. Hindenberg replaced Friedrich Ebert, the Social Democrat who had been the first president of the Weimar Republic. If the Republic was somewhat more acceptable to conservatives, they still refused to give it their enthusiastic support. Intellectuals, artists, academics, and all educated Germans followed these political events with an involvement and concern that had been unknown in the Germany of the old order.

Scene with Convertible Architecture, Tower (Stage Design for "Murderer, Hope of Women"). (1921). Watercolor. 8½ × 11½ in. Oskar Schlemmer Theater Estate, Collection UJS. [Cat. no. 105-a].

Weimar Culture

In retrospect it may seem puzzling and ironic that an environment so charged with the pain of military defeat, economic uncertainty, political polarization, ethnic prejudice, psychological distress, class hostilities, and general social flux, should also have been the setting for a flourishing and innovative cultural life. Paradoxical though it may be, the years of the Weimar Republic were filled with exciting artistic advances. They were also some of Schlemmer's most creative and productive years, marked by the beginning in 1920 of his position on the teaching staff of the Bauhaus, first in Weimar (1920–1925) and then in Dessau (1925–1929). It was a time of several of his most fruitful collaborative undertakings. In 1920–1921, while Schlemmer produced stage designs for Oskar Kokoschka's *Murderer, Hope of Women*, Paul Hindemith set the piece to music. Later, in 1925–1926, Hindemith composed the music for Schlemmer's *Triadic Ballet*. In 1929 Schlemmer produced highly imaginative stage settings for Igor Stravinsky's fairy tale operas, *The Nightingale* and *The Fox* (both performed in Breslau), and in the following year he created the designs for a production of Arnold Schönberg's *The Lucky Hand* at the progressive Kroll opera house in Berlin.

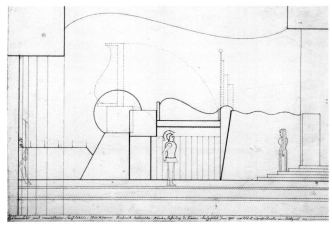

Stage Design with Convertible Architecture (for "Murderer, Hope of Women"). (1921). Ink. 11⅝ × 16⅞ in. Oskar Schlemmer Theater Estate, Collection UJS. [Cat. no. 105-b].

The intellectual and creative ferment of the Weimar years was deep and genuine, suggesting that cultural productivity may thrive better in times of intense conflict than of idyllic tranquility. To be sure, the idea of "Weimar Culture" has also been romanticized and mythologized to some degree, a consequence of the fact that its life was

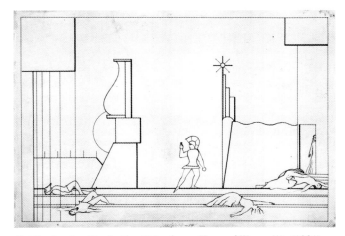

Set Design for Finale (for "Murderer, Hope of Women"). (1921). Ink. 12⅜ × 17¹⁵⁄₁₆ in. Oskar Schlemmer Theater Estate, Collection UJS. [Cat. no. 105-c].

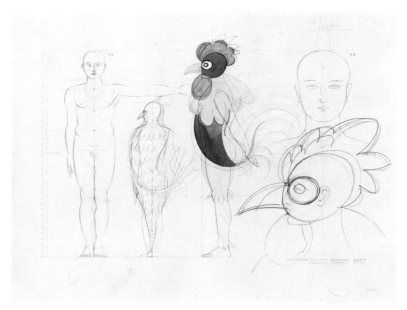

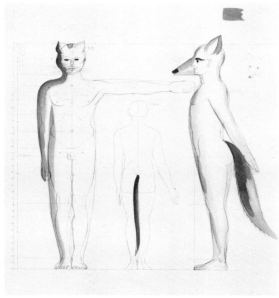

Costume Design for ''The Fox'': Study for the Rooster. 1929. Pencil and watercolor. 19⅝ × 25⅝ in. Oskar Schlemmer Theater Estate, Collection UJS. [Cat. no. 177-a].

Costume Design for ''The Fox'': Study for the Tomcat and the Fox. (1929). Pencil and watercolor. 19⅝ × 17⅝ in. Oskar Schlemmer Theater Estate, Collection UJS. [Cat. no. 177-b].

cut short by the brutal assault of National Socialism. In metaphorical language we can say that ''Weimar Culture'' was martyred and, like martyrs at other times, its meaning became more significant in death than in life. As Henry Pachter, himself a young Weimar intellectual, has eloquently argued, the intellectual and artistic emigrés did much to create a paradisiacal image of their former cultural life in Weimar.[13] The truth in that insight, however, does not deny the fact that the years of the Weimar Republic were exceptionally exciting and fruitful.

One of the features that distinguished the Republic from the previous political system was the high visibility of what have been called the ''left-wing intellectuals.'' Intensely critical of the Social Democratic reluctance to push for a thoroughgoing socialist revolution in 1918–1919, and often scornful of the weaknesses of the Weimar Republic, these left-wing intellectuals seldom found a political party with which they were comfortable. Negativism was one of their hallmarks. Kurt Tucholsky, editor and constant contributor to the influential journal, *Die Weltbühne*, believed that negativism was inevitable in that environment.[14] The left-wing intellectuals found in Marxism a system of thought with strong cerebral appeal, and that went along with their professed sympathy for the working class. A substantial number of them thus flirted with the Communist party, but its strict discipline and narrow intellectual outlook were seldom satisfying in the

long run. Only a few, such as Johannes Becher, were able or willing to subordinate their aesthetic values to the political priorities set by the Communist party. Despite their strong political preoccupations, most left-wing intellectuals were politically homeless.

In addition to the close intermingling of cultural life and politics, ''Weimar Culture'' was characterized by the most vigorous experimentalism. The Dadaists began it with reckless abandon. Others were more systematic. In the theater, Erwin Piscator, in addition to his left-wing political predilections, was an accomplished proponent of the trial-and-error system. He employed new and advanced stage machinery, set up simultaneous stages, and introduced film as one of his most imaginative innovations. Schlemmer's stage designs and his *Triadic Ballet* were no less innovative and experimental, and without the leftist political message imposed by Piscator. Kurt Schwitters, the talented and individualistic Hanover artist, built his renowned ''Merz Construction'' from the most diverse materials, including discarded objects from the streets. The list could go on. Innovation, experimentation, newness—these were important cultural dimensions of the Weimar years.[15]

It would be erroneous and misleading to try to reduce the richness of culture during the Weimar Republic to a limited set of ideas and trends. There were right-wing intellectuals as well as those on the left. There were pro-

Yellow-Red, Mural Study II and *Brown-Red, Mural Study I.* (1928).
Oil. Each, approx. 39½ × 9 in. Staatliche Kunstsammlungen Kassel:
Schlemmer Family Estate Deposit. [Cat. nos. 24–23].

war advocates as well as pacifists. There were conventional dramatists as well as radical innovators like Ernst Toller, Georg Kaiser, and Bertolt Brecht. There were the new Existentialists, notably Martin Heidegger, as well as the Marxists of the Institute for Social Research in Frankfurt. The complexity of the era should warn against simple generalization.

Still, the strength of some currents is incontestable. Despite the seeming irrationality of mankind as demonstrated by the meaningless slaughter of the First World War, stressed so vehemently by the Dadaists, the confidence that society and culture could be refashioned in accordance with rationality remained strong throughout these years. It was a fundamental assumption in the work of the Bauhaus, notwithstanding the presence there of certain mystical tendencies. The effort to affirm rationality was embedded in Bertolt Brecht's didactic theory of the theater. And it can be seen as well in Arnold Schönberg's development of the twelve-tone system in the early 1920's as a way to overcome the chaos that had been created by his subversion of tonality.

With few exceptions, Schlemmer was in basic harmony with what have been identified here as the broad modernist characteristics of "Weimar Culture." The major exception concerned politics. At nearly every turn his life was directly affected by political reality—during the war and the revolution, in 1925 when the Bauhaus had to leave Weimar for Dessau, and after 1933 when the Nazi regime denounced him and destroyed the basis for his livelihood. But through it all he tried to remain aloof from direct or even indirect political involvement. The political orientation of other painters, such as Otto Dix, Georg Grosz, Käthe Kollwitz, and Max Pechstein, went counter to his personal temperament and artistic values. In the years immediately after the war several of the people who were associated with the Bauhaus, including Walter Gropius, had been deeply involved with the *Novembergruppe* and the *Arbeitsrat für Kunst*, but not Schlemmer. Only in 1918–1919, and then with obvious reluctance, had he ventured into public view in a role other than that of the creative artist. Nonetheless, the atmosphere in Germany was so politically polarized that the innovative artistic work of the unpolitical Schlemmer was anathema to cultural traditionalists, right-wing conservatives, and Nazi racists.

From Weimar into the Third Reich

Only a few months after Schlemmer left the Bauhaus in the autumn of 1929 to take a new position at the Staatliche Akademie für Kunst und Kunstgewerbe (State Academy for the Arts and Crafts) in Breslau, the foundations of the Weimar Republic began to crumble and an environment that had encouraged progressive artists turned increasingly hostile. The worldwide depression brought an end to the years of prosperity and, once again, by the middle of 1930 an economic crisis was intensifying the social and political conflicts that favored the electoral growth of Hitler's National Socialists on the right and, to a lesser extent, the Communists on the left. As productivity dropped and unemployment rose, state revenues declined, threatening the financial viability of everything from welfare systems to cultural institutions.

The shortage of funds prompted the Prussian state government to cut back its support for art academies. Of the five major art academies in Prussia, only two, Berlin and Düsseldorf, would continue, and they on sharply reduced budgets. The Akademie in Breslau, which Schlemmer had joined only in 1929, closed in the spring of 1932. Schlemmer found a position in the Vereinigte Staatsschulen für Kunst (United State Schools for Art) in Berlin, and moved there in the summer of 1932, at the same time that the Bauhaus, under constant attack by Nazis on the Dessau municipal council, was being dissolved. The Bauhaus also moved to Berlin the same autumn. But within only a few months Nazi political advances once again uprooted both Schlemmer and the Bauhaus. The appointment of Adolf Hitler as Chancellor on January 30, 1933, led directly to the imposition of cultural policies more destructive than even the most pessimistic observers had imagined possible.

Schlemmer had been among the pessimists by late 1930 as he witnessed the weakening of the Republic, the political polarization, the growing strength of the National Socialists, and the aggressiveness with which they promoted their racist, supernationalist, and antimodernist cultural views. His work had already fallen victim to their vicious prejudices in 1930 when Nazi pressure in Thuringia led to the removal or destruction of the materials of the 1923 Bauhaus exhibition in Weimar. Schlemmer's murals and reliefs were either removed or painted over.[16]

Schlemmer viewed National Socialism with alarm and repugnance. In the middle of 1932 he wondered why the Germans had to make "such a to-do over . . . nationality," and he could see clearly that "National Socialism . . . holds a terrible threat for our cultural life."[17] As a loyal citizen of Germany, a veteran of the First World War, and a basically unpolitical artist, he viewed his creative work as a natural and integral part of the broader German cultural world. Modernism had a rightful place in his view of German society. But the xenophobic nationalism of the political right took the opposite view,

Design Submitted in the Competition for the Decoration of the Congress Hall in the Deutsches Museum, Munich: Wall Section in Scale of 1:5. (1934). Pencil and chalk. 36⅛ × 71⅜ in. Family Estate of Oskar Schlemmer. [Cat. no. 206-a].

Design Submitted in the Competition for the Decoration of the Congress Hall in the Deutsches Museum, Munich: Enlarged Detail from the Lengthwise Wall. (1934). Pastel. 50¾ × 78 in. Family Estate of Oskar Schlemmer. [Cat. no. 206-b].

as he noted, with a certain astonishment, that "it almost looks as though modernism will now be considered unpatriotic."[18] What seemed a vague possibility in August 1932, became a harsh reality in less than six months. Immediately after coming to power, the Nazis began to dismiss progressive and modernist artists, as well as Jews, Communists, and Social Democrats, from state institutions. Although Schlemmer still remained aloof from all political involvement, by early April he too expected to be dismissed at any moment from his teaching position.[19] His apprehension was warranted. Already in the middle of March the Nazis had banned an exhibition of his art in the Stuttgart *Künstlerbund*; on April 30 he was suspended temporarily from his new position, and in August his dismissal was final. Hundreds and thousands of other Germans shared the same fate.

The intense hostility of most National Socialists to modernism only identified their enemy, but did not in itself spell out the artistic goals that the regime wanted to achieve or the aesthetic principles on which these were to be based. As a regime that claimed to embody the true German spirit, National Socialism also desired to promote its racist and parochial conception of German art as well as to purge the country of every residue of what it hated. But initially Nazi cultural commentators themselves did not always agree on their positive principles, and this lack of a well-defined artistic program encouraged some progressive artists to believe that the most reactionary anti-modernists would not necessarily gain absolute dominance in Germany. Although Schlemmer had no hope after 1933 of regaining a teaching position in a state-supported academy, and although creative work was impossible for many months, he began to paint again in 1935–1936. During 1936, the year of the Olympic games in Berlin, the Nazis, for reasons of public relations, relaxed somewhat their open aggression against modernist art. Some of Schlemmer's work appeared in 1936 in Hamburg in an exhibition of German painting and sculpture, and early in 1937 the Ferdinand Möller Gallery in Berlin sponsored a show of his new painting. His prospects for creative work seemed to be improving. In February 1937 he even thought that if he could find a decent studio that "things will look up."[20] But this hope was quickly crushed.

In 1937 the *Reichskulturkammer* (Reich's Chamber for Arts and Culture) renewed its vicious attacks on modernist art, and confiscated some 15,997 works of art from galleries, museums, and other collections. Many of these confiscated pieces, including nine by Schlemmer, were then assembled in the exhibition that the Nazis entitled "Entartete Kunst" ("Degenerate Art").[21] It opened on July 19, 1937, in several rooms of the Hofgarten arcade in Munich. Henceforth, it was absolutely clear that Schlemmer and every other artist included in the "Degenerate Art" exhibition had no hope whatsoever of making a living as an artist in Germany. The National Socialist party had succeeded in imposing its will on all of the arts. Schlemmer and his family thought about emigrating, as so many other Germans had done, but that prospect too had disadvantages. In the following years, Schlemmer eked out an existence as a house painter in Stuttgart (1938–1940), and then worked in a Wuppertal paint laboratory (1940–1943) whose owner employed a number of artists defamed by the Nazi regime.

The drastic changes in Germany during Schlemmer's lifetime had been both stimulating and devastating for creative artists. From the late nineteenth century to the early 1930's modernist trends seemed to gain steadily in strength and popularity, but almost always in the shadow of those who viewed such currents with intense resentment and hostility. Conflict and rivalry were often stimulants to cultural productivity, but that too ended with the years of Nazi tyranny when nationalist hysteria, racist hatred, and brute force silenced, exiled, or annihilated many of Germany's most creative spirits. The renewal of cultural life in Germany after the fall of Hitler's Third Reich, and the revival of much of the modernism of earlier decades, belong to another chapter of recent German history.

VERNON L. LIDTKE

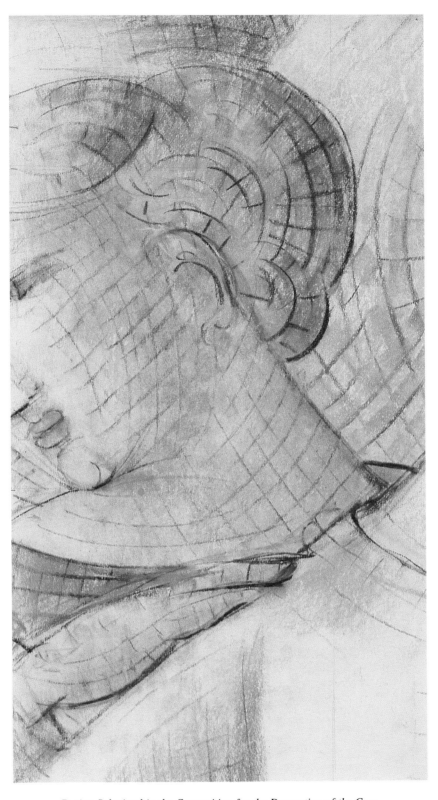

Design Submitted in the Competition for the Decoration of the Con-
gress Hall in the Deutsches Museum, Munich: Girl's Head Facing
Left, with her Hand on the Shoulder of Another Figure. (1934).
Pastel. 18⅞ × 10 in. Staatsgalerie Stuttgart. [Cat. no. 206-c].

Design Submitted in the Competition for the Decoration of the Congress Hall in the Deutsches Museum, Munich: Head Looking Up.
(1934). Pastel. 14¾ × 11⅝ in. Family Estate of Oskar Schlemmer.
[Cat. no. 206-d].

Notes

1. Gerhard Ritter, *The Sword and the Scepter: The Problem of Militarism in Germany*, trans. Heinz Norden, 4 vols. (Coral Gables: University of Miami Press, 1969), vol. 2, chap. 5; Gordon A. Craig, *The Politics of the Prussian Army 1640–1945* (1955; reprint ed., New York: Oxford University Press, 1964), chap. 6.

2. See Roger Chickering, *We Men Who Feel Most German: A Cultural Study of the Pan-German League 1886–1914* (Boston, London, and Sydney: George Allen & Unwin, 1984).

3. Thomas P. Hughes, *Networks of Power: Electrification in Western Society, 1880–1930* (Baltimore: Johns Hopkins University Press, 1983), chaps. 1, 7.

4. Karin von Maur, *Oskar Schlemmer: Monographie und Oeuvrekatalog der Gemälde, Aquarelle, Pastelle und Plastiken*, vol. 1 (Munich: Prestel-Verlag, 1979), pp. 17–29.

5. Maur, *Schlemmer Monographie*, pp. 63–67; Joan Campbell, *The German Werkbund: The Politics of Reform in the Applied Arts* (Princeton: Princeton University Press, 1978), chaps. 1–3.

6. See Peter Paret, *The Berlin Secession: Modernism and Its Enemies in Imperial Germany* (Cambridge, Massachusetts and London: Harvard University Press, 1980), and Peter Vergo, *Art in Vienna 1898–1918: Klimt, Kokoschka, Schiele and their contemporaries* (Ithaca: Cornell University Press, Phaidon, 1975), chap. 1.

7. See, for example, Fritz Stern, *The Politics of Cultural Despair: A Study in the Rise of the Germanic Ideology* (Berkeley: University of California Press, 1961); Shulamit Volkov, *The Rise of Popular Antimodernism in Germany* (Princeton: Princeton University Press, 1978); and Gary D. Stark, *Entrepreneurs of Ideology: Neoconservative Publishers in Germany, 1890–1933* (Chapel Hill: University of North Carolina Press, 1981), especially chap. 3.

8. Quoted in Koppel Pinson, *Modern Germany: Its History and Civilization* (1954; reprint ed., New York: Macmillan Company, 1966), p. 349.

9. Quoted in Robert G. L. Waite, *Vanguard of Nazism: The Free Corps Movement in Postwar Germany 1918–1923* (1952; reprint ed., New York: W. W. Norton & Company, 1969), p. 42.

10. Hans Richter, *Dada: Art and Anti-Art* (New York and Toronto: McGraw-Hill Book Company, 1965), pp. 122–123.

11. Karin von Maur, *Oskar Schlemmer und die Stuttgarter Avantgarde 1919* (Stuttgart: Staatliche Akademie der bildenden Künste Stuttgart, Institut für Buchgestaltung, 1975), pp. 7–15.

12. Statement by Frieda Wunderlich, quoted in Gerhard Bry, *Wages in Germany 1871–1945* (Princeton: Princeton University Press, 1960), p. 225.

13. Henry Pachter, *Weimar Etudes* (New York: Columbia University Press, 1982), chap. 3. On Weimar culture, see also Peter Gay, *Weimar Culture: The Outsider as Insider* (New York: Harper and Row, 1968), and Walter Laqueur, *Weimar: A Cultural History 1918–1933* (New York: G. P. Putnam's Sons, 1974).

14. Harold L. Poor, *Kurt Tucholsky and the Ordeal of Germany, 1914–1935* (New York: Charles Scribner's Sons, 1968), pp. 67–68. Also, Istvan Deak, *Germany's Left-Wing Intellectuals: The Political History of the Weltbühne and its Circle* (Berkeley: University of California Press, 1968).

15. On experimentalism, see especially John Willett, *Art and Politics in the Weimar Period: The New Sobriety, 1917–1933* (New York: Pantheon Books, 1978), which is not restricted to Germany, but treats trends throughout Europe.

16. See Schlemmer's diary entries for mid-November 1930, 27 November 1930, and his letter of 1 December 1930, to Otto Meyer. Oskar Schlemmer, *The Letters and Diaries of Oskar Schlemmer*, selected and edited by Tut Schlemmer, trans. Krishna Winston (Middletown, Connecticut: Wesleyan University Press, 1972), pp. 272–275.

17. Schlemmer to Otto Meyer, 7 May 1932, in Schlemmer, *Letters and Diaries*, pp. 290–291.

18. Schlemmer to Otto Meyer, 26 August 1932, in Schlemmer, *Letters and Diaries*, p. 300.

19. Schlemmer to Willi Baumeister, 2 April 1933, in Schlemmer, *Letters and Diaries*, p. 309.

20. Schlemmer to Hermann Müller, 5 February 1937, in Schlemmer, *Letters and Diaries*, pp. 358–359.

21. On the exhibition "Degenerate Art," see Bertold Hinz, *Art in the Third Reich*, trans. Robert and Rita Kimber (New York: Pantheon Books, 1979), pp. 23–44.

Fig. 1. *Five Figures in a Room (Classical Style)*. 1925. Oil. 38³/₁₆ × 24³/₈ in. Kunstmuseum Basel, Öffentliche Kunstsammlung. [Not in exhibition].

The Art of Oskar Schlemmer

Schlemmer as Painter

In recent years Schlemmer has been associated so exclusively with the Bauhaus that as a painter he has been identified almost entirely with paintings like *Five Figures in a Room (Classical Style)*, 1925 (fig. 1), done during his Bauhaus period. Although these Bauhaus paintings indisputably belong among his masterpieces, such a view of the artist neglects large and important aspects of his oeuvre. During the more than thirty-year span of his creative life, Schlemmer's painting and his concept of form changed in significant stages, opening up ever new modes of expression. These transformations coincided for the most part with the stages of his life: student, soldier, master at the Bauhaus, professor at the art academy, victim of persecution, and paint researcher.

The influence of Schlemmer's professors at the Stuttgart Akademie der bildenden Künste (Academy of Fine Arts) is evident in his work only until about 1910. The two artist-teachers of whom we can see traces are the Swabian painter of laborers and landscapes, Friedrich von Keller (1840–1914), and the open-air painter, Christian Landenberger (1862–1927). Shaped as it is by the French masters, Landenberger's cultivated, meditative style appealed to Schlemmer more than Keller's vehement, powerful, impasto painting, although it was Keller who took Schlemmer on as his master pupil in late 1909 or thereabouts. Then around 1910 Schlemmer learned how to merge color and structure in his paintings by studying the work of Vuillard and Cézanne. In 1911–1912, the year Schlemmer studied in Berlin, he was exposed to many modernist styles, with Expressionism, Futurism, and Orphism among them. But only early Cubism, as exemplified by Picasso's or Derain's paintings from the years 1908–1910, represented a standard to him, for the work of these artists corresponded perfectly to Schlemmer's desire for "system and basic artistic laws."[1] Schlemmer's thinking was also stimulated by Herwarth Walden's journal *Der Sturm*, by Kandinsky's essay "On the Spiritual in Art," and by the almanac of the *Blaue Reiter* (Blue Rider) school. The "internal necessity" of the work of art (Kandinsky) and capturing the "mystical inner construction" (Franz Marc) became more important than reproducing the world of outward appearances.[2] Schlemmer's first painting done in Berlin, the 1911 *Hunting Lodge in Grunewald* (fig. 2), shows how masterfully the Stuttgart art student could already handle a specific subject, here a hunting lodge built in 1542 by the Hohenzollerns. He selected a few significant motifs from the actual building, using these suggestions of structure to create an unusually harmonious pictorial architecture that derives its vitality from the juxtaposition of cube-like structural forms, curving tree trunks, and the two figures, whose standing and reclining poses likewise embody a structural principle. On May 11, 1912, Schlemmer wrote from Berlin to his fellow student Willi Baumeister, "Judging by my present work, people will perhaps assign me to the Cubists." At that time he was working on the painting *Outside the Cloister* (see the 1912 preliminary study, fig. 3), so rigorously structured that it dispenses entirely with painterly effects and with narrative motifs.

Schlemmer's determination to exclude anything fortuitous or emotional, his striving for an objectification and Cubist clarity which could transform the individual into the generic, become particularly obvious in his self-portrait of 1912, which Schlemmer significantly titled *Male Head I* (fig. 5). It is certainly no coincidence that this self-portrait and a variation done a short time later—the two most important of four self-portraits that Schlemmer painted—were completed in Berlin; they express a growing sense of his own worth, the result of his recognition that he had found his own artistic path. The radical reduction

Fig. 2. *Hunting Lodge in Grunewald*. (1911). Oil. 25 × 19½ in. Staatsgalerie Stuttgart. [Cat. no. 1].

of the palette to a few shades of gray and brown and the equally radical simplification of the forms intensify the expressiveness of the image: the shoulders drawn up bastion-like, the nose prominent, the eyes attentive, the gaze from the corners of the eyes searching, the chin energetically sculpted—all these features emphasize the wish-persona of a solemn, combative, decisive young man who seems determined to assert himself in an unwavering dedication to his goal. This was the last time that Schlemmer used himself as a model for a painting. (Aside from a small self-portrait from 1906 that shows him laughing, we know only of a larger watercolor, painted twenty years later in response to a request by his tailor.) The fact that he so rarely undertook self-portraiture testifies to his horror of any form of psychologizing or expression of personal feelings in art. What now followed was a systematic effort to eliminate individual attributes in order to achieve a supra-personal type. We can see what icon-like concentration Schlemmer achieved that same year (1912) if we examine his *Female Head in Gray* (fig. 4), a tall oval head with some features in light, others in shadow. It could be the painted counterpart of sculpted

heads by Brancusi like the *Sleeping Muse* (1910) or *A Muse* (1912).[3] It is unlikely that Schlemmer knew either work, but both the painter and the sculptor strip away all inessential elements to create an abstract head that resembles Cycladic figures, symbolic of life suspended between awakening and extinction.

Around 1912–1913 Schlemmer completed the transition from pre-Cubism to its analytic phase which, however, assumed different form in his work than in that of French (or Spanish) Cubism. He began by infusing stronger light which seems to dematerialize the objective context from within, dynamizing it and emphasizing certain forms while others recede into the background, with a resulting rhythmic alternation between plane and depth. He developed a sort of "X-ray technique," which employed light that seemed to penetrate a solid body to reveal its skeletal structure. The two versions of the painting *Stove and Arm Chair*,

Fig. 3. *Houses (Cloister Garden)*. 1912. Pencil and watercolor. 7½ × 5⅛ in. Staatsgalerie Stuttgart: Schlemmer Family Estate Deposit. [Cat. no. 72].

40

Fig. 4. *Female Head in Gray*. (1912). Oil. 22⅝ × 15⅜ in. Private
Collection. [Cat. no. 2].

Fig. 5. *Male Head I (Self-Portrait)*. 1912. Oil. 17⅞ × 13⁵⁄₁₆ in.
Staatsgalerie Stuttgart: Hugo Borst Collection. [Cat. no. 3].

both of 1914 (figs. 6 and 7), document the growing tendency "to single out colors and forms."[4]

Much has been made of the influence of Adolf Hölzel (1853–1934) on Schlemmer's development. The charming Austrian was appointed to his position at the Stuttgart Akademie in 1905; his painting and his revolutionary theories on pictorial harmony soon placed him at the forefront of abstraction, attracting hordes of German and foreign disciples. But Schlemmer did not become Hölzel's master pupil until after his year in Berlin, that is, until late 1912 or early 1913; by that time he had attained a level of independence that made a close discipleship out of the question. It may well be, however, that Hölzel's theories on the primacy of pictorial means and on a constructivist approach to composition helped Schlemmer move more quickly in the years before the First World War toward his own emphasis on formal elements in painting. Yet in the end, the conclusions Schlemmer drew from Hölzel's teaching took him in a very different direction from his master. While Hölzel gradually blurred and veiled the network of lines with which he plotted the structure of a painting, Schlemmer worked in the opposite

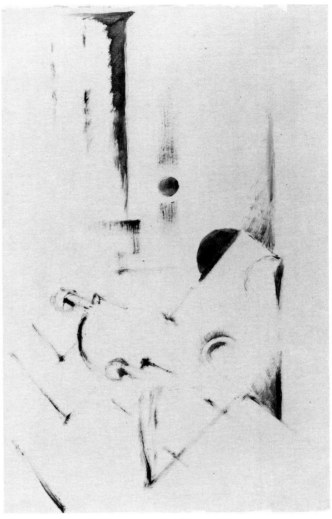

Fig. 7. *Stove and Arm Chair IV*. (1914). Oil on paper. 17¾ × 10⅞ in. Staatsgalerie Stuttgart. [Cat. no. 7].

Fig. 6. *Stove and Arm Chair III*. (1914). Oil on paper. 13⅛ × 10⅜ in. Ulm Museum: on indefinite loan from the State of Baden-Württemberg. [Cat. no. 6].

direction: he began intuitively, allowing himself to be guided by the resonance of the object, in order to bring out the "full force of the artistic media themselves,"[5] to reveal structures and to define them with greater precision. In the end, the work of Schlemmer is entirely different from Hölzel's. In the older man's paintings we find intricate ornamental curves and complexity of line, whereas in Schlemmer's we see just a few clear, geometrically simplified structures. Hölzel uses intense warm colors, preferably red, while the younger man uses spare, secondary shades or renounces color altogether, restricting himself to light-dark contrasts. The approximately twenty paintings from the years 1911–1914, of which some are preserved only in photographs, show Schlemmer to be one of the few representatives of Cubism in Germany—an aspect of his work that has been little recognized.

Fig. 8. *Brown Houses*. (1913–1914). Oil. 23¼ × 17½ in. Family Estate of Oskar Schlemmer. [Cat. no. 5].

Abstract and Figurative Plans

From 1915 Schlemmer pursued two directions concurrently: liberation from the object, and application of abstraction to the human figure. Even before the war he had already explored the abstract potential in planar pictorialism, as seen in compositions like *Brown Houses*, 1913–1914 (fig. 8). The pictures done in 1915–1916, after almost two years of military service during which he did not paint, reveal substantive advances toward both goals. With *Composition on Pink Ground* (fig. 9) of 1915 or 1916, originally titled ''Relationship of Three Figures,'' Schlemmer boldly introduced a system of schematized figuration that was paradigmatic for his future work. A highly stylized, silhouetted profile figure slants diagonally across the picture plane. It is flanked contrapuntally by a

geometrically disjointed figure in the upper left and a miniature, rigidly vertical mannequin-like figure in the lower right. In this painting Schlemmer demonstrated a new conception of the human figure, antithetical to that of the Expressionists: in place of agitated gestures and fractured human form, Schlemmer concentrated expression in a formulaic outline; instead of using the figure as a vehicle for expression, he refined it to essential geometric elements that could serve as modules for pictorial composition. In its schematic abstraction, however, there is retained sufficient figural reference to relate to the forms as living beings. Consequently, the painting is suffused with the perception of impending action: the disjointed figure must be made whole, the falling figure must right itself, the mannequin must explode from its fixed rigidity. Movement seems irresistibly imminent, and the forms thus assume human characteristics not specified in their

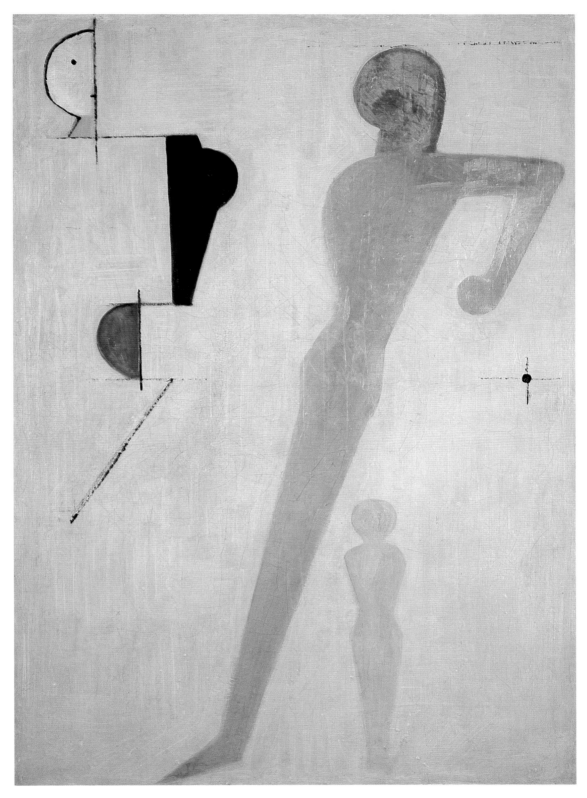

Fig. 9. *Composition on Pink Ground—Relationship of Three Figures.*
(1915 or 1916). Oil and collage. 51⅜ × 36⁷⁄₁₆ in. Private Collection.
[Cat. no. 8].

Fig. 10. *Composition on Pink Ground (Second Version)*. 1930.
Enamel on canvas with wood relief. 51⅛ × 38 in. Museum moderner Kunst, Vienna: Schlemmer Family Estate Deposit. [Cat. no. 9].

schematic outlines. That this approach to composition was quintessentially architectural can be seen not only in the version of the painting done in 1930 in wood (fig. 10), with the central figure mounted in relief, but also in the recurrence of similar figural types in the murals done in 1923 for the Bauhaus workshop building. While working on such figural inventions, Schlemmer continued to ex-plore—independently of the human figure—the laws of pure abstraction. Of the few compositions he did in this vein only one survives in the original, *Painting K* (fig. 11) of 1915 or 1916; of the others we have only unsat-isfactory photographs.

"The hour of the manifesto is past; . . . the dividing lines [have been] drawn; now it is time to take stock, and the German method of bringing order out of chaos can come into play," Schlemmer wrote in April 1919 in his diary.[6] This desire for construction, consolidation, and clarification shaped his 1919 *Scheme with Figures* (fig. 12), in which his early figural studies are recalled as examples and integrated into a planar-tectonic scheme of

subdivisions. Coordination of complete or partial motifs, the alternation between points of concentration and empty spaces, of structured and unstructured surfaces, of volume and line, give rise to a fugue-like rhythm which prefigures the polychrome wall reliefs.

The few surviving compositions from the years 1914–1919 (including the painted reliefs) place Oskar Schlemmer at the forefront of the European avant-garde during and after the First World War. He created a type of figural constructivism free of veristic reference that is unique, at least in Germany, for its radical consistency. Baumeister, who arrived at a similar conception in 1919–1920, moved on to a form of analytic abstraction in which the figural element played a subsidiary role, whereas in Schlemmer's work the figural element remained potent, indeed decisive. Schlemmer's constructivism is not only anthropomorphic but also anthropocentric, and this distinguishes him fun-damentally from similar tendencies that can be found in France, for instance in the work of Fernand Léger. While

Seated Youth. 1925. Oil. 24 × 18½ in. Private Collection. [Cat. no. 21].

Fig. 11. *Painting K*. (1915 or 1916). Oil. 23⅜ × 29⅞ in. Private Collection. [Cat. no. 10].

Fig. 12. *Scheme with Figures*. (1919). Oil and collage. 36⅝ × 51⅛ in. Staatsgalerie Stuttgart. [Cat. no. 14].

Schlemmer's work of the Stuttgart period should be viewed in connection with related post-Cubist currents, it is true that he found his own way to a reformulation of goals. In this connection the opinion of art critic and museum director Paul Ferdinand Schmidt remains valid after more than half a century. Schmidt stated in 1920 that Schlemmer had "advanced the farthest along the road to planar abstraction and that similar attempts in Germany and the rest of Europe lacked the immaculate purity of Schlemmer's solution to the problem."[7]

Within the context of easel painting Schlemmer's exploration of figural potential left only three possibilities: to continue to do variations on earlier work; to abandon figural motifs entirely, as Baumeister did; or, the very opposite, to enrich the concept of the human form by taking into consideration its spatial and volumetric realities. By choosing the latter course, Schlemmer could integrate his experience of planar tectonics with the repertory of fundamental types he had already developed. He could admit the principles of architecture into his studio.

The Magic of Space

In 1923, after a hiatus of several years, Schlemmer presented recent paintings at the Bauhaus exhibition in Weimar. A metamorphosis had occurred. Schlemmer had left behind pure studio art. In these years he devoted himself intensely to sculpture, the theater, and architectural decoration—genres that suggested a more comprehensive context. It was a time during which he was deeply absorbed in the Bauhaus program and the artistic currents that fed it. After a period of bold abstraction and an analytic approach to form, Schlemmer moved closer to visible reality in his portrayal of figures in space, at the very time when his Bauhaus colleagues, under the leadership of Kandinsky, Moholy-Nagy, and their Weimar neighbor van Doesburg, were seeking revelation in a canon of form that was both abstract and universally applicable.

In line with the Bauhaus policy that the craft workshops should generate models for products, Schlemmer wanted the fine arts to produce models as well, both in the realm of ideas and in the realm of forms. Schlemmer determined to create pictorial prototypes which could convey elemental concepts of man as a function of spatial environment. These pictorial prototypes were to be images of inspiration for the architecture of the future and the human beings who would inhabit it. In November 1922, Schlemmer wrote "I should not direct myself toward building houses,

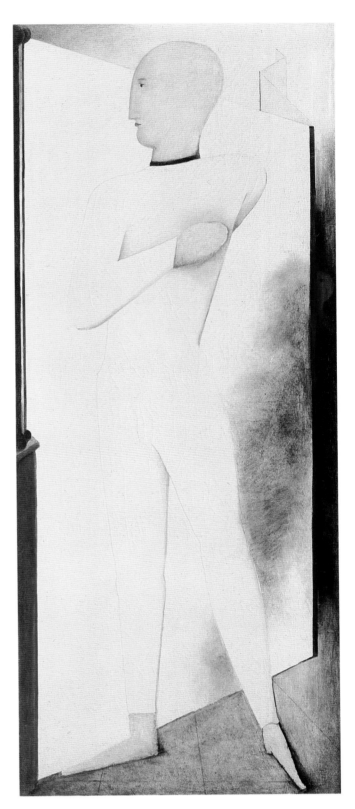

Fig. 13. *The Dancer*. 1923. Oil. 69 × 27¾ in. Staatsgalerie Stuttgart. [Cat. no. 15].

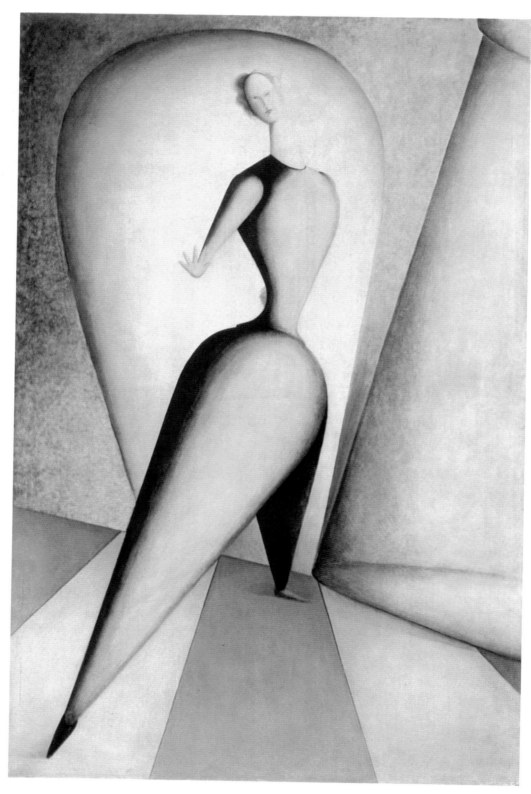

Fig. 14. *The Gesture (Dancer)*. (1922). Oil. 78¾ × 51³⁄₁₆ in. Neue Pinakothek, Munich: Bayerische Staatsgemäldesammlungen. [Not in exhibition].

except the ideal house which my paintings imply and anticipate."[8] After thus claiming for art an archetypal role, Schlemmer turned once more to painting, but had to concede that his concept could be put into practice only if he partially renounced his previous abstract treatment of surfaces.

What Schlemmer gained from his much criticized reintroduction of depth perspective is easily discerned in a comparison of his last Stuttgart paintings with his first Bauhaus paintings. Instead of a metrically divided, transparent "differentiated man," Schlemmer presented a figural outline worked out as a body. Instead of aligning figures on a plane, he grouped them to suggest spatial depth. Instead of figures sketched as abstractions, they are given tone and value (thus, volume), thereby giving the painting new viability as a model for the real world. By renouncing modernity in form, Schlemmer gained recognizable imagery, a sense of life, general validity, and—in the alliance he sought between "perfection of form and profundity of thought"[9]—classical balance.

It is not coincidental that the series of Bauhaus pictures began with the two paintings *The Gesture (Dancer)* (fig. 14) and *The Dancer* (fig. 13) of 1922 and 1923. It was not merely theoretical consideration that led Schlemmer to treat space in his pictures, but the experience of a painter who had become a dancer and choreographer and was now trying to express in painting his sense of the body in space. He had discovered that "the human figure, plucked out of the mass and placed in the separate realm of the stage (the picture) is surrounded by an aura of magic and thus becomes what one might call a space-bewitched being."[10] It is thus no accident that the figure of the female dancer in *The Gesture (Dancer)* bears a resemblance to the figurine called "The Abstract" from the closing segment of *The Triadic Ballet* (fig. 15). The female dancer confronts the observer in an almost challenging manner, with her club-shaped leg thrust forward, while at the same time her hand wards off intrusion. *The Dancer*—a stylized self-portrait of the artist—stands in a collected pose, the profile view expressing reserve, before a screen perhaps intended to represent a mirror, behind which space opens up only minimally. Frontal view and side view, self-confident confrontation and reflective reserve—with these two postures Schlemmer created a complementary pair that embodied the duality within him. This pair turns up repeatedly throughout his work, in many variations.

Schlemmer returned to the frontal view in 1923 with a powerful, immovable, parabolic image of the sixteenth-century Swiss-born alchemist, physician, and philosopher Paracelsus (fig. 16), a profound thinker who postulated that our understanding yields mere images locked into

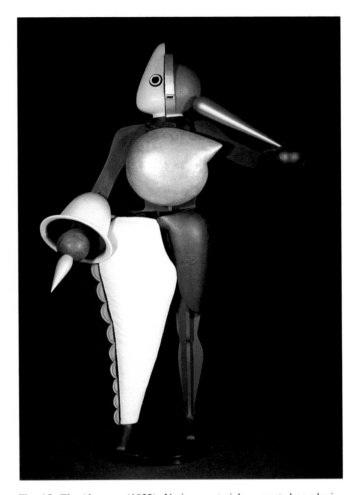

Fig. 15. *The Abstract*. (1922). Various materials, mounted on plexiglas armature. 79½ in. high. Staatsgalerie Stuttgart. [Not in exhibition; see cat. no. 60].

time and space, but who also perceived man as a microcosm of the macrocosm, recognizing that the basis of man's existence is ultimately inexplicable and that his being is mystically linked with the universe. The persuasive dogmatic element in *Paracelsus (The Lawgiver)*—the symmetrical frontality, the dark mass of the torso, the masklike form of the head with its hypnotic eyes, the raised left index finger, and the braced right fist—was entirely retracted, veiled, and shifted into a shadowy, unreal realm in the delicate *Head with Cup* (fig. 17), also of 1923, distantly reminiscent of the metaphysical still lifes of Carrà or Morandi, but lacking their veristic precision.

Whether he approached the human figure from the front, the back, or the side, Schlemmer discovered a new way to lend dimension to space, a possibility he exploited in both exemplary and magical fashion in his first group picture, the 1923 *Company at Table* (fig. 18). As if infused

Fig. 16. *Paracelsus (The Law-Giver)*. 1923. Oil. 39 × 29⅛ in.
Staatsgalerie Stuttgart. [Cat. no. 17].

Fig. 17. *Head with Cup*. 1923. Oil on paper. 22⁷⁄₁₆ × 15 in.
Daimler-Benz A.G., Stuttgart. [Cat. no. 16].

Fig. 18. *Company at Table*. 1923. Oil. 25³⁄₁₆ × 39⅞ in. Private
Collection. [Not in exhibition].

with the intoxication of discovery, everything in the picture appears heightened: the dominating, almost silhouetted form of a seated woman viewed from the rear; the enormous white table surface receding into the depths; in the background, a ghostly little figure dissolved in light, confronting both the woman and the viewer with a hypnotic stare. Between these two figures, on the left side of the long table, there is the figure of a boy, behind which a more distant figure seems to float out of the wall, raising its hand imploringly. Spatial positions, directions of gaze, and vanishing lines are reinterpreted to form an invisible net of psychic lines of force. Alternately, Schlemmer may completely retract the magical, menacing tension and the exaggerated depth and instead fix his subjects to the painted plane, as in *Women at Table* (fig. 19) of 1923 or in the lost picture *The Passerby*, of which we can get a sense from the watercolor of the same title of ca. 1924–1925 (fig. 20). Here the figure, viewed from the rear and concentrated into a dark parallelogram, is pinned to the surface in the motion of passing by; but behind it, visible only in the upper left of the picture, appear the illuminated backs of heads and faces of other figures, turned toward the nude boy who can be seen at the extreme left edge,

Fig. 20. *The Passerby*. (ca. 1924–1925). Pencil and watercolor. 9⅜ × 8½ in. Staatsgalerie Stuttgart: Collection Karin and U. Jaïna Schlemmer Deposit. [Cat. no. 140].

almost as a picture within a picture. Static and dynamic elements, depth and surface interact in a complex system of directional relations and juxtapositions, so that the picture becomes a section cut out of the surrounding space.

From now on, the increasingly dominant motif in Schlemmer's paintings is the figure viewed from the rear, usually standing on a central vertical, its shoulders at the intersection of the axes, as, for example, in *Lounge*, 1925 (fig. 21), a symmetrical configuration focused on a window whose mysterious emptiness and brightness exercise a powerful suction effect. Space, which in *Company at Table* still receded into indefinite depths, is limited and defined by architectural motifs in the paintings after 1925, but in such a way that a prospect, an opening, is always retained. Interior space in the picture, suggested by architectural elements reminiscent of a stage set, and natural space, of which only a slice is visible, enter into a triadic relationship with the observer's empirical field of perception. Thus the space portrayed in the picture becomes an imaginary station between real space and a free space that can only be divined, so that the transition from reality to transcendent reality occurs in stages, leading from the limited to the unlimited.

Fig. 19. *Women at Table*. 1923. Oil. 28¾ × 24 in. Kunstsammlung Nordrhein-Westfalen, Düsseldorf. [Not in exhibition].

Fig. 21. *Lounge*. 1925. Oil. 43⁵⁄₁₆ × 35⁷⁄₁₆ in. Staatsgalerie Stuttgart.
[Cat. no. 19].

This perspectivized space also has a temporal aspect, for the transfixed figures are tempted to move through the space toward the vanishing lines. In this fashion a curious ambivalence is created between temporal movement and timeless duration, an ambivalence particularly evident in a picture like *Lounge*. The stationary poses of the figures seem a momentary pause, as if captured shortly before the grouping shifts as one figure enters and another departs. This dialectic between time and space is shaped and emphasized by the use of those architectural features specifically designed to convey traffic from one space to another, such as corridors and stairways. In the compositions of 1925, particularly *Five Figures in a Room (Classical Style)*, the pictorial space becomes more ambient and less foreshortened; the figures are placed so that they relate to one another in multiple ways, and their gazes probe the space multidirectionally.

If space earlier had an isolating, alienating effect, in 1925 it became a framing motif, providing a setting in which each figure is assigned a suitable place for its own existence, but also a particular function within the group. This new vision certainly reflected Schlemmer's experience of the communal life at the Bauhaus, and from this vantage point his multifigured spatial pictures could be interpreted as a reflection of his intensified involvement with others. In any case, the inhabited world of Schlemmer's pictures stands in stark contrast to the abandoned streets, public squares, and interiors in the work of de Chirico and Carrà, whose figures almost always appear in isolation, surrounded only by objects resembling stage props. In their paintings the human element—at least up to 1919—is suppressed to such an extent that the people themselves become reified as mannequins, anthropomorphic torsos, or interchangeable elements in figural montages. Schlemmer's figures, on the other hand, seem full of life, in spite of their stereometric simplification and archetypicality. The magical suggestiveness of his paintings emanates not from motifs, from disconcerting figures or objects, but rather from minutely intertwined spatial and figural relations. As Schlemmer renounced enigmatic motifs (like the ghostly figure in *Company at Table*) and exaggerated recession into space, he moved away from the lifeless menace and *solitudine* of the Italian *pittura metafisica* and gained that classical calm and capacity for life that characterize *Five Figures in a Room (Classical Style)*. When art critics sometimes link Schlemmer's pictures from the first Bauhaus period to the Italians' "metaphysical painting," what they may overlook is the fact that Schlemmer's paintings grew out of experiences and perceptions all his own, and that they form a coherent part of his development. Achieving a synthesis of figure and architecture had been his primary concern from the outset, manifest in his work from his early explorations of Cubism to the figural plans of 1919. Schlemmer's adoption of depth and volume, his evolution from planimetric to stereometric figures, reflect an inner necessity, an outgrowth of his experiences as a dancer and his preoccupation with the Bauhaus program.

It was the concept of structure that mattered to Schlemmer, not one-point perspective, as can be seen when he renounced traditional perspective for the 1925 painting *Concentric Group* (fig. 22). Here the attempt to integrate volumetric figuration with constructivist planar organization resulted in concentrated mass. From the juxtaposition of deep space at the center of the picture, where the heads are densely clustered around the coordinate axes, and planimetric integration toward the edges of the picture, there emerges a columnar statuary effect focused on the illuminated nude figure. The relief-like profile treatment of figures at the center of a surface divided in four is reminiscent of earlier compositions, particularly the 1919 *Ornamental Sculpture on Divided Frame* (see fig. 84), except that by 1925 everything had been translated into figural motifs and pure painting. *Concentric Group* also demonstrates how masterfully Schlemmer employed color for planar-spatial syncopation. While the dark sections, arranged diagonally, seem optically opaque and thus close to the surface, the light parts recede, letting the plane expand, until it finally throws open an imaginary space, glimpsed in a flash through the door-like aperture above.

Schlemmer's unique position vis-à-vis similar currents in European painting of the early 1920's rests chiefly on his extraordinary ability to resolve divergent impulses. In his pictorial world the physical and symbolic alienation of human figures, the menacing isolation so evident in the work of his Italian contemporaries, are gradually diminished as each figure becomes part of an orchestrally organized group. The individual figure plays its own role in creating spatial and metaphysical dimensionality, creating "community" while preserving its own viability. In 1925, shortly before his move to Dessau, Schlemmer painted his last picture, *Contemplative Figure* (see the watercolor, *Contemplative Figure I*, fig. 23), as a sort of "renunciation" of painting, before he threw himself entirely into theatrical endeavors.[11]

Fig. 22. *Concentric Group*. 1925. Oil. 38⅜ × 24⅜ in. Staatsgalerie Stuttgart. [Cat. no. 18].

Fig. 23. *Contemplative Figure I.* (1925). Watercolor over pencil.
10¾ × 8⅝ in. Staatsgalerie Stuttgart: Schlemmer Family Estate
Deposit. [Cat. no. 143].

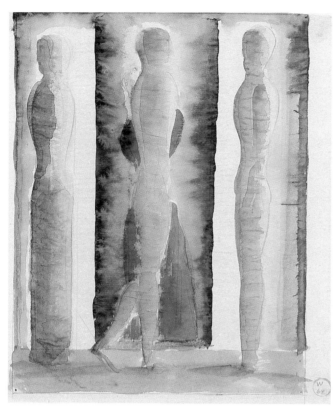

Fig. 24. *Triptych III*. (1925). Pencil and watercolor. 10½ × 8⅞ in. Staatsgalerie Stuttgart: Schlemmer Family Estate Deposit. [Cat. no. 150].

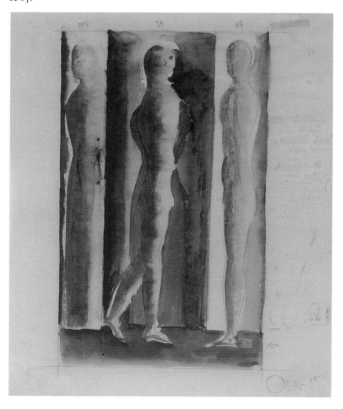

Fig. 25. *Triptych V*. 1925. Pencil and watercolor. 9¼ × 5½ in. Staatsgalerie Stuttgart: Schlemmer Family Estate Deposit. [Cat. no. 151].

The Dynamic Element and the Cycle

Schlemmer returned to painting only three years later, motivated by a commission from the Museum Folkwang in Essen. These first paintings done in 1928 reveal a number of divergent impulses. Some of them, like *Triptych* (see figs. 24 and 25), take up where his Weimar compositions left off, retaining their clear, taut concept of space and figure. In contrast to the archaic, statuesque quality of this row of column-like figures, reminiscent of ancient Greek kouroi, the painting *Idealistic Encounter* (fig. 26), also from the year 1928, seems full of dynamic tension. Here Schlemmer introduced dramatic diagonal relationships and light-dark contrasts to create an imaginary space, out of which the two figures rise up as in a dream. The surreal qualities of this composition were not, however, repeated in other pictures of this last Bauhaus period, when Schlemmer returned to more strictly tectonic configurations.

Schlemmer's major preoccupation during the last year in Dessau and the early Breslau period was his work on the cycle of murals for the fountain room in the Museum Folkwang. His first experimental panel for the project, the 1928 *Four Figures and a Cube* (fig. 27), proved to have such a monumental effect that in the relatively small rotunda it overpowered Georg Minne's fountain. In later versions Schlemmer took greater pains to adapt to the existing architectural conditions, which were quite restrictive. He struggled with the commission for three years, and produced three different versions—a total of twenty-four compositions as well as a series of related trial panels and paintings and drawings in various sizes (figs. 28 and 29). Using the theme of "instruction" as his point of departure for the first version, Schlemmer painted five panels with multiple figures and four large panels with single figures, intended to flank the doors (see figs. 30 and 31, *Fallen Figure with Column* and *Blue Painting*). All but two panels of this version have been preserved. When the nine panels were hung, Schlemmer was not entirely satisfied with the relationship between the series of figures emerging ghostlike from foggy backgrounds and the large, fully articulated nudes. He therefore decided to use only nude figures in the second version, of which only the pastel cartoons are preserved (see figs. 32, 33, 34). He used one single nude; eight groups of two to five

Fig. 26. *Idealistic Encounter*. 1928. Oil. 36⁷⁄₁₆ × 23¹³⁄₁₆ in. Collection of Rolf and Margit Weinberg, Zurich. [Not in exhibition].

Fig. 27. *Four Figures and a Cube*. (1928). Oil. 96⅝ × 63 in. Staatsgalerie Stuttgart. [Cat. no. 25].

youths performing rhythmic gymnastic movements; and architecturally-suggestive motifs such as stairs, railings, rectangular fields, and, once, a symbolic circle. The bright, weightless effect of these pastels at first seemed ideal, but it was again feared that the Minne fountain would suffer by comparison.

With heavy heart Schlemmer set to work in Breslau on the third version, of which only pastels have been preserved. He returned to his formula for the first version, combining four large individual figures with five panels containing three to five figures. But he generated completely new compositions for this version (figs. 35–38). He abandoned the earlier concentrically arranged groups in favor of asymmetrical triangular arrangements of clothed and unclothed planar figures, suspended in rectangular fields of graduated colors, layered in planes. In contrast to the five gray-toned panels with their cut-out-like figures,

Fig. 29. *Folkwang Group IV: Group with Figures Ascending Staircase.* (1928). Tempera. 20¹⁵⁄₁₆ × 13⅜ in. Staatsgalerie Stuttgart. [Cat. no. 174].

the four large nudes floated, almost translucent, against a reddish-violet background done with a spray technique. When this last version of the Folkwang cycle finally went on display in the Schlesischen Museum in Breslau in 1930, before being shipped for installation in Essen, Schlemmer spoke in a radio interview of the conception underlying the commission:

> I resisted the temptation to portray an allegory of life; even though that would have seemed the obvious and conventional approach in such a case. I wanted to respond to the simple gesture of the figures in Minne's fountain by portraying the simple existence of figures, without pathos, without dramatic movement, without telling stories! For the painter or sculptor, simple acts of the human figure, such as inclining the head, raising an arm, gesturing with the hand, moving a leg, provide such an expressive richness that themes such as standing, coming, going, turning, and the like would suffice to occupy an artist's lifetime.[12]

Fig. 28. *Folkwang Group I: Instruction.* (1928). Watercolor. 18⅝ × 12⅝ in. Staatsgalerie Stuttgart. [Cat. no. 173].

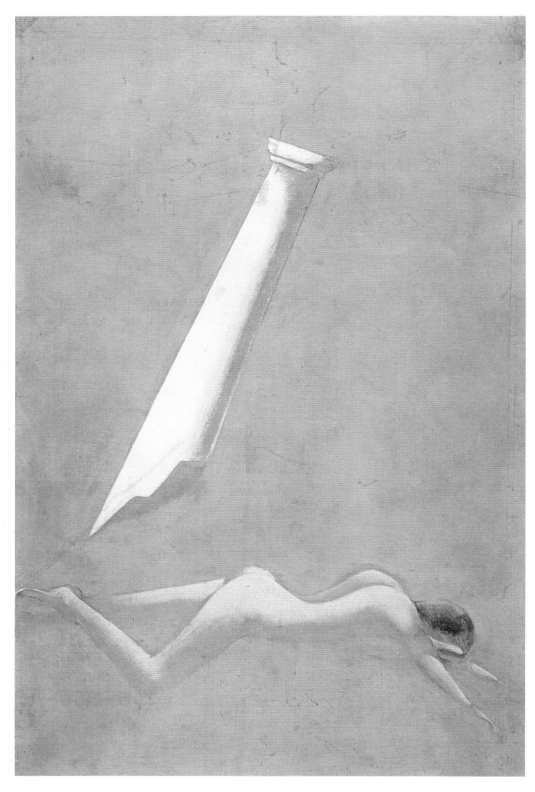

Fig. 30. *Fallen Figure with Column*. (1928/1929). Oil. 94⅛ × 61 in.
Staatsgalerie Stuttgart. [Cat. no. 28].

Fig. 31. *Blue Painting*. 1928. Oil. 49⅜ × 46¼ in. Öffentliche
Kunstsammlung Basel: Private Collection Deposit. [Cat. no. 22].

Fig. 32. *Folkwang Cycle II: Stepped Group of Four with Angular Arm Gestures.* (1929–1930). Pastel over charcoal. 90 × 60⅝ in. Staatsgalerie Stuttgart. [Cat. no. 181].

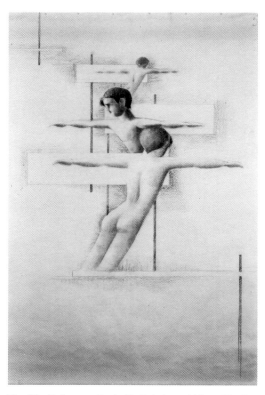

Fig. 33. *Folkwang Cycle II: Echelon of Three Youths with Outstretched Arms.* (1929–1930). Pastel over charcoal. 88⅝ × 59 in. Staatsgalerie Stuttgart. [Cat. no. 179].

Fig. 34. *Folkwang Cycle II: Floating and Stretching Youth in a Circular Form.* (1929–1930). Pastel over charcoal. 91⅛ × 60⅞ in. Staatsgalerie Stuttgart. [Cat. no. 180].

This programmatic statement summarizes Schlemmer's most fundamental artistic aspirations. Just as he stripped the human figure of all expressive and personal attributes, he also excluded all illustrative, mimetic, and allegorical references, so that he could restrict himself to elemental, absolute form that would yield a new symbolic meaning. Here Schlemmer's intentions coincide with those of Hans von Marées (1837–1887): both considered the human figure the painter's "supreme challenge," and to both of them the human figure was not an individual model but a general type, not a vehicle of expression but a formed organism whose structural principles had to be made visible. Both of them created canonical figures, fundamental types distinguished only in their poses and movements, for both painters considered the human figure the "first and foremost means of shaping space" (Marées). Posture and gesture, form, color, and light all served to shape surface and depth within the picture. Each individual movement and juxtaposition was necessarily related to every other and was subordinated to overall pictorial structure. The only difference was that as a child of the new century and as beneficiary of the Cubist experience, Schlemmer was free to experiment more radically with that "primary object," man, in relation to the tectonics of abstract space.

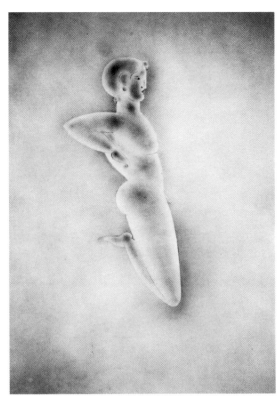

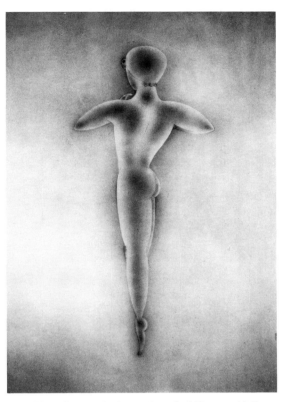

Fig. 35. *Folkwang Cycle III: Figure of a Youth with Bent Knees, Seen from the Side.* (1930). Sprayed casein. 92½ × 63 in. Whereabouts unknown.

Fig. 36. *Folkwang Cycle III: Stretched Figure with Bent Arms Raised, Seen from Behind.* (1930). Sprayed casein. 92½ × 63 in. Whereabouts unknown.

Fig. 37. *Folkwang Cycle III: Group of Three, One above the Others.* (1930). Oil. 92½ × 63 in. Whereabouts unknown.

Fig. 38. *Folkwang Cycle III: Group of Five with Central Nude Figure.* (1930). Oil. 92½ × 63 in. Whereabouts unknown.

Fig. 39. *Group of Fourteen in Imaginary Architecture*. 1930. Oil. 36 × 47⁷⁄₁₆ in. Museum Ludwig, Cologne. [Not in exhibition].

Human Architecture and Banister Scenes

In compositions done around 1930, during and after his taxing three-year preoccupation with the Folkwang panels, Schlemmer effortlessly mastered large formats and complex arrangements of figures; organically-shaped nudes increasingly came to the fore. In multifigured pictures like *Group of Fourteen in Imaginary Architecture*, 1930 (fig. 39), or *Group of Fifteen*, 1929 (fig. 40), a certain expansiveness and a tendency to round the body are evident. These paintings demonstrate how intent Schlemmer was on bringing out the "imaginary inner structure" of the nude. The "architecture" of the human body is beginning to supplant the "architecture" of constructed pictorial space. An unmistakable component of these

1929–1930 works is a new awareness of the body and a tendency to vitalize figuration, a more generalized artistic phenomenon in Europe in the late 1920's.

Expressionism, Cubism, and Futurism had deformed, dismembered, or obliterated the human image; now artists began to feel the need to find their way back to a harmonious, integrated portrayal of man. This development can be observed in the work of Picasso, Léger, Derain, Carrà, Severini, Carl Hofer, Baumeister, Rudolf Belling, Archipenko, and others. In part, the impulse grew out of the naturopathic movement that began shortly after the turn of the century, and the attempt to liberate and perfect natural human beauty through hygiene, sports, and dance. The proponents of this movement wanted to instill in man not only a new awareness of his own body, but also a new sense of life and of community, with nature and spirit functioning together as equals. Thus the

Fig. 40. *Group of Fifteen*. 1929. Oil. 70⅛ × 39⅜ in. Wilhelm-Lehmbruck-Museum der Stadt Duisburg. [Cat. no. 30].

Fig. 41. *Group with Ecstatic Figure in Blue*. 1931. Oil. 47⅞ × 26
in. Hamburger Kunsthalle. [Cat. no. 35].

German writer Hermann Kasack declared in 1925 that sports were the "contemporary manifestation of the spirit," and the "great athletic events of the twentieth century will create a new 'community' whose faith, ecstasy, sense of harmony with the world will be more compelling and more apparent than that of a church, a nation, or a political party."[13] And it was Léger who in 1932, viewing the new production of *The Triadic Ballet* and other works by German dance troupes at the international dance competition in Paris, spoke enthusiastically of the birth of a "new choreographic order," reminiscent of athletic processions and military parades, whose disciplined formations had swept away classical ballet's obsolete leaps and toe-dancing.[14]

Since *The Triadic Ballet* of 1922 Schlemmer had largely given up stereometric camouflaging of the human figure, and in his painting he had been moving ever closer to the living model; increasingly in both painting and the dance, the human figure was, for Schlemmer, both the derivation and the expressive vehicle of his formal invention. It is

hardly surprising, therefore, that he enunciated this change of style in a lecture in 1929 in Darmstadt under the manifesto-like title, "Man the Beautiful in Contemporary Art"; he spoke of the dawning of a "renaissance in the portrayal of man," and of a rebirth of the ideals of "artistically beautiful man"—ideals which he defined as "creations born of the combination and the ideal balance of abstraction, proportion, and law on the one hand and nature, feeling, and idea on the other."[15] Schlemmer's 1929 painting *Clothed and Unclothed Figures in Architecture*, fig. 42 (which won him a gold medal in Darmstadt and was destroyed by fire during the war), and the works of other sculptors and painters document neoclassical tendencies in European art of the time; a few years later such tendencies would be co-opted by the Nazis, who bent them to their own ideological, racist purposes. In their work of this period Schlemmer and his contemporaries clearly evidenced a strong desire for centering and order, in response to an era made chaotic by political radicalization, emergency decrees, and mass unemploy-

Fig. 42. *Clothed and Unclothed Figures in Architecture.* 1929. Oil. 35⅝ × 59¼ in. Destroyed in World War II.

ment. There can also be no question that Hitler knew how to harness this latent desire for order in the service of his own political aims.

Schlemmer did not tarry long with the athletically inspired forms of the 1929–1930 paintings. The next year the pictorial tensions of his human "architectures" began to relax. He spoke of a heightened sense of life that wants "to break out of the old shell and rigidity and flow outwards."[16] Certainly the agreeable atmosphere at the Staatliche Akademie für Kunst und Kunstgewerbe (State Academy for Art and the Crafts) in Breslau, where he went to teach in 1929, and the Baroque architecture in Silesia proved stimulating. In any case, what he himself described as his "baroque phase" culminated in the spring of 1931 in paintings like *Group with Ecstatic Figure in Blue* (fig. 41). Instead of statuary concentration and clarity we suddenly see a flowing, wave-like rhythm which surrounds and erodes the figures, underscored by a sonorous chromatic chord in blue, violet, red, and ocher, out of which the faces emerge vividly, like bright fanfares. The dignified pathos of the gesture of the focal "Ecstatic Figure in Blue," illuminated by flickering reflections of light, heightens the drama of the scene; the composition reminds one of Schlemmer's fondness for Handel.

To discipline his baroque impulses, Schlemmer again turned to schematized architectural motifs. They no longer compartmentalize space like backdrops; they are stair and banister motifs which, instead of spatial layering, provide a framework in which to arrange figures on the same plane in order to fill the entire picture surface. In modified form Schlemmer was following his intention to relate plane and volume, figure and architecture, except that now the space is more filled by the figures—indeed, often completely obscured by them. One of Schlemmer's most compelling series of pictures was painted with these stair and banister motifs in 1931–1932 (see figs. 43, 44, 46, 47).

There are probable psychological reasons for Schlemmer's sudden attraction to staircase motifs after his period of baroque indulgence. Although in the early 1930's he felt at the height of his powers and at the high point of his career as both an artist and teacher, he consciously forced himself to restrain his desire to let forms and colors flow freely, precisely because he was aware of the dangers of indulging himself. The "scaffolding" or banister motifs provided him with support and stability in the face of what he felt to be irrational subconscious forces, a structure both literal and pictorial to channel those forces into rationality. In the Breslau paintings Schlemmer's "plunging into the fullness of life" (Goethe) on the one hand and his use of staircase forms on the other express the profound dualism of feeling and reason, of Dionysian and

Fig. 43. *Group at Banister*. 1931. Oil. 36⅜ × 23¹³⁄₁₆ in. Kunstsammlung Nordrhein-Westfalen, Düsseldorf. [Not in exhibition].

Apollonian impulses, whose tension he experienced throughout his life and attempted to resolve through his art. A number of paintings, notable among them the 1932 *Staircase Scene* (fig. 44), are marked, for all their beauty, by this struggle for self-control, which lends them both a compulsive and a compelling character.

Thus it happened that on the eve of Hitler's assumption of power Schlemmer urgently called upon "measure and law" as salvation from chaos, while he also warned insistently against blind submission: "Experience has taught me that proportion and the basic laws signify something very noble in art, but also something very dangerous. . . . The initial impulse should be emotion, the stream of the unconscious, free, unfettered creation. The more latitude feeling receives, the more readily it will gravitate toward precision, compressing the picture into final form without help from the laws of proportion or measurement."[17] This goal of purification and clarifi-

Fig. 44. *Stairway Scene*. 1932. Oil. 47⅝ × 22¹⁄₁₆ in. Hamburger
Kunsthalle. [Not in exhibition].

Fig. 45. T. Lux Feininger (German, born 1910). *Gunta Stölzl, head of weaving workshop, with students, Bauhaus stairs*. (ca. 1930). Photograph. 4½ × 3⅜ in. Courtesy Prakapas Gallery, New York. [Not in exhibition].

the window at center right. An artistic reality is here held up as exemplary contrast to everyday life: the Bauhaus, understood as a symbol of youth's aspiration to a brighter future.

Banister Scene, 1932 (fig. 46), Schlemmer's last painting before his move to Berlin, reveals an easy synthesis of human and architectural forms. Organization of space according to the rules of Euclidean geometric perspective is modified here in order to suggest infinitely extensible imaginary space. Both figure and architectural setting lose their firm contours; they are bathed in fluid striations of light and dark. In several watercolors from the Breslau period, Schlemmer took particular advantage of the medium to produce lovely effects by layering bundles of colored rays over the depicted figures (see fig. 48). He

cation was an unending struggle to achieve harmony between these two realms, a harmony Schlemmer captured to monumental effect in his most significant compositions. His success is particularly striking in his best known painting, *Bauhaus Stairway* (fig. 47), on which he was working in the summer of 1932 when word reached him in Breslau that the Bauhaus in Dessau had been closed. Out of the building blocks of memory, he recreated the transcendent architecture of the staircase in the Dessau Bauhaus building (see fig. 45), creating a pictorial structure that recapitulated all the essential elements of his painting from the 1920's: the arrangement of figures, which corresponds to the movement of the painting's verticals and diagonals; slices of figures at the canvas edges that lead the eye toward the center of the picture and emphasize that the scene represents a segment of a whole; the triadic central group, which organizes both the surface and the depth; the countermovement of the tiny figure descending the staircase at the upper right, of the figure seemingly suspended on the landing, and the figure glimpsed through

Fig. 46. *Banister Scene*. (1932). Oil. 41½ × 27¾ in. Staatsgalerie Stuttgart. [Cat. no. 37].

Fig. 47. *Bauhaus Stairway*. (1932). Oil. 63⅜ × 44½ in. The
Museum of Modern Art, New York: Gift of Philip Johnson. [Cat.
no. 38].

Fig. 48. *Seated Figure, in Colored Stripes in front of Checkered Background*. 1932. Watercolor. 22 × 16½ in. Staatsgalerie Stuttgart: Schlemmer Family Estate Deposit. [Cat. no. 203].

achieved a similarly transparent modulation of light and dark in *Banister Scene* by applying oil paint in a glaze technique. This transparency contributes to the metaphysical, visionary aspects of the picture. In Schlemmer's earlier work color contributed primarily to establishing tensions between plane and depth, as is still the case in *Bauhaus Stairway*; more often in this period, however, color modulation served to meld figure, space, surface, and light, which were thus brought into a constantly shifting relationship.

It was not only Schlemmer's painting of this period that tended toward dematerialization, with light playing a decisive part. His sculpture, too, manifests this tendency. The open-work, weightless, shadow-casting wire construction he produced for a wall in Zwenkau in 1931 (see figs. 112–115), and the *Banister Scene* of 1932 in which the figures are illuminated and made transparent, equally show the artist whisking his image of man off to safety in a transcendent realm at the very time when his person and his art were most threatened as victims of defamation.

Fig. 49. *Conversation*. (1935). Oil on paper. 16⅝ × 23⅛ in. Daimler-Benz A.G., Stuttgart. [Cat. no. 40].

Pictures Out of Darkness

In 1937, after several years of suppression, Schlemmer was able to exhibit his most recent pictures at the Ferdinand Möller Gallery in Berlin and the Valentien Gallery in Stuttgart. They were to be his last lifetime exhibitions. Once more his paintings had undergone apparent change. Instead of the bright clarity and color of his last Breslau compositions, the new pieces were immersed in darkness, and the figures seemed to press close together against an undefined background. Schlemmer now aimed for a kind of painting that could convey unfathomable depths purely by means of scrubbed coloration. Unable to obtain canvas, he began to use oilpaper, which did not need priming,

could easily be hidden from unwelcome visitors, and with its smooth, gleaming yellowish finish provided a warm, glowing surface on which to paint.

In paintings like *Conversation*, 1935 (fig. 49), or *Gray Women*, 1936 (fig. 50), Schlemmer created a conspiratorial atmosphere by orchestrating varied gray and violet tones against the light background of the paper. In 1936 at Whitsuntide he produced the surprising series of abstract symbol pictures, called *Arabesques* (see fig. 52), those "aesthetic births" and "eruptions" that Schlemmer explored as an "act of liberation."[18] In contrast to the eccentric, almost whimsical *Arabesque* abstractions, Schlemmer next painted a group of pictures in which closely cropped figures viewed from the rear almost claustrophobically dominate the composition, like *Seated Figure at Table (Seen from Behind)*, 1936 (fig. 51), obscuring the depicted setting and merely hinting at the

Fig. 50. *Gray Women*. (1936). Oil on paper. 26½ × 19¾ in.
Collection of U. Jaïna Schlemmer. [Cat. no. 43].

existence of something beyond by means of a lightening of color. That Schlemmer considered such isolated figures turned toward the interior of the picture as reflections of both personal and political events of the times can be seen from statements such as, ''To create heroic solitudes— that, too, is an image of the times!''[19]

In the summer of 1937 Schlemmer's pictures were removed from German museums and pilloried in the exhibition of ''Entartete Kunst'' (''Degenerate Art''). Once again Schlemmer gave up painting for three years, while he tried to support himself and his family. Although his job conducting technical research with a Stuttgart painting contractor had some superficial connection with his own calling, the compromises he was constantly forced to make cut him off from his artistic identity more than an entirely unrelated job might have. Not until 1940, when Baumeister arranged for him to work at Dr. Kurt Herberts' paint factory in Wuppertal, where a number of artists were employed, did he find his way back to his own art, at least intermittently.

Fig. 52. *Arabesque (with Circle and Rectangle)*. (1936). Oil on paper. 25⅜ × 18⅞ in. Family Estate of Oskar Schlemmer. [Cat. no. 42].

Fig. 51. *Seated Figure at Table (Seen from Behind)*. (1936). Oil on paper. 29⅝ × 23⁵⁄₁₆ in. Museum Folkwang Essen. [Not in exhibition].

New Artistic Paths

The most striking features of Schlemmer's painting during his last two years in Wuppertal are their miniature formats and their prescient stylistic elements. Schlemmer drew inspiration for these endeavors partly from his contact with new painting techniques, particularly the use of lacquer paints, but also from his readings in Oriental philosophy and art. For quite some time Schlemmer had explicitly incorporated in his art chance discoveries from his surroundings or from nature. He now strove to capture an art ''from somewhere,'' an art that would look as though it had not been created by human hands, an art with ''no trace of the wretched paint brush.'' While engaged in this search, he discovered the technique of making blot prints, which allowed him to achieve unexpected effects ''from somewhere.'' He had been leafing through a 1936 issue of the *Minotaure* and had come upon reproductions of *décalcomanies* by the French Surrealists. He promptly tried his hand at this technique (fig. 53).[20] That was the beginning of his series of monotypes or "splotchographics," as he called them, a term he borrowed from the Romantic writer Justinus Kerner.[21] The blots of paint seemed to form themselves into figures. These are pictures of a delicate, flowing vividness, ethereal modulations in which the figures dissolve into irreality. Yet Schlemmer regarded this work as dabbling; for what he considered his serious work, he still wanted to stay with the visible world. Whereas Baumeister greatly admired the symbolic quality of the late Klee, Schlemmer found in the drawings of Seurat confirmation of his conviction that the visible world had to remain his point of departure. Perhaps he also sensed that he did not have much more time, and that he could no longer afford the risky adventure of seeking "the unknown in art." This insight spurred him to new activity, and in the space of four months, between April and July 1942, his last works came in a flood of intense activity.

Fig. 53. *Tilted Head I.* (1941). Monotype. 7⅛ × 4¹/₁₆ in. Family Estate of Oskar Schlemmer. [Cat. no. 213].

Window Pictures

The visible world, to which Schlemmer now dedicated himself with new fervor, was close at hand in his immediate surroundings. He had only to look out of the window of his room in Wuppertal (at Döppersberg) to see down below the flood canal of the Wupper River, and on the far side a high, gray wall, with the arched windows of a Baptist church hemmed in by the rear façades of five-story tenements. Schlemmer was fascinated by this view, which reminded him of Venice. Every evening he sat at the window, "like a hunter in a blind," and recorded in his sketchbook a flurry of motifs. He filled page after page with stenographic notations for his *Fensterbilder* ("window pictures"): pencil or ink sketches, with notes and indications of color for the final versions. Then he went to work on the paintings, turning out one after the other on cardboard or oilpaper, each piece no larger than a sheet of stationery, with brush, crayon, and oils applied in transparent glazes and subtle mixes, sometimes washed out again in stripes, so that a fine texture seemed to veil the figures (see figs. 54 and 55). He used a whole variety of muntin arrangements, behind which everyday domestic scenes could be glimpsed: a woman cooking or ironing, partially obscured by curtains or laundry hanging on the line; a family at the supper table, suggested rather than clearly illustrated behind the window frame. Seen thus from a distance, the perceived images coalesce into a fabric of color and form that imagination alone could scarcely have generated.

Schlemmer painted in a state of intoxication; he had never felt so much in harmony with himself and his art, so sure of having found the synthesis in which reality and abstraction, natural and artistic truth were effortlessly united. In a letter to Julius Bissier written in May 1942 he first mentions this blissful condition:

> I am a painter, after all, and have recently completed a series of pictures, inspired by what I see right around me: views from my window into the neighboring window, done in the evening between nine and half-past nine, shortly before the blackout. When night is falling and clashes with the scraps of interior beige-orange-brown-white-black, it produces amazing optical effects. I am experiencing with unfamiliar intensity the mystic force that resides in the optical effects of nature, and I observe that with the passing years one keeps learning to see in new and different ways.[22]

But this renewed joy in creating did not necessarily result in especially cheerful pictures. On the contrary, the window pictures radiate a restrained melancholy, fed perhaps by Schlemmer's longing for his family and domestic security. The wall and the coordinate axes of the windows, which establish order but also distance, make the figures appear far-off and shadowy: the artist is standing outside, no longer actively involved in the lives of others. In spite of, or perhaps precisely because of, that separation, these fragments of everyday reality revealed to the wistful artist a symbolic glimpse of the world as a whole and the "miracle of the visible."[23]

This vision gave Schlemmer his answer to the question of abstraction and surrealism—they could be perceived in reality and portrayed through reality. In this spirit he wrote to Bissier: "Nowadays, when I no longer believe in the infallibility of Picasso-style abstraction and also cannot find the courage to applaud the moderns of those days, I find the world of the visible opening up to me in a remarkable fashion, in all its density and surrealistic mystique."[24] Preference for the window motif, which can

Fig. 55. *Window Picture III: Living Room with Standing Woman.* (1942). Oil. 12⅞ × 9 in. Öffentliche Kunstsammlung Basel: Schlemmer Family Estate Deposit. [Cat. no. 49].

Fig. 54. *Window Picture XII: Room with Seated Woman in Violet Shadow.* 1942. Oil. 12 × 8⅛ in. Öffentliche Kunstsammlung Basel: Schlemmer Family Estate Deposit. [Cat. no. 50].

be traced through all of Schlemmer's work (see *Lounge* of 1925 [fig. 21]), rests not only on a formal interest in the structure provided by the window muntins or in the geometric clarity of a rectangular section of light; rather, it reveals Schlemmer's pervasive aspiration to see beyond tangible things, to make the invisible visible, to bring another, unknown world into view, a transcendent realm opening up behind the immanent world of appearances. On May 23, 1942 Schlemmer wrote in his diary: "When the creative spirit comes over one . . . one becomes nothing but a medium, a tool . . . a transitional agent."[25] He saw himself as transitory in the most cosmic sense of being, a personal philosophy related to Oriental spiritualism and reflected in his last pictures in their interpenetration of man, light, and space. Schlemmer's final diary entry was a quotation from Rainer Maria Rilke: " . . . to consider art not a piece plucked out of the world, but the complete and utter transformation of the world into pure glory. . . ."[26]

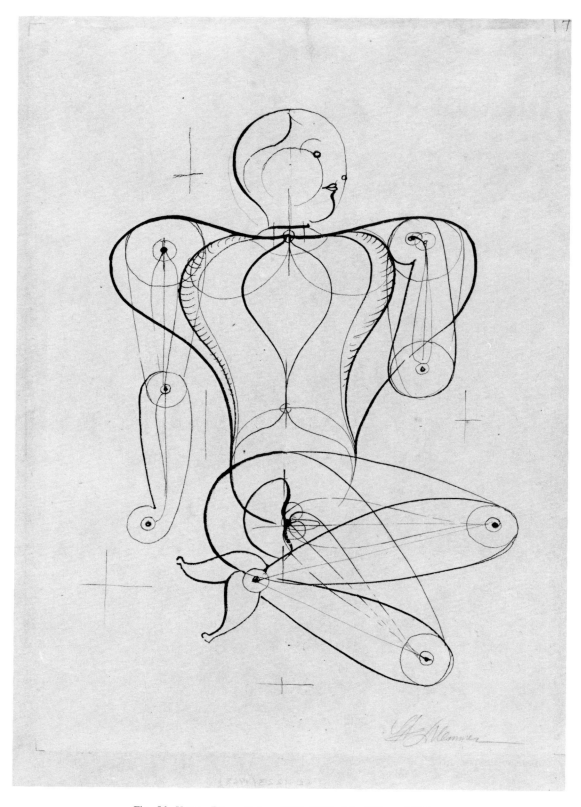

Fig. 56. *Homo, Figure T.* (ca. 1920–1921). Ink. 16¼ × 11⅜ in. Staatsgalerie Stuttgart: Schlemmer Family Estate Deposit. [Cat. no. 101].

Schlemmer's Drawings and Graphics

Oskar Schlemmer's drawings, like those of many other artists, often provide the most direct access to the faceted evolution of his work. The drawings comprise a record of both major and minor preoccupations. Working in pencil or pen and ink, chalk, watercolor, or pastel allows a kind of spontaneity that can capture the original artistic impetus. Schlemmer's works in these mediums document the often extended genesis of the large paintings. Yet they also develop so independently over the years that we find—particularly among the watercolors—many fully realized compositions that were never turned into paintings, and often were not intended to be.

The specific choice of medium in various periods reveals Schlemmer's changing stylistic interests and his highly developed sensitivity to the expressive possibilities and limits of each. In the Stuttgart years Schlemmer displayed a decided preference for India ink. In his painting before 1920 he renounced three-dimensional modeling, spatial perspective, and strong color in favor of tightened planar relations; likewise in his drawings of the time he confined

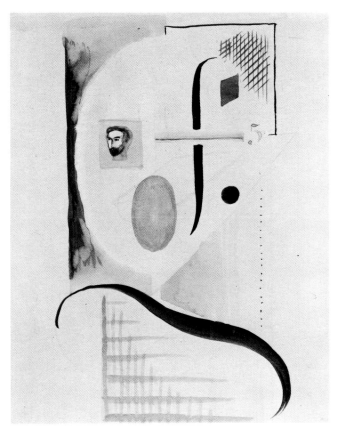

Fig. 57. *Abstraction with Figure 5 and Head.* (ca. 1915). Watercolor. 11 × 8⅜ in. Family Estate of Oskar Schlemmer. [Cat. no. 77].

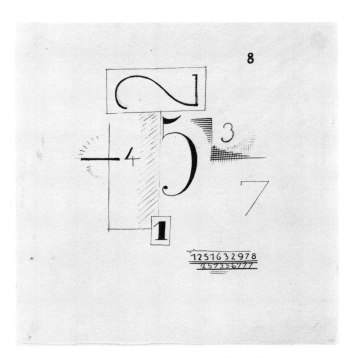

Fig. 58. *Numerology with 5.* (1919). Ink. 13¼ × 12⅝ in. Staatsgalerie Stuttgart: Schlemmer Family Estate Deposit. [Cat. no. 97].

Fig. 59. *Numerology with 8.* (1919). Pencil and ink. 13⅜ × 12¾ in. Staatsgalerie Stuttgart: Schlemmer Family Estate Deposit. [Cat. no. 98].

himself to refinements of line. Thus Schlemmer noted in his diary on September 2, 1915, speaking of his young German contemporaries, "They lack a unifying line. Sharpness, ruggedness, precision. The magnificence of any conception depends on the clarity with which it is perceived."[27] The finality of drawing in India ink, the harsh contrast between the black contours and the white paper, the brittle quality of the medium, all accommodated his desire for precision and imposed an artistic form. In both intention and ultimate significance the early drawings are preparatory drafts, sketches of ideas, formal experiments, often merely tentative first steps on the way to a new language of form and a distinctive style. The fine line of the sharp pen, confined to a single contour, looks engraved, the figure fixed in curiously rigid, unrhythmic outlines. If his figural abbreviations seem depersonalized, the artist also concealed his own personality behind the spare, formulaic style, deliberately eschewing "cute little artistic tricks" in order to limit himself to "registration of the necessities."[28] What he saw served merely as a springboard, allowing him to discover the basic formula

Fig. 60. *Four Figures in Stereo-Perspective.* (ca. 1924–1925). Watercolor. 10½ × 8⅝ in. Staatsgalerie Stuttgart. [Cat. no. 139].

Fig. 61. *Two Standing Figures and a Figure on a Narrow Staircase.* (ca. 1924–1925). Watercolor. 10¾ × 8⅝ in. Staatsgalerie Stuttgart. [Cat. no. 141].

through a step-by-step reduction process. With increasing decisiveness he employed strict linearity and planarity as "obligatory forms" and "weapons" to achieve the desired "systematic depersonalization" and renewal of form, in accordance with his maxim: "Form provides the guise and the framework within which the idea manifests itself. I would like to devote myself completely and absolutely to pure form until I have it at the beck and call of the idea."[29]

One can see the extent to which he achieved pure abstraction from the little group of number diagrams from about 1915–1919 (figs. 57, 58, 59), which at that time were comparable, if at all, only to certain typographical experiments by the Italian Futurists. Schlemmer deployed these forms as structural devices, using the numeral as a graphic element, though at the same time undeniably endowing it with cabalistic significance and numerological mystery. Gradually he evolved a repertory of typified yet protean figural motifs that were arranged in a plane into figural schemes fully independent of literal references.

The result was transparent, taut, layered, or colliding line—formations that stand almost in relief against the white paper, like transparent grilles against the emptiness of space. It was around 1920 that Schlemmer finally hit upon the definitive conception of a new type of artistic creature, the "differentiated man": in the drawing *Homo, Figure T* (fig. 56), which—half jointed doll, half archaic deity—may be seen as the symbolic representation of this first, analytic phase of his creative life. He would return to it a decade later for his Zwenkau wire sculpture. A distinct feeling for graphic contour, for weightlessness and filigree effects, and for precision, characteristics of his early ink drawings, ultimately led him naturally to sculptural creations in wire, a medium which can delineate and contain space and materialize contours.

During the Bauhaus period, when Schlemmer introduced sculptural figures into his painting, his graphic work consisted chiefly of pencil studies and watercolors that bear witness to a different set of preoccupations. Pencil drawing makes possible a modulated use of shading, which suited a body-oriented conception of figuration. The important "gallery pictures" of the years 1923–1925 were primarily prepared in watercolor; the colorful tonal values were added as elements to convey mood; formal structure is more relaxed. The result was a series of blooming watercolors on tissue paper whose sensitive language of brush and light, transparent color creates an evanescent effect. When the watercolors were translated into oils, this quality was sacrificed for tightly structured tectonic effects, and the character of the picture often changed markedly. Watercolor studies like *The Passerby*, ca. 1924–1925, or *Contemplative Figure I*, 1925 (see figs. 20 and 23), are all the more valuable to us because the oil paintings based on them fell victim to the vandalism practiced against "degenerate art" under the Nazis.

Gradually the watercolor became a genre Schlemmer cultivated for its own sake, and the pictures he did in this medium showed increasing complexity in the treatment of space. In *Four Figures in Stereo-Perspective* (fig. 60) and *Two Standing Figures and a Figure on a Narrow Staircase* (fig. 61), both of ca. 1924–1925, space is pushed back in sequential steps toward the background, like a stage set, creating cells of space that hug the outlines of the figures. Never before had Schlemmer's pictures displayed such fusion of man with space; but despite the almost archaic reserve of the figures, the interior of the picture is marked by powerful tension, the result of a new element to which the entire configuration conforms: direct recession of space into depth, portrayed in boldly truncated perspective, whether as a narrow passageway or as a staircase leading to an illuminated doorway, on whose threshold the silhouette of a dark figure appears.

The print shop at the Bauhaus, under Lyonel Feininger's direction, stimulated Schlemmer to design his most handsome graphics. When the *Neue europäische Graphik* series was introduced in 1922, the first portfolio contained fourteen pages of work by masters at the Bauhaus, including two lithographs by Schlemmer, *Figure H2*, a variation on the homo motif, and *Design with Figures K1*. A year later a portfolio was issued to coincide with the Bauhaus exhibition; Schlemmer contributed his only engraving, still another variation on the homo motif. But the high point of Schlemmer's graphic oeuvre is the series of six color lithographs published in October 1923, *Play with Heads* (see figs. 63, 64, 65). Here he tried a spray technique for the first time, achieving a curious synthesis of structural clarity, seen in the almost mathematical

Fig. 62. *Dancer*. 1923. Lithograph. 24¼ × 17⅛ in. Staatsgalerie Stuttgart. [Cat. no. 219].

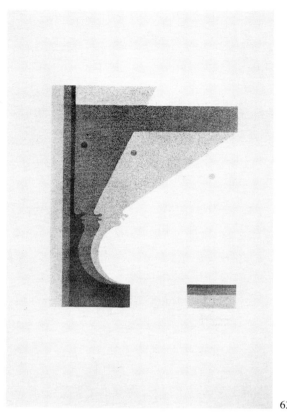

63

64

Fig. 63. *Three Ascending Profiles, Between the Vertical and the Diagonal.* 1920. Lithograph. 18 × 11½ in. Staatsgalerie Stuttgart. [Cat. no. 217].

Fig. 64. *Three Profiles, the Middle One Vertical.* (1920). Lithograph. 18 × 11⅝ in. Staatsgalerie Stuttgart. [Cat. no. 216].

Fig. 65. *Three Profiles in Vertical Lines, One Turned to the Right.* (1920). Lithograph. 18¼ × 11¾ in. Staatsgalerie Stuttgart. [Cat. no. 218].

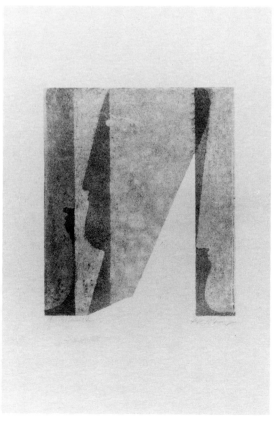

65

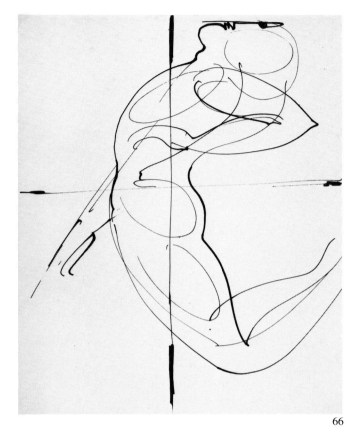

66

67

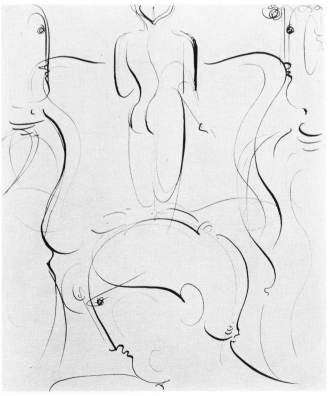

68

Fig. 66. *Figure Bending Backward in System of Coordinates.* (1931). Ink. 11¼ × 8⅝ in. Kunstmuseum Düsseldorf Graph. Sammlung: Schlemmer Family Estate Deposit. [Cat. no. 187].

Fig. 67. *Two Figures in Motion.* (1931). Ink. 11¼ × 8⅝ in. Staatsgalerie Stuttgart. [Cat. no. 191].

Fig. 68. *Group of Figures.* (1931). Ink. 11 × 8⅝ in. Staatsgalerie Stuttgart: Schlemmer Family Estate Deposit. [Cat. no. 188].

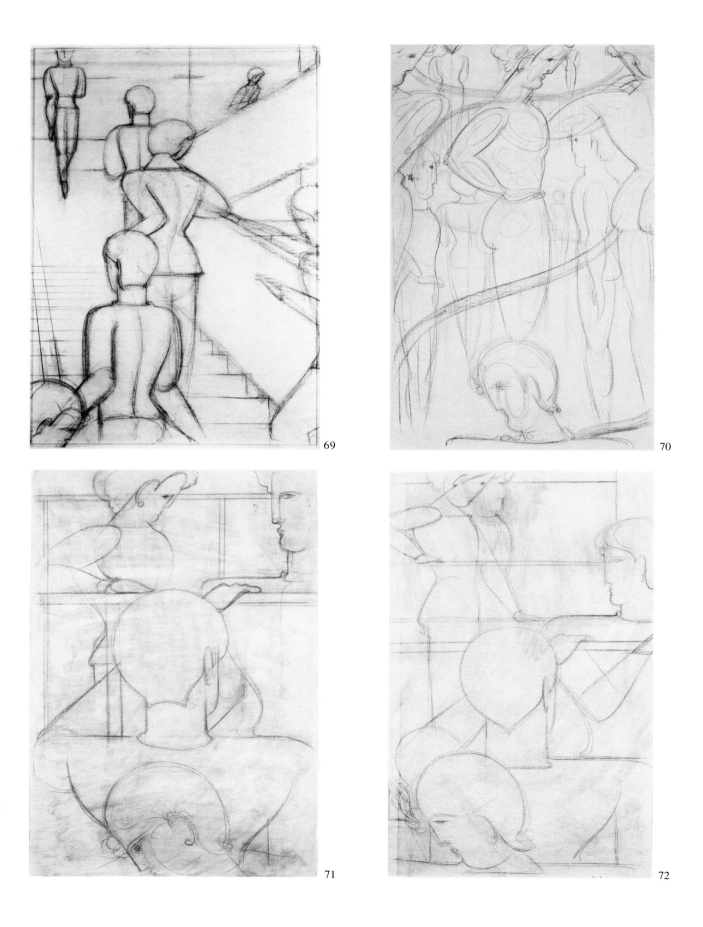

69

70

71

72

73

74

Fig. 69. *Bauhaus Stairway*. 1932. Charcoal. 63 × 43⁵⁄₁₆ in. Bauhaus-Archiv, Berlin. [Cat. no. 198].

Fig. 70. *Nude at Spiral Banister, Men's Steps*. (1931). Charcoal and chalk. 61¾ × 38 in. Family Estate of Oskar Schlemmer. [Cat. no. 196].

Fig. 71. *Group at the Banister*. (1931). Charcoal and chalk. 36⅜ × 24½ in. Family Estate of Oskar Schlemmer. [Cat. no. 194].

Fig. 72. *Scene at the Banister*. (1931). Charcoal. 40½ × 25⅞ in. Family Estate of Oskar Schlemmer. [Cat. no. 195].

Fig. 73. *Blue Group of Women*. 1931. Charcoal and chalk. 61¼ × 47¼ in. Family Estate of Oskar Schlemmer. [Cat. no. 193].

Fig. 74. *Banister Scene*. (1931). Charcoal and chalk. 40¼ × 27¾ in. Family Estate of Oskar Schlemmer. [Cat. no. 192].

Fig. 75. *Three Facing Shadows*. 1932. Charcoal and chalk. 31¼ × 23¾ in. Staatsgalerie Stuttgart: Schlemmer Family Estate Deposit. [Cat. no. 197].

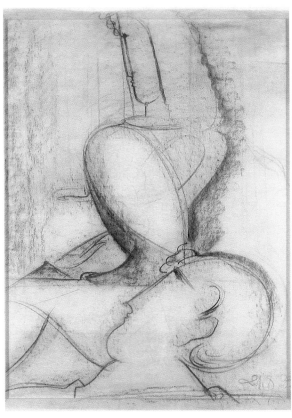

75

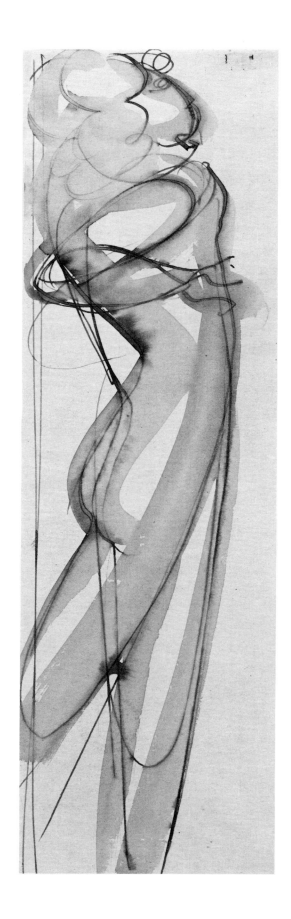

variations of three heads in profile, and symbolic spiritual dematerialization. This series was preceded in 1922 by a single print, apparently issued in a very small edition, on the theme of Faust, which shows Schlemmer's attraction to the work of Seurat. In this lithograph, which shows Faust and Gretchen taking their Easter stroll, Schlemmer achieved a pointillist texture not by using his spray technique but by rubbing chalk on the paper. A second print from the Weimar period was *Dancer* (fig. 62), a 1923 variation on his 1922 painting *The Gesture (Dancer)*, in which the voluminous figure of the painting is translated into a precise contour drawing in black ink on white Chinese paper.

When Schlemmer resumed painting again in 1928 after almost three years of abstinence, his drawings as well as his paintings revealed an increasingly dynamic quality in the figure groupings, perhaps as a result of his theater work. Figures engaged in boldly criss-crossing diagonal movement disrupt and activate the calm, static equilibrium of other, contrasting figures and inject an element of tension that seems to break through the frame of the picture. This new vitality is also manifest in strong light-dark effects and in the sketchy thrust of the lines. Schlemmer's most lovely images of the human body are caught in sweeping, liberated movement by the bamboo pen and brush drawings of leaping, swinging, and floating youths (see figs. 66, 67, 68) of 1931. Whereas in 1916 the floating figure was captive in a continuous, schematized outline, the figure now seems to come into being before our very eyes, evolving out of the rhythmic ebb and flow of linear arabesque. These works show a mastery in drawing the human body that can only have been acquired through years of experience in drawing nudes and working in the dance.

Paintings from the Breslau period display an unusually pronounced tendency toward roundness and fullness, both in color and in form; from 1931 on, these "baroque" impulses were once more contained and tectonically ordered through the use of staircase motifs. Several full-scale transfer drawings from 1931 (see figs. 69–75), found among the materials in Schlemmer's estate, document how carefully he proceeded when composing these paintings, most of which are large-scale. As with the Folkwang panels, Schlemmer used charcoal or colored chalk to establish the primary lines of the painting on tracing paper the same size as the projected painting. On the reverse side of the paper he darkened in the outlines with soft charcoal; thus he could attach the sketch to the easel and

Fig. 76. *Female Nude Stretching Upward*. (1931). Ink. 10⅞ × 3⁷⁄₁₆ in. Staatsgalerie Stuttgart. [Cat. no. 186].

Fig. 77. *Scene with Nude at Banister*. (1931). Ink. 11 × 8⅝ in. Staatsgalerie Stuttgart: Schlemmer Family Estate Deposit. [Cat. no. 190].

Fig. 78. *Profile in Diagonals*. 1932. Watercolor. 16⅜ × 21⅛ in. Staatsgalerie Stuttgart: Collection Karin and U. Jaïna Schlemmer Deposit. [Cat. no. 202].

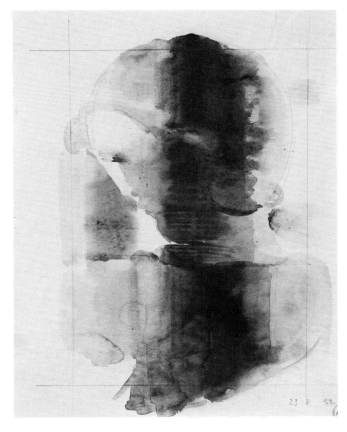

Fig. 79. *Girl's Head in Vertical Stripes*. (1932). Watercolor. 11 × 8⅝ in. Staatsgalerie Stuttgart. [Cat. no. 201].

transfer the outline to the canvas, after which he immediately set to work applying paint.

There is a distinct relaxation of pictorial tension in certain works of 1931, particularly evident in a group of colored ink pictures (see figs. 76 and 77) which seem to grow directly out of the flowing medium, that is, out of light-dark transitions and the fluidity of the ink. With a light touch the artist followed the lead of the ink blots, to which he gave specific figural quality. Schlemmer promptly noted the transformation he felt here: ''A baroque period!? . . . desertion of strictness, of static-constructivist structure, in favor of dynamism, intense feeling, resulting perhaps in romantic ecstasy . . . my own impulses. Perhaps pre-spring impulses to break out of the old shell and rigidity and flow outwards.''[30] Blue ink, which Schlemmer loved, intensifies the reflective, relaxed atmosphere of these pictures.

Schlemmer's ''baroque'' phase culminated in 1932 in a series of watercolors, most of them large, in which the paint has taken on such luminescence and autonomy that it frees itself from literal description of forms and develops independently. Heads or torsos appear like ghosts behind analysis cannot be determined any more definitely than whether they played a role in inspiring the Breslau watercolors. Although most of these twenty or so watercolors have disappeared since the Schlemmer exhibition in London in 1937, those that have survived demonstrate Schlemmer's ability to modulate and manipulate pure color, causing figures and space to resonate in a color chord. The rhythmic alternation between shadow and illumination can intensify to produce extraordinary dynamism and monumentality, as in *Profile in Diagonals* (fig. 78), or it can produce lyrical, reflective effects as in *Girl's Head in Vertical Stripes* (fig. 79), both of 1932. Thus space is no longer an architecturally defined receptacle but the aura and emanation of a spiritual mood.

The Breslau period, the high point of Schlemmer's career as an artist and a teacher, also resulted in one of only four known self-portraits, the 1931–1932 watercolor created at the request of Schlemmer's tailor who accepted

Fig. 80. *Heads on Top of Each Other*. 1935. Ink and oilstick. 25¾ × 13⅝ in. Staatsgalerie Stuttgart: Schlemmer Family Estate Deposit. [Cat. no. 208].

an atmospherically illuminated, shimmering veil of color, sometimes looking as if they had been caught only incidentally. Here Schlemmer captures those "infinitely varied effects" of "imaginary space" that Lissitzky described in 1925 in the *Europa-Almanach*: "The stereoscopic effects produced by movement when it passes through colored media. The color impressions that result from layering colorful bundles of rays, polarization, etc. . . ."[31] Whether Schlemmer read these directives on the artistic application of effects based on spectrum

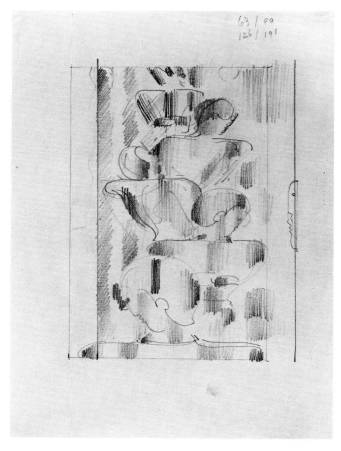

Fig. 81. *Theme: Confrontation*. (1932). Pencil. 11⅝ × 8¼ in. Staatsgalerie Stuttgart: Schlemmer Family Estate Deposit. [Cat. no. 204].

the depths (of figures)."[32] Swept away from the realm of the real, the figures seem to be surrounded and penetrated by a cosmic fluid of rays (see figs. 80–83).

In contrast to these mostly large and painting-like chalk drawings and monotypes, Schlemmer adopted a miniature format in his last Wuppertal period. One can discern an increasingly dominant tendency to dissolve the human figure ethereally into tachist configurations of spots—this approach is particularly evident in the washed sheets of these years that lead up to the window pictures of 1942.

Viewed together, Schlemmer's drawings and watercolors reveal a richness of nuance, a variety of figural invention, and a mastery of a wide range of mediums that confirm Schlemmer's significant place within the graphic arts of the twentieth century.

Fig. 82. *Wool and Weaving: Two Girls with Red Thread*. (1936). Oilstick. 25¾ × 19¾ in. Staatsgalerie Stuttgart. [Cat. no. 211].

Fig. 83. *Four Girls' Heads in Echelon*. (1936). Oilstick. 25⅝ × 19⅝ in. Staatsgalerie Stuttgart. [Cat. no. 209].

art works in payment for suits (fig. 117). The watercolor, perhaps inspired by a Bauhaus photograph of the artist in a similar pose, shows that even when Schlemmer took himself as a model, he was interested in the subject only as a symbolic and universal motif—in this case the artist who teaches and loves fundamental principles.

During his last decade, when he was in what later came to be called "inner emigration," Schlemmer developed a particular fondness for the texture of paint. On the backs of yellowed printed materials from the Bauhaus he recorded his "inner visions" in the tactile mediums of oil crayon and pastel. In spite of the official defamation of his art, which he could not understand, he portrayed man as a disembodied, spiritualized being. Heads and bodies well up from a colored ground, shaped out of light and intermeshed with the space around them, which seems to shimmer into infinite distance. In the colored chalk drawings of 1935–1936 the strictly constructed ensemble of the earlier compositions has been replaced by a swaying structure of dully glowing linear networks. Schlemmer created "brightnesses born of the depths, breaking into

Fig. 84. *Ornamental Sculpture on Divided Frame*. 1919/1923.
Painted wood. 35⁷⁄₁₆ × 26¾ × 1¹¹⁄₁₆ in. Kunstsammlung Nordrhein-
Westfalen, Düsseldorf. [Not in exhibition].

Schlemmer as Sculptor and Relief Muralist

Schlemmer's chief work as a sculptor dates from the years 1919–1923. During this brief period he completed four reliefs (and several polychrome variations), two free-standing sculptures, a series of studies for sculptures that were never executed, and finally the relief mural for the workshop building at the Weimar Bauhaus, which combined elements of both painting and sculpture. In later years, he turned only occasionally to sculpture, for instance in 1931 with the wire relief mural for the Rabe house in Zwenkau, and in 1942 with a series of miniature plaster reliefs. Although his sculptural works are few in number, their intensity and originality make them an important part of his oeuvre, and they decisively enriched and influenced sculpture in the first half of this century.

Schlemmer's concern with sculptural problems originated at the time of the First World War; Schlemmer was reading a good deal in his spare time and giving much thought to artistic questions as he tried to determine what path he should follow amid the competing stylistic currents of the day. "Join forces with the idealists of form. Lehmbruck and Archipenko in sculpture, the Cubists in painting. They form a bridge to architecture, for their paintings are constructed."[33] Long before the founding of the Bauhaus, before the advent of Dutch De Stijl and Russian Constructivism, Schlemmer opted for the constructive principle in both sculpture and painting, at the same time emphasizing their connection with architecture, which he saw as the more elevated artistic union. This recognition played no small part in his resolve to move away from "the geometry of the surface to the half-sculptural relief" when he resumed his artistic work after the end of the war.[34] His exploration of the substantiality and malleability of sculptural material (mostly plaster or wood) gave him an opportunity to articulate three-dimensionally his desire for tectonic form, and by so doing to incorporate that form directly into a reciprocal relationship with the surrounding wall surfaces and the room they enclosed.

Reliefs

In the fruitful months following the end of the war, Schlemmer completed his first relief sculptures; they were displayed in October 1919 in the Stuttgart "Herbstschau Neuer Kunst" ("Autumn Salon of Contemporary Art"), and immediately triggered a crossfire of contradictory reviews. The cautious Fritz Schneider saw these sculptural works as "spiritual skeletons" and "scientific experiments rather than artistic creations," whereas the progressive Konrad Düssel emphasized their "strong sense of the functional, of the structure and elaboration of form as an expression of function."[35]

Presumably it was the *Ornamental Sculpture on Divided Frame* (fig. 84), lost and then rediscovered in 1975 in Holland, which marked the beginning of the 1919 series of reliefs. It consists of a complex arrangement of cylindrical forms, much like organ pipes, standing out against the coordinate axes of a vertically positioned wooden panel divided into colorful sections by different types of molding. The unusual structure and palette of the piece reveal a close relationship to earlier paintings such as the 1915–1918 *Divided Figure* (fig. 85) or *Scheme with Figures*. Both the sculpture and the paintings incorporate four-part segmentation, at whose intersecting point the motifs cluster, split, and interpenetrate. The divided plane serves simultaneously as a supporting framework and dominant system of order, integrating at the center the various messages inherent in the forms. As a whole, *Ornamental Sculpture on Divided Frame* is a montage of painted and sculpted elements, some of which are found objects; in this montage the aims of Dada and Constructivism are united in a unique creation.

With *Relief JG in Bronze* (fig. 86), also of 1919, anthropomorphic figuration manifests itself in Schlemmer's sculptural work as it had already in his painting. Along the vertical axis of an upright, rectangular panel, a frontally-positioned figure is assembled from divergent sculpted parts—a doll-like hand, a geometricized thigh, a sculptural half-circle. The relief bears a clear resemblance to the painting *Man with Fish* of 1916 (fig. 87). In several polychrome versions (see figs. 88 and 89) Schlemmer played through the interpretive possibilities of the basic sculptural model: first in small segments, with portions painted in pointillist and hatched techniques, and metallic parts; later in softer coloration, which allows the structural aspects of the figure to emerge. At the same time, these variants suggest symbolic expressive values: while the bronzed elements of the Stuttgart version emphasize its idol-like character, the broken tonal values of the Düsseldorf version emphasize the reserved, hermetic aspect of this figural montage. There is no definitive explanation of the meaning of the letters in the relief's title. Available sources do not point to their being someone's initials. It seems more likely that the form of the letters J and G is connected with the dominant forms in the relief: the raised

Fig. 85. *Divided Figure*. (1915–1918). Oil. 38⁹⁄₁₆ × 28¹⁵⁄₁₆ in.
Staatliche Kunstsammlungen Kassel: Private Collection Deposit.
[Cat. no. 11].

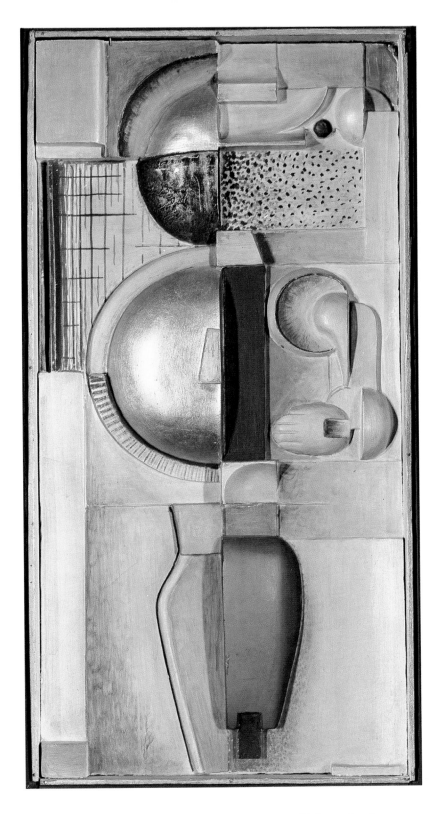

Fig. 86. *Relief JG in Bronze*. (1919). Plaster, with bronzed and painted wood. 26⁹/₁₆ × 12¹³/₁₆ in. Staatsgalerie Stuttgart. [Cat. no. 55].

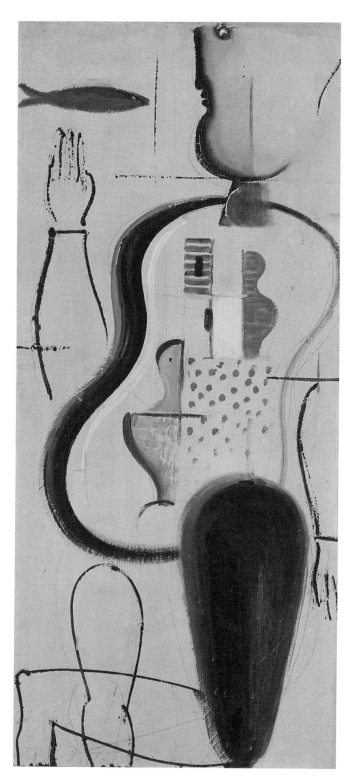

Fig. 87. *Man with Fish*. 1916 (1918?). Oil. 36⅛ × 15¾ in. Museum moderner Kunst, Vienna: Private Collection Deposit. [Cat. no. 13].

half-circle at center left could be seen as a reference to the letter G, and the geometricized thigh as a J. But these references are not obvious, as is the case with *Painting K*, where the letter is depicted. Perhaps Schlemmer had some other purpose in mind when he cited these particular letters—the exclusion of illustrative references to reality, a reminder of the tectonic and cryptographic quality of his forms—which are to be "read" in a new way, indeed, spelled out?

In contrast to the emphasis in *Relief JG* on montage of small, distinct elements, *Relief H* (fig. 90) is composed of larger segments, like building blocks, both linked and separated by the powerful vertical of the central figural image. In the figure's exaggeratedly prominent chin, molded with the neck and chest to produce a bulbous, abstract outline, Schlemmer's art of stylizing organic forms is fully revealed. The otherwise abstract figure conveys identity as living form because of the antithesis between the hard, sharply cut straight lines and angles of its surround, and its own soft indentations and curvaceous forms, which are further enlivened by tactile surface effects—rough sections contrast with smooth ones. The profile view, of which Schlemmer was fond, accentuates distanced, generic perception. The contrast between planar and relief elements, particularly evident in the earlier sculptures, is diminished in *Relief H* where the figure emerges from the plane but remains continuously joined to it. A bronzed version of *Relief H* (fig. 91) recently came to light, revealing the extent to which the totemistic magnetism of this work can be enhanced by color; the unpainted plaster casts seem symbolically neutral by comparison.

In the Germany of 1919 Schlemmer's polychrome reliefs represented a bold advance into uncharted territory. But, within the larger European avant-garde community (from France to Italy to Russia), the relief montage technique itself reflected developments that had been underway for some years. Painters and sculptors alike were experimenting with new materials and expanding conventional genres to unprecedented limits. Illusionistic representation of reality was gradually giving way to assemblage. Along with Picasso, Boccioni, Laurens, Arp, Tatlin, Gabo, and others, it was primarily Alexander Archipenko who, since 1912, had been combining diverse materials in what he named his "sculpto-paintings," and who reintroduced color to sculpture as a dynamic, spiritualizing "energy."[36] The melding of painterly and sculptural elements of form and expression fit in well with Schlemmer's interest in structure as a way toward artistic renewal. Although no documented connection with Archipenko's work can be found, one may assume that Schlemmer drew inspiration for his polychrome reliefs from the Russian, who was

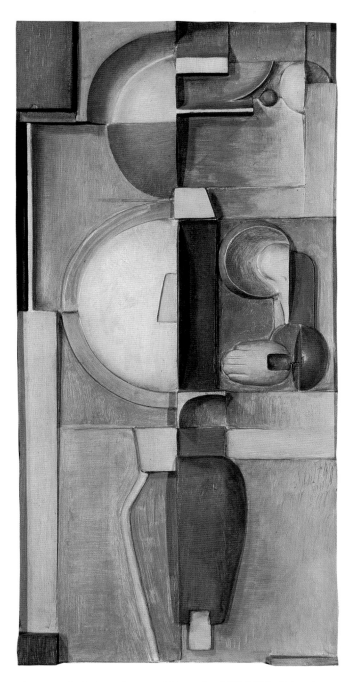

Fig. 88. *Relief JG (with Painted Mount I)*. (1919/1921). Painted plaster. 27¾ × 15³⁄₁₆ in. Nationalgalerie, Staatliche Museen, Berlin, German Democratic Republic. [Not in exhibition].

Fig. 89. *Relief JG (with Painted Mount II)*. (1919/1921). Painted wood. 26⁹⁄₁₆ × 12¹¹⁄₁₆ in. Kunstmuseum Düsseldorf. [Not in exhibition].

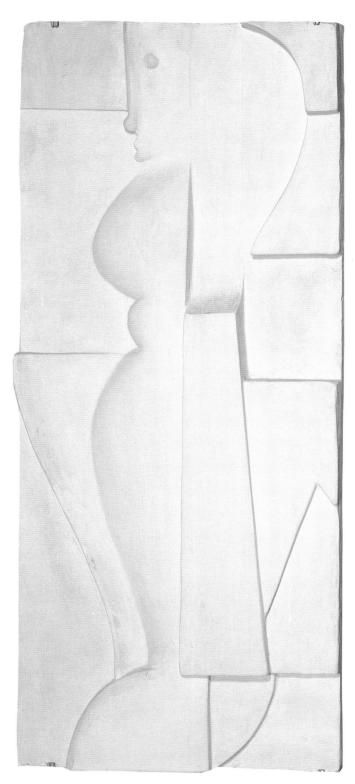 

Fig. 90. *Relief H.* (1919). Plaster. 26⅜ × 11⅛ × 1⅛ in. Galerie Beyeler, Basel. [Cat. no. 53].

Fig. 91. *Relief H, Bronzed.* (1919). Plaster, with bronze finish. 26½ × 11 × 1¼ in. Sammlung und Archiv für Künstler der Breslauer Akademie, Kassel. [Cat. no. 54].

living in France and exhibited his work in January 1918 in Herwarth Walden's Der Sturm gallery. Perhaps Schlemmer even saw the exhibition in Berlin when he was attending his officer-training course there.

Around the same time (in 1919–1920) Schlemmer's studio neighbor Willi Baumeister adopted a similar technique in his "wall pictures" which, however, were not yet exhibited, as Schlemmer's reliefs were at the 1919 "Autumn Salon." Baumeister continued to work on his "wall pictures" for several years, but for Schlemmer this colorful mixture of genres represented only a transitional stage on his way to high relief and three-dimensional sculpture. But for both artists "sculpto-painting" later found an echo in mural designs. Schlemmer's series of reliefs of 1919 culminated in *Constructed Sculpture R* (fig. 92), with which he largely abandoned both polychrome treatment and assemblage elements. Very similar to *Relief H* in conception, along the axis of the narrow vertical rectangle of *Constructed Sculpture R* rises the figure of a youth facing to the right, his slim outlines reduced to basic geometric elements. The figure's proportions generate a system of stacked rectangular units, balanced on either side of the central vertical axis, which serves as both the figure's spine and as the most powerful structural element of the composition. The plane is graded to varying depths by the rhythmic alternation of concave and convex. In this fashion Schlemmer creates a clear, differentiated ensemble of box-like hollow forms, incised contours, sharp-edged ridges, and molded protuberances. Here light takes the place of color in providing accents that activate the forms; with each change of light, there are dramatic, shifting contrasts between the illuminated and shaded sections, a dynamic tension that promotes equilibrium between plane and volume. Schlemmer had found his symbol for man as the measure in art and a new architecture. *Constructed Sculpture R* exemplifies what Schlemmer said of his paintings of about the same time: they extend beyond their frames, "becoming part of a large surface, a larger space than themselves, thus actually becoming part of an ideal architecture. Compressed in them, reduced to a miniature scale, is what should furnish the laws and form of their surroundings. In this sense: Tablets of the Law."[37]

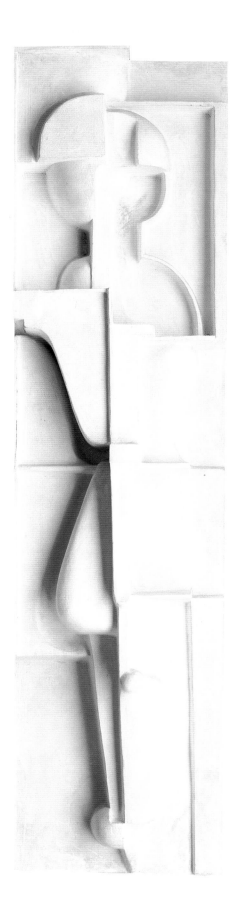

Fig. 92. *Constructed Sculpture R*. (1919). Plaster. 39⅜ × 9⅞ × 3⅞ in. Städtische Kunsthalle Mannheim: Schlemmer Family Estate Deposit. [Cat. no. 51].

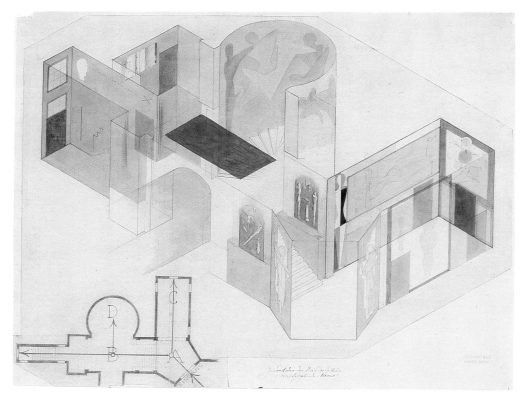

Fig. 93. *Master Plan of Mural Painting inside the Workshop Building of the Weimar Bauhaus.* (1923). Pencil and watercolor. 16⅞ × 21⅝ in. Staatsgalerie Stuttgart: Schlemmer Family Estate Deposit. [Cat. no. 128].

Fig. 94. *Three Mural Studies for the Workshop Building of the Weimar Bauhaus.* (1923–1928). Pencil, ink, and watercolor. 15⅞ × 21⅝ in. Family Estate of Oskar Schlemmer. [Cat. no. 129].

Wall Designs in the Weimar Bauhaus, 1923

In 1923 Schlemmer's work became a literal part of architecture when he was given the opportunity to decorate Henry van de Velde's workshop building at the Weimar Bauhaus with designs combining sculpture and painting (see figs. 93 and 94). Aiming for the essential and for coherence, Schlemmer interpreted the walls, corridors, stairwells, and niches in the sprawling building as clean slates on which he could lay out a universal grammar of human types in both relief and colored line (see figs. 95 and 96). The elemental was to be the measure, not only in the motifs but also in style: "The elemental colors of the color wheel, the elemental forms of geometry (point, line, rectangle, circle, ellipse, Golden Section, Pythagorean formula), and 'elemental sculpture' in regular forms such as the cube, the pyramid, the sphere, the cylinder, and their interpenetration."[38]

The designs for sculptural reliefs in plaster and mortar, which Schlemmer executed with the help of Josef Hartwig, were concentrated in the entry hall, painted in a "stabilizing," calming blue. To the right and left of the entrance, two enormous, stylized figures served as "guardians of the temple," as Schlemmer called them, the male figure characterized by stark verticals and horizontals, the female by softer, more rounded forms. On the ceiling three overlapping figures marked the main axes of the building. The space that opened up to the right, with a high rear

Fig. 96. *Man-Hero Line Figure (Mural Painting inside the Workshop Building of the Weimar Bauhaus)*. (1923). Fresco, no longer extant.

wall, was dominated by a "masculine heroic linear figure," in the spirit of the 1920–1921 *Homo* drawing. It embodies Schlemmer's vision of anatomical-metaphysical man. The staircase to the left of the entrance provided a setting for figural representations in full relief. Placed vertically, horizontally, and diagonally, these marionette-like figures painted in metallic tones stood out against the English-red background of the wall alcoves, exemplifying fundamental postures and movements such as standing, floating, or falling. The figures in the semi-circular stairwell leading to the upper story took yet another form; they were large torsos in limpid colors, arranged in a fresco frieze full of dance-like movement, against a pale violet ground. The walls and ceilings of the other spaces were painted with calligraphic contour figures or friezes of heads in pastel colors.

Thus Schlemmer used this rather dark building for the creation of a painterly-sculptural *Gesamtkunstwerk*, a total work of art. Will Grohmann's description of it as a "first attempt at a contemporary form of monumental painting" is still apt. With extraordinary sensitivity Schlemmer

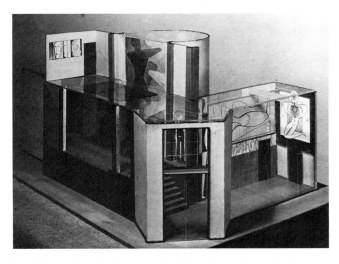

Fig. 95. *Model of the Workshop Building of the Weimar Bauhaus.* (1955 reconstruction). Bauhaus-Archiv, Berlin. [Not in exhibition].

integrated his figures with the building's proportions, orientation, and unique spaces, bringing them into harmony with the measure "that the artist carries within himself." Out of the ensemble arose numerical relationships and correlations that surprised even him: "Quite by accident the numbers 3, 5, and 7 cropped up in a great variety of forms and combinations in the painting of the workshop building. Instinct decided, and reason confirmed it ex post facto. The same applies to the forms and the colors. The trinity of primary colors, red—blue—yellow, increased to five by the addition of the non-colors white and black, and the resulting numerical series of combinations have their counterparts in the basic forms of the surface and the reliefs, but they suggest only the rough dimensions of the incalculable dynamics of the whole."[39] A polychromatic symphony with variations based on the theme of man as the measure and the mean had been created. At the same time, the murals for the Weimar Bauhaus constituted the first major communal achievement of the Bauhaus, for in the actual execution of the designs not only Schlemmer and Hartwig were involved but also the students from the mural-painting and sculpture workshops.

Sculpture

In 1923 Schlemmer also completed his only free-standing sculptures, the *Grotesque* (see fig. 97) and the *Abstract Figure*, intended for the Bauhaus exhibition. They represent two fundamental types: a figure in profile with a rigid silhouette effect, and a frontally conceived figure organized of differentiated parts.

In the wood sculpture, which Schlemmer dubbed the *Grotesque*, one finds a figural concept similar to that of *Relief H*, here transposed into a sculpture standing free in space. The head and belly of this figure are drawn together in a sweeping S-curve, at whose midpoint a heart-shaped mouth is situated, while the eye, an ivory disk with a metal button, is placed high up in the rounded head section. The result is a fabulous anthropomorphic creature, floating on a metal rod, which in turn is anchored in a large, club-like foot so that the figure can be swiveled. The foot can thus be pointed along the figure's sight line or, producing a playfully ironic effect, it can be pointed backwards, as a counterweight to the expansive curves of the head and rump; the latter arrangement seems to lend the figure greater abstraction and formal elegance. The fine grain of the sculpture's nutwood creates a tracery of

Fig. 97. *Grotesque II*. (1923). Walnut, ivory, and metal. 22 × 9¼ × 4⅛ in. Staatsgalerie Stuttgart. [Cat. no. 56].

Fig. 98. *Abstract Figure*. (1961, from 1921/1923 plaster). Nickel-plated bronze. 41½ × 24⅝ × 8⅜ in. The Baltimore Museum of Art: Alan and Janet Wurtzburger Collection. [Cat. no. 57].

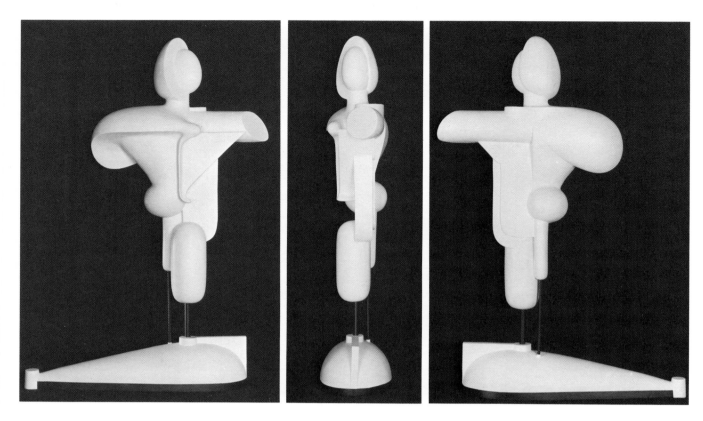

Fig. 99. *Abstract Figure*. (1921/1923). Plaster. 42⅛ in. high. Staats-galerie Stuttgart: Schlemmer Family Estate Deposit. [Not in exhibition].

lines over the polished surface, highlighting the curves and enlivening the figure.

In the final analysis, *Grotesque* is born of creative deformation of the human figure; characteristic elements of the body undergo a subtle and largely unconscious process of simplification, omission, and amalgamation, to yield a novel artistic entity. The result is a bird-like creature that seems to step out with stiff dignity and real seriousness, but with a scamp hidden inside. For Schlemmer's imagination bristles with a grotesque sense of irony, the source of some of his most inspired ballet inventions, such as the *Figural Cabinet*, the first parts of *The Triadic Ballet*, or the *Musical Clown*. The fascinating juxtaposition of odd body form and human bearing, of mask-like immobility and organic consistency, places *Grotesque* in the realm of the surreal. Yet in Schlemmer's work this surreal aspect is always more controlled, concealed, and subtle than it is, for example, in the creatures of Max Ernst.

Oskar Schlemmer's work as a sculptor culminates in the large piece originally called "Free-standing Sculpture G," which became known as *Abstract Figure* (fig. 98). It too was completed in 1923, as can be seen from the

catalogue to the Bauhaus exhibition. *Abstract Figure* poses majestically in a frontal view. The head is divided into a face and a helmet, like a kernel in a shell. The mighty shoulder emerges on the left in a generously rounded form, and to the right it thrusts out horizontally, ending abruptly in a plane sliced on an angle. The rump, divided in half by a bulging ridge, is formed on the left side from a rounded form, which pitches to a ball formation below, while the right side consists of a sharp-edged triangular surface with a lengthwise surface layered behind it. The cylindrical round form of the leg ends in a metal rod which, as in *Grotesque*, is fixed in an enormous clubfoot shape.

The center of action is the powerful torso. All the dynamic force is gathered on the right side—in its sharp diagonal, in the purposeful swelling of the middle, and in the abrupt, brute cylindrical thrust of the arm. The sweeping curve of the left shoulder offers a sight line to the opposite pole: the steadfast, protective, sheltering element. The vertical thrust of the figure is counter-weighted by the parallel horizontals of shoulders and "feet," which anchor the figure's tendency to float on its metal rod.

The contrasting forces of energy and composure perceived when the sculpture is viewed frontally pervade the entire figure, which offers two very different profiles and an asymmetrical rear view. A sequence of varied aspects is thus created, visible only when one walks around the sculpture, which yields its total significance only when taken as a whole, in the round (fig. 99). While the wooden sculpture *Grotesque* could be grasped essentially from one vantage point, *Abstract Figure* embodies in exemplary fashion Schlemmer's conception of "true sculpture," as he described it in a note written in January 1924:

> Sculpture is three-dimensional (height, breadth, depth). It cannot be grasped in any given moment; rather it reveals itself in a temporal succession of vantage points and views. Since a piece of sculpture does not yield a total impression from one angle, the spectator is obliged to move, and only by walking around and adding up his impressions does he eventually grasp the sculpture. Thus

any piece of plastic art which does not offer the viewer a series of surprises as he walks around it, but merely repeats one segment (and this is true of all stereometric bodies), has no validity as sculpture. . . . In fact, the sculptural quality of any sculpture can be measured by the number of individual facets that can be viewed.[40]

Since Schlemmer was artistic director of the wood and stone workshops at the Bauhaus during these years, one may ask why he did not work in stone, like his pupil Kurt Schwerdtfeger, for instance, and whether he may not have contemplated executing his *Abstract Figure* in marble, for which the plaster version could have been a full-scale model. The possibility is certainly conceivable, and what speaks in its favor is the fact that this particular sculpture occupied a prominent foreground position in a photograph of the stoneworking shop at the Bauhaus in 1923 (fig. 100). But executing the sculpture in stone would have required the aid of a skilled stoneworker like Hartwig,

Fig. 100. Stoneworking Shop at the Weimar Bauhaus, 1923.

who had in fact helped with the wooden *Grotesque*. If Schlemmer planned to do the *Abstract Figure* in stone— and no references to such a plan can be found in Schlemmer's diaries—the tremendous workload imposed first by the workshop murals and then by Schlemmer's new position as director of the Bauhaus theater would have put an end to the project. And after 1923, Schlemmer turned his mind from sculpture to other things.

But Schlemmer's small body of executed sculptures cannot be seen as his complete sculptural oeuvre. The costumed figurines for *The Triadic Ballet* of 1922, for instance, should also be considered polychromatic sculpture; he himself called them ''the first consistent demonstration of costume in a spatial-plastic mode.'' Furthermore, Schlemmer's drawings from the Bauhaus period indicate that he had conceived an entire series of sculptures, in great detail. There is evidence of as many as twenty such projects. Drawings known to be intended as studies

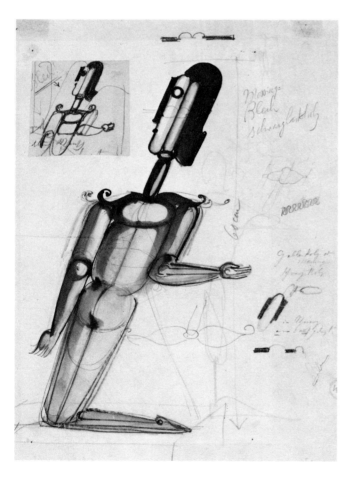

Fig. 101. *Ivo, Design for a Sculpture.* (ca. 1922–1923). Pencil, ink, and watercolor. 11⅛ × 8¾ in. Private Collection, Stuttgart. [Cat. no. 118].

for sculpture are of particular interest. Schlemmer dwelled on one sculptural figure that he called Ivo (see fig. 101); it is a kneeling figure, androgynous in character. Schlemmer's handwritten notes on the watercolor study indicate that the sculpture was to be executed in materials of contrasting colors: sheet brass, light-colored wood, and black lacquered wood. Its height was initially conceived to be 60 centimeters, but in the final version it was increased to 110 centimeters, which would have made the sculpture taller than *Abstract Figure*. In the turned joints, for instance in the head and neck section, Schlemmer emphasized the marionette-like quality of the figure. As in his ballet figurines he wanted to make visible the ''apparatus of limbs with its marvelously precise functions.'' He had come to the conclusion that art (including theatrical art and the dance) could be cured of obsolete illusionism in the imitation of reality only by conscious emphasis on its ''made'' quality, its artificiality. ''The medium of every art is artificial, and every art gains from recognition and acceptance of its medium. Heinrich [von] Kleist's essay *Über das Marionettentheater* [On the Marionette (Theater)] offers a convincing reminder of this artificiality, as do E. T. A. Hoffmann's *Phantasiestücke* [Fantasy Pieces] (the perfect machinist, the automata). Chaplin performs wonders when he equates complete inhumanity with artistic perfection.''[41]

Wire Sculpture

Along with plaster, wood, and glass, Schlemmer soon came to see metal and wire as his most important sculptural materials. Until 1923 he was Form Master of the metalworking shop, along with Johannes Itten. Work Master Christian Dell, who possessed outstanding technical skill, assisted him. Schlemmer, himself the grandson of a goldsmith, doubtless was stimulated by this workshop experience to consider wire and metal as materials suitable for sculpture, not merely for useful objects (such as the clock he designed). Making shapes in wire especially appealed to him because it was the ideal way to materialize one important aspect of his art—graphics—and to transform planar drawing to spatial drawing. Wire combined properties of elasticity, tautness, density, stability, and precision with a minimum of weight and mass; as such, it was particularly suited to translate his explorations in graphics, of which the pen and ink drawings are prime examples, into three-dimensional form. A series of sketches torsos that could easily be executed as sculpture. A number of factors point in this direction: the relatively large format of the studies (about 50 x 30 centimeters), which probably corresponds to the proportions of the projected works; the precision of contour in the drawings; and the use of tracing paper, which is often employed to transfer a design onto the chosen material.

There is also evidence that the composition *Mythical Figure* (fig. 106) of 1923 was originally intended not as a picture in its own right but as a template for a relief, planned but never executed: a preliminary sketch from 1922–1923, which is inscribed "Sculpture with Brass Limbs and Wires"; a collage illustrated in the publication *Staatliches Bauhaus Weimar 1919–1923*, with the title "Figural Composition. Working Drawing"; and the strict planarity and abstraction of the figure, so characteristic of the oil paintings of the Stuttgart period but later on

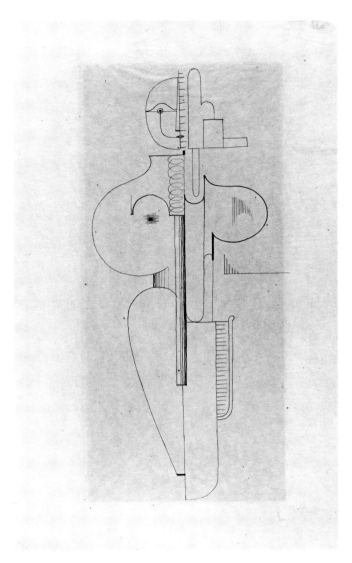

Fig. 102. *Abstract Figure, Frontal*. (ca. 1921). Ink. 20¾ × 12½ in. Staatsgalerie Stuttgart: Collection Karin and U. Jaïna Schlemmer Deposit. [Cat. no. 102].

and studies for sculpture reveals that between 1921 and 1924 Schlemmer was intensely preoccupied with the idea of using wire and metal bands for sculptural purposes. First came a group of detailed pen and ink drawings of profile heads or torsos, probably studies for wire reliefs (see figs. 102–105). This conclusion is bolstered by a comparison of these drawings with a page of apparently casual sketches that are actually important studies for the Bauhaus murals. On the left side of the page is a large, linear head in profile, with a revealing notation on materials: "Wire lines and glass on wood." Among the pen and ink drawings there is a series of similar heads in profile, worked out in greater detail, as well as stylized

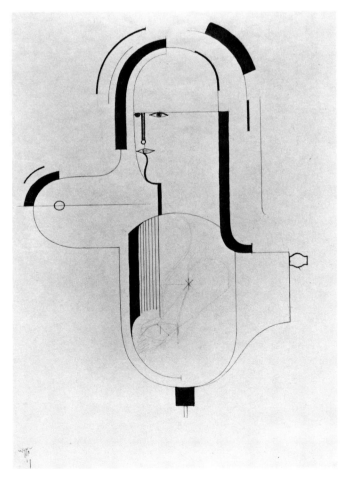

Fig. 103. *Torso with Accentuated Black Lines*. (1923). Pencil and ink. 21¾ × 15⅞ in. Staatsgalerie Stuttgart: Collection Karin and U. Jaïna Schlemmer Deposit. [Cat. no. 132].

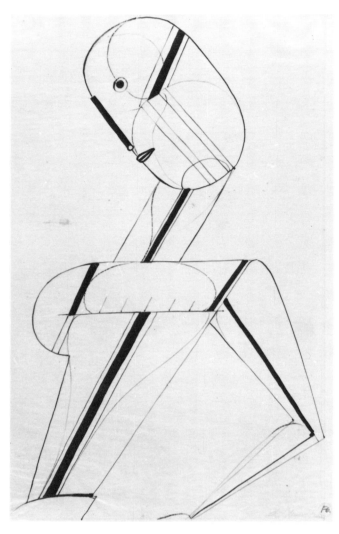

Fig. 104. *Abstract Torso*. 1923. Ink. 20¼ × 12⅝ in. Staatsgalerie Stuttgart: Collection Karin and U. Jaïna Schlemmer Deposit. [Cat. no. 120].

the material or, alternatively, found the only material suitable for a specific concept. In these works he materialized his formula "nature x material x concept." Mass is subjugated to the spiritualization of the human form, with symbolic concentration on the head. At least one of these sketches was actually realized as a sculpture; according to the artist's widow Tut Schlemmer, it was on display in their Eichberg apartment in 1936 but somehow disappeared in the course of the move to Sehringen. It was a head in profile, about 50 centimeters high, constructed of circles, straight lines, and tiny spheres. The full-scale working drawing (fig. 110) is preserved, with detailed instructions on material that have made it possible to reconstruct the wire sculpture (fig. 109). In these designs for radically simplified, transparent wire forms floating above their base on rods, the heads become

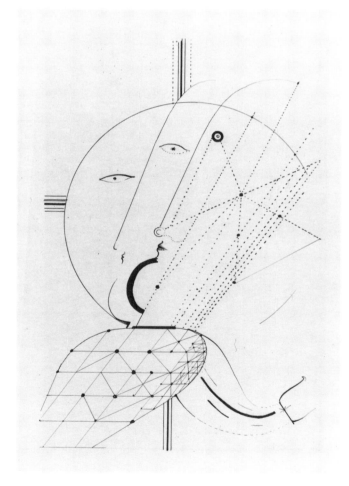

Fig. 105. *Profile with Dotted Lines*. 1924. Ink. 21¾ × 15 in. Staatsgalerie Stuttgart: Schlemmer Family Estate Deposit. [Cat. no. 137].

found only in the murals. Possibly Schlemmer had in mind a relief made of marquetry (a craft he learned in his youth), with the figure outlined in wire and bits of metal. Later he renamed the collage *Mythical Figure* and cited it as numbering among the few works he would not want to see omitted from a retrospective exhibition of his works.[42]

Looking further at Schlemmer's projects conceived for the wire medium, there is a group of three designs for sculptures that are clearly labeled with the materials Schlemmer planned to use (figs. 107–109). They, too, use the motif of the stylized head in profile, but they are conceived as free-standing wire sculptures attached to bases. These projects demonstrate how Schlemmer derived the concept of a work of art from the inherent nature of

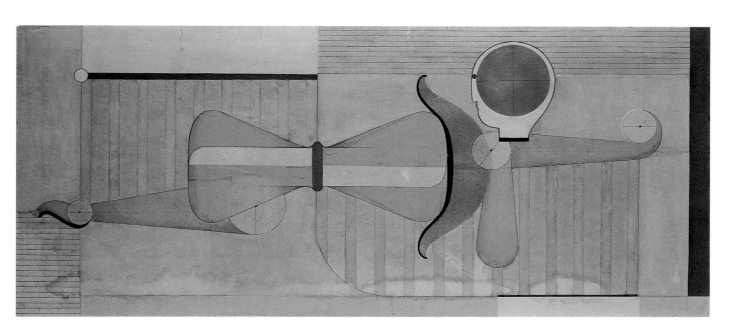

Fig. 106. *Mythical Figure*. (1923). Ink and collage. 29½ × 68⅛ in.
Staatsgalerie Stuttgart. [Not in exhibition].

paradigmatic symbols of the spirit. In 1920 the brothers Naum Gabo and Antoine Pevsner declared in their *Realistic Manifesto*, ''We exclude physical mass from sculpture as a sculptural element.''[43] By 1921 Schlemmer had already reached this stage of extreme reduction of mass and volume, at least conceptually, and had achieved the ideal of completely perforate sculpture.

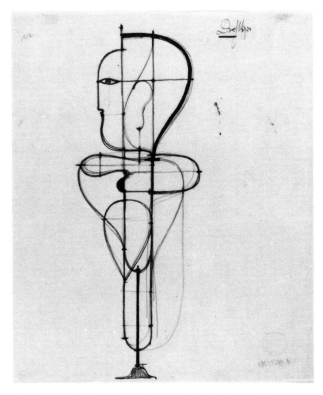

Fig. 107. *Wire Figure*. (1921–1922). Pencil. 12 × 9⅜ in. Staatsgalerie Stuttgart. [Cat. no. 108].

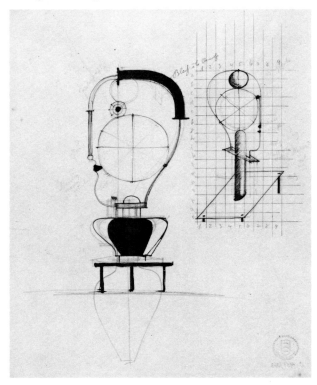

Fig. 108. *Two Constructional Heads: Design for a Metal Sculpture*. (1921–1922). Pencil and ink. 12 × 9⅜ in. Staatsgalerie Stuttgart. [Cat. no. 107].

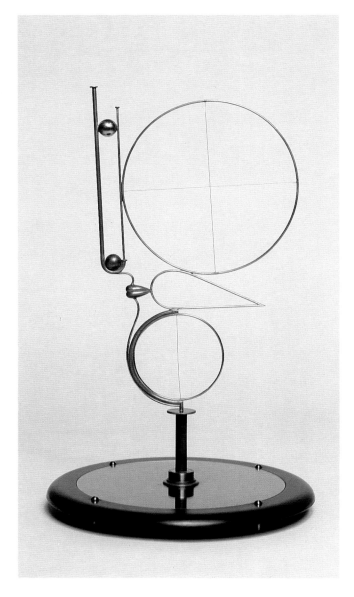

Fig. 109. *Abstract Head (Reconstruction)*. (1973, based on a 1923 working drawing). Copper wire and nickel-plated chromium wire. 16½ in. high. Collection of C. Raman Schlemmer, courtesy Nicholas Wilder, New York. [Cat. no. 58].

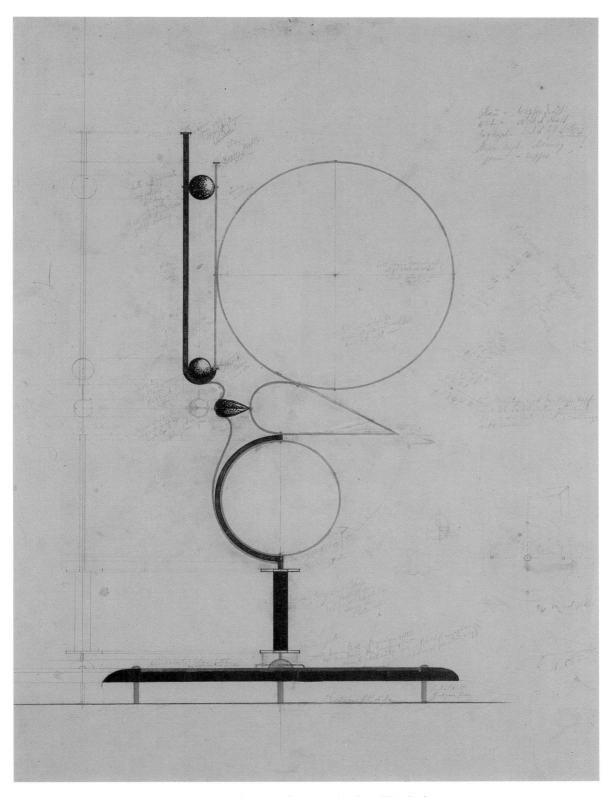

Fig. 110. *Abstract Head: Working Drawing for a Wire Sculpture.*
(1923). Pencil and ink. 22⅜ × 16⅝ in. Staatsgalerie Stuttgart. [Cat.
no. 119].

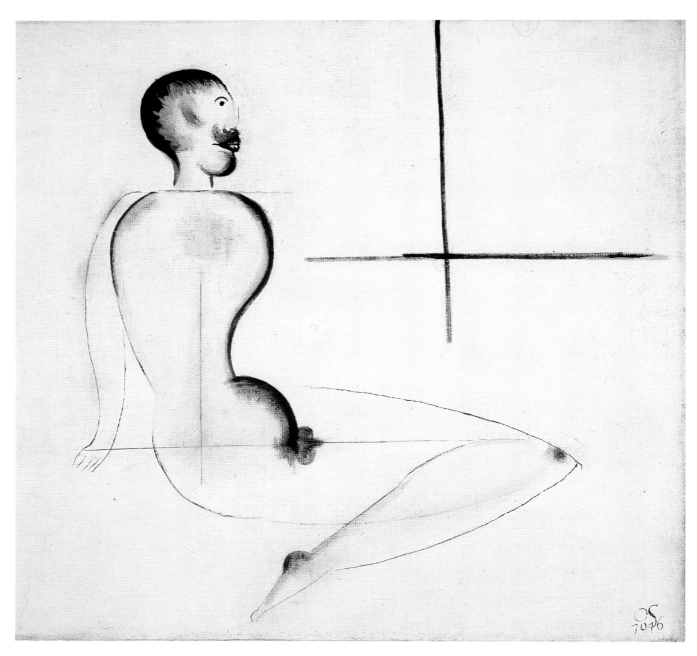

Fig. 111. *Homo*. 1916. Oil. 17⅞ × 18⅞ in. Private Collection.
[Cat. no. 12].

"Metallurgy" in Leipzig (Zwenkau), 1930–1931

In 1930 Schlemmer received a commission for a monumental wall design, to be mounted in the private house of Dr. Rabe built in Zwenkau by the architect Adolf Rading. Schlemmer immediately recalled his designs for wire sculpture from the Weimar years. Here was his chance not only to realize the vision of floating wire sculpture that he had "carried around with him for ten years," but, even more significantly, to do so within the framework of contemporary architecture. At a time when his painting had entered a new, baroque phase, with a softening of contours and spatial boundaries, Schlemmer used the mural projects as an opportunity to materialize his abstract-constructivist ideas from an earlier period. It was in this spirit that he wrote to Otto Meyer-Amden: "I imagine I shall eventually reach a new form of abstraction via the specifications of the architects, which involve not painting as such but compositions in material. . . . The

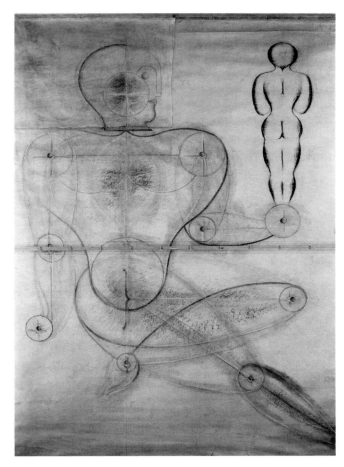

Fig. 113. *Seated "Homo" with Back-View Figure on its Hand.* (1930). Charcoal and chalk. 121⅝ × 89⅜ in. Staatsgalerie Stuttgart. [Cat. no. 183].

clear distinction between 'painting' and 'composition in material' suits me very well."[44]

And so Schlemmer reverted to the figure he had worked out in detail in about 1920, *Homo, Figure T*, and used it as the basis for the Zwenkau wall design (see fig. 112 for replica). This homo was the final figure in a series of analytic figure studies whose prototype could be found in the seated man placed at the intersection of the three axes in the painting *Homo* done in 1916 (fig. 111). In this painting, but also in a number of drawings and lithographs, Schlemmer had developed a planar, stylized figure, shaped according to principles of planar geometry, which he called "differentiated man." Since man is "both an organic and a mechanical construct," he wanted to establish a basic figure formula that would capture the laws of this dual reality. The outer shell, patterned after a jointed doll, demonstrates the mechanical functions of human body structure and of the proportions of the limbs; curving lines extending in arabesques throughout the

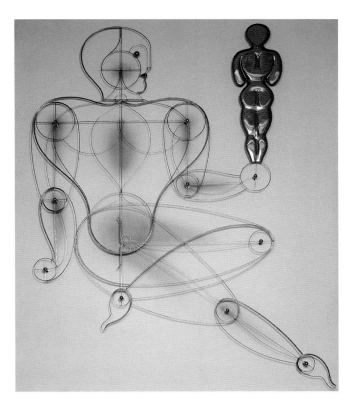

Fig. 112. *Homo Wire Figure with Back-View Figure on its Hand.* (1968 reconstruction, based on a 1930–1931 installation). Steel wire and silver-plated zinc cast. 121⅞ in. high. The Museum of Modern Art, New York: The Riklis Collection of McCrory Corporation (fractional gift). [Cat. no. 59].

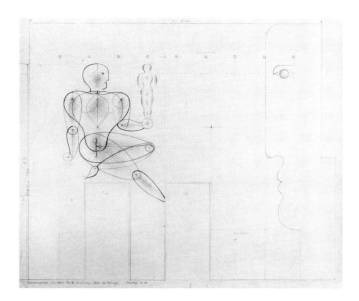

Fig. 114. *Master Plan for the House of Dr. Rabe*. (1930). Pencil. 22¼ × 26¼ in. Family Estate of Oskar Schlemmer. [Cat. no. 182].

interior of the body make visible the organic, animating rhythm of circulation. Weightlessness and transparency combined with hieratic monumentality of stature lend this figure some of the "severity and greatness" of those Egyptian portrayals of the pharaohs that Schlemmer had always admired.[45]

The pen and ink drawing and the working drawings (see figs. 113 and 114) for the Zwenkau project reveal how Schlemmer transposed the *Homo* drawing into a format of three square meters, materializing it in copper, brass, and nickel wire of varying gauges, and adapting it to fit the existing wall and space conditions. The wall was painted olive green. It measured 5.3 by 6.5 meters, had two doors, and was located in a spacious living area with a large window in the opposite wall and only a few pieces of furniture, in tubular steel. Rading's emphatically functional architecture, flooded with light, provided the ideal setting for Schlemmer's "metallurgy." The task was to transform the calm, self-contained homo figure of the pen and ink drawing so that it could serve as one segment of a wall design containing several figures. Since the sculpture was supposed to levitate above the doors on the left side of the wall, elements were added that could reach out toward the right side: the drawn-up arm is bent into a perpendicular and balances on its circular hand a female figure viewed from the rear, made of embossed nickel sheeting. In the original conception the figure's legs were tucked under; here one leg was stretched out on the diagonal toward the door. This two-figured homo group is balanced on the right side by an enormous profile face in copper banding that casts a shadow, the profile

taking up the entire height of the wall. As a connective element Schlemmer positioned at the wall's center a metal piece made up of concentric circles of wire with a ball-shaped core on a coordinate axis of wire, in which the fundamental formal elements of circle, horizontal, and vertical are recapitulated (see fig. 115). Shortly after it was installed, Schlemmer described the mural to Baumeister: "The project for the figures in metal really looks fantastic. Photographs do not do them justice. . . . The wire sculpture, or better, 'Composition in Metal,' a figural composition made of different kinds of metal wire, consists of three figures: the large figure carries a smaller one in its hand; to the right of the wall in relation to the first figure is the metal profile of a face, over fifteen feet high. The figures stand out three inches from the wall, and the changing light creates interesting shifting shadows (on the sundial principle)."[46]

This simple but effective device of using shadows to project the sculpture's outlines onto the wall took advantage of the daylight entering the room from the left to penetrate and enliven the sculpture, to modify or dematerialize it. Although Schlemmer nowhere ascribed symbolic significance to this work, references to the Creation, Adam and Eve, and the unity of man and cosmos are unavoidable. It is fitting that here, in the house of a

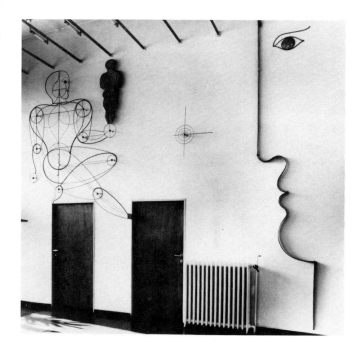

Fig. 115. Homo Wire Figure Installation in the House of Dr. Rabe, Zwenkau, 1930–1931.

doctor, Schlemmer had the opportunity to register his vision of a ''transcendent anatomy of man.''[47]

Schlemmer's Zwenkau ''metallurgy'' and his wire projects of the early 1920's were pioneering efforts. In his own unique style he completed the last three stages of sculptural development from mass to movement outlined by Moholy-Nagy: the perforated stage, the floating stage, and at least the beginnings of light-kinetic sculpture—in his use of light to transform the wire shapes into a linear shadow play.[48]

Sculptural Miniatures

A year before his death, after a ten-year break, Schlemmer returned to sculpture, but this time in an entirely different, reticent, intimate form (see fig. 116). Simultaneously with the miniature *Fensterbilder* he created ''little plaster statues, modelled in plasticine in the negative, and then cast straight off in plaster, which is then painted.''[49] They are significant as a parallel to the development in his painting during this final phase, characterized by ''confining oneself to a small but certain sphere,'' by concentration on the smallest possible format into which everything is to be packed, and by introspection.[50] These delicately colored plaster reliefs reveal the mysterious traces of their genesis in the sensitive modeling, the hesitant coalescence into form, and the organic connection between the figures and their background. In this last period Schlemmer was seeking artistic form that ''appears to be a piece of nature, perceived and formed by a phenomenon. A strange by-product of what we call 'nature'! I wish I could paint it as if it came 'from somewhere' and not from the human hand.''[51] These sculptural miniatures, created in the premonition of approaching death, provide a coda to a development that much earlier inclined to integration in an expanded realm of activity. Thus the Weimar reliefs and the wire sculpture projects fed into the Zwenkau ''metallurgy,'' while the plastic, mobile figurines of *The Triadic Ballet* liberated Schlemmer's free-standing sculptures from static fixity and contextual constraints.

Fig. 116. *Group of Eight Plaster Reliefs*. (1942). Painted plaster. Various sizes, from approximately 4 to 10 in. high. Oskar Schlemmer Family Estate. [Not in exhibition].

Fig. 117. *Self-Portrait with Raised Hand*. (1931–1932). Watercolor.
21¼ × 15½ in. Collection of Peter Kamm, Zug, Switzerland. [Not
in exhibition].

Schlemmer's View of Man

"Oskar Schlemmer's painting vibrates with a new spatial energy. . . . In the mind of the observer it awakens a premonition of a future holistic culture, a culture that will reunite all the arts."

Walter Gropius, 1961

It would be difficult to find a twentieth-century artist who could rival Oskar Schlemmer in the unfaltering intensity with which he functioned as painter, sculptor, muralist, choreographer, set designer, and teacher. Such was Schlemmer's creativity that he left an indelible impression on each of the fields in which he was active. From the outset his work displayed a passion for synthesis, totality, and universality. In his first mural (1911) and dance projects (1912) Schlemmer can already be seen striving to overcome the narrow confines of the individual, discrete work, to reach out and integrate the work in a more comprehensive context. This lifelong preoccupation accounts for the extraordinary range of his oeuvre.

Despite his great versatility, Schlemmer's work manifests an unusual degree of iconographic concentration. At first viewing this concentration might suggest a limited imagination, but closer scrutiny reveals Schlemmer's astonishing capacity for evolution. In Schlemmer, one discovers a Faustian search for binding themes, for a bridge between the visible world and the metaphysical, for an "ethical grounding" and a "grasp on the metaphysical," for a way of portraying ideas through visual images.

Schlemmer found his chief image in the human gestalt which, he was convinced, still offered "the great symbol for the artist." Unlike the Expressionists, who viewed the human form merely as a vehicle for expression, Schlemmer viewed it as a vehicle of structure. Man for him was not a cipher for spiritual turmoil but an icon of the absolute, ruled by the higher laws that govern tectonically organized space. What Schlemmer envisioned and invested in his forms was a synthesis of formal renewal and profundity of thought, of mathematics and metaphysics. He was not content merely to develop a new language of forms, a repertory of abstract figural motifs, and to vary them in his "figure designs" of the Stuttgart period; he wanted these forms to approach absolute meaning, to carry a message, a utopian vision that corresponded to the Bauhaus concept: "I should not direct myself toward building houses, except the ideal house which my paintings imply and anticipate."[52]

Many years later Schlemmer declared, "I am interested in creating human types, not portraits . . . and I am interested in the essence of space, not in 'interiors.' "[53] With this lapidary statement he articulated not only his own guiding principle but also an intellectual goal that he shared with other artists of his generation. Franz Marc, for instance, declared that he wanted to look through things, not just at them, in order to discover "the mystical inner construction of the world."[54] Paul Klee wanted to press on "from the model image to the primal image,"[55] and Kasimir Edschmid, the author of "On Expressionism in Literature," proclaimed in 1917, "All things are concentrated into their essence: the simple, the general, the essential" and "the figure becomes typical. . . . Anything inessential is stripped away. What is important is imparted by the idea: no longer a thinker, no: thinking itself."[56]

Understood thus, art acquires an epistemological function, making archetypal images visible. When Schlemmer purified the human form "in the crucible of abstraction" and reshaped it into a timely and timeless image of man, he was working within a German tradition that went back to ideas formulated primarily by the great Swabian writers, Schiller and Hölderlin. Their aesthetic, derived from transcendental idealism, was modified and applied to painting and sculpture by their contemporaries, Gottlieb Christian Schick (1776–1812) and Johann-Heinrich von Dannecker (1758–1841). Schiller defined the "rational concept of beauty" thus: out of the "individual and changing manifestation" of single human beings, we ought to seek "to derive the absolute and permanent."[57] It is as though Schlemmer, with his concept of man as a canonical figure, shaped by form and mind, a symbol and a standard, had captured to the letter what Schiller says elsewhere: "Every individual is that much less a human being the more he is individual. Only by discarding accidental features and cultivating pure expression of the essential can we achieve greatness of style."[58] This transcendental approach so characteristic of German art grew out of the postulate that behind visible reality could be found a hidden *Ding an sich*, Kant's term for reality independent of the human observer. This view tended to result in disdain for the visible world. Schlemmer too wished to portray not a specific individual but the underlying essence, the primal form, the prototype, and not a specific interior but the "essence of space."[59]

But Schlemmer's classical tendencies were not out of touch with his times and his world; his creations, for all their ideal character, display contemporary traits and are molded by elements of the "new structural thinking" of the 1920's: pragmatism, elimination of the inessential, rationality, precision, and constructive qualities. In spite of Schlemmer's consciously rational optics, his figures are neither lifeless nor soulless; rather they bear the psychic stigmata of modern life.

Within Schlemmer's pictorial space, the posture, placement, orientation, and movement of the figures assume a mental and spiritual dimension, as well as a spatial one. The frontal, profile, or rear view signify basic human attitudes: self-confident confrontation, reflective reserve, or complete withdrawal from the observer, a turning inward. Standing becomes "withstanding," walking becomes "walking through" space, in an existential as well as physical sense. In this realm everything becomes ambiguous: proximity, serial arrangement, opposition, positioning behind, figures passing each other, the isolation or massing of figures. Similarly, the relationship between space and figures can project expressive dimensions. There is an emptiness, a lack of atmosphere, a suction effect in such pictures as *Company at Table* or *Lounge* that project a menacing aspect like that of the monochrome vacuum of the earlier pictures, *Homo* or *Scheme with Figures*. Paraphrasing a statement of Max Beckmann's, Schlemmer might have said, "One must place the figure against the emptiness of space in order not to see its horrifying depths so clearly."[60] Such a formulation expresses a magical experience of space, an experience that corresponds to Beckmann's experience of existence, and Schlemmer himself speaks, in connection with the theater, of the "aura of magic" that transforms man into a "space-bewitched being."[61]

Although in Schlemmer's painting that recession into mysterious depths gradually gives way to a rapprochement between space and figure, Schlemmer remained loyal throughout his life to certain motifs and stylistic forms: reification of the figures, the attempt to freeze their outlines, emphasis on axial structure, support and staircase motifs, even the statuesque composure of the figures. In the early 1930's Schlemmer's figures began to fill the entire picture plane with their plasticity; the dimension of depth is sensed only as an uncertain potential somewhere behind the figures. It is not indefensible to see this new style as deliberate self-assertion that seeks to hold the menace at bay. Retaining and repeating familiar, controlled motifs and techniques also suggest a magical function: taming, disciplining, warding off the chaos of the irrational.

That Schlemmer's image of man was not merely an eccentric allegory but a reflection of experience and contemporary events becomes evident in his dark-toned oilpapers done in the late 1930's. There concealment, camouflage, and withdrawal find tragic expression. And, at the end of his life, his "window pictures" seem premonitory with their view into "the other house," which, though perceived in this world, seems to belong to the realm of the beyond. For Schlemmer, his art was existential necessity: "We need number, measure, and law as armor and as a weapon, lest we be swallowed up by chaos."[62] These words, uttered on the eve of Hitler's seizure of power, carry the urgency of a warning cry, and they attribute an almost eschatological significance to his striving for order and form: art is a means of mastering life, a refuge, a salvation. Schlemmer met the standard enunciated by Nietzsche in the year of Schlemmer's birth: "The greatness of an artist can be measured by the degree to which he approaches great style. . . . To master the chaos within you, to compel your chaos to become form: logically, simply, unambiguously, to become mathematics, law."[63] Thus Schlemmer joins the ranks of that avant-garde of European artists in the first half of the century who took the elements of disorder and the fragments of a disparate reality and drew out of them fictive "order-pictures,"[64] in which the dissonances were preserved but controlled and thereby transcended.[65]

KARIN VON MAUR
Translated from the German by Krishna Winston

Notes

1. Diary entry, July 1913, Oskar Schlemmer, *The Letters and Diaries of Oskar Schlemmer*, selected and edited by Tut Schlemmer, trans. Krishna Winston (Middletown, Connecticut: Wesleyan University Press, 1972), p. 12.

2. Wassily Kandinsky, *Über das Geistige in der Kunst* (1912 [actually 1911]; reprint ed., ed. Max Bill, Bern-Bümpliz: Benteli-Verlag, 1952), p. 120. Franz Marc, "Geistige Güter," in *Der Blaue Reiter*, eds. Wassily Kandinsky and Franz Marc (Munich: R. Piper, 1912), p. 3.

3. See Sidney Geist, *Brancusi: A Study of the Sculpture* (New York: Grossman, 1968), pp. 34–35; cat. nos. 56, 57, and 66; pls. pp. 34–35 and 41.

4. Diary entry, October 1919, Schlemmer, *Letters and Diaries*, p. 73.

5. Diary entry, October 1919, Schlemmer, *Letters and Diaries*, p. 73.

6. Diary entry, 30 April 1919, Schlemmer, *Letters and Diaries*, p. 69.

7. Paul Ferdinand Schmidt, *Saarbrücker Zeitung*, 20 August 1920.

8. Diary entry, mid-November 1922, Schlemmer, *Letters and Diaries*, p. 134.

9. Notes for a lecture delivered 16 February 1923 at the house of the philosopher and art critic Eberhard Grisebach in Jena, printed with the erroneous dating "Spring 1925," in Schlemmer, *Letters and Diaries*, p. 165.

10. Manuscript of the lecture "Formale Elemente der Bühne," delivered 4 March 1933, p. 14.

11. Diary entry, 13 July 1925, Schlemmer, *Letters and Diaries*, p. 171.

12. Radio interview, broadcast on 30 November 1930 on the "Schlesische Funkstunde," printed in part in Karin von Maur, *Oskar Schlemmer: Monographie und Oeuvrekatalog der Gemälde, Aquarelle, Pastelle und Plastiken* (Munich: Prestel-Verlag, 1979), vol. 1, p. 194.

13. *Europa-Almanach*, eds. C. Einstein and P. Westheim (Potsdam: G. Kiepenheuer Verlag, 1925), p. 271.

14. Fernand Léger, "Concours chorégraphique international au théâtre des Champs-Elysées. Juillet 1932." *Cahiers d'art* 7 (1932), p. 288.

15. Catalogue for the exhibition "Der schöne Mensch in der Neuen Kunst" (Städtische Ausstellungsgebäude, Darmstadt, 1929), p. 54.

16. Diary entry, 18 March 1931, Schlemmer, *Letters and Diaries*, p. 277.

17. Diary entry, 30 October 1930, Schlemmer, *Letters and Diaries*, pp. 271–272 (the dating is questionable, since the content is closely connected with the "Perspektiven" address—see note 47).

18. Diary entry, 31 May 1936, Schlemmer, *Letters and Diaries*, p. 353.

19. Diary entry, 17 May 1936, in Maur, *Schlemmer Monographie*, p. 276.

20. Diary entry, 8 July 1941, Schlemmer, *Letters and Diaries*, pp. 389–390. The published version omits the reference to the source, the *Minotaure* 3, no. 8 (June 1936), in which André Breton's article "D'une décalcomanie sans objet préconçu" reported on the Surrealist experiments.

21. *Klecksographien von Justinus Kerner, mit Illustrationen nach den Vorlagen des Verfassers* (Stuttgart, Leipzig, Berlin, Vienna, 1890). Similar experiments were undertaken by Victor Hugo and Christian Morgenstern, and in 1921 the Swiss Hermann Rorschach developed his technique for using ink blots in psychiatric diagnosis. There was a close connection with the Surrealist principle of *écriture automatique*.

22. Schlemmer to Julius Bissier, 11 May 1942, Schlemmer, *Letters and Diaries*, p. 399.

23. Diary entry, 12 May 1942, Schlemmer, *Letters and Diaries*, p. 400.

24. Schlemmer to Julius Bissier, 11 May 1942, Schlemmer, *Letters and Diaries*, p. 399.

25. Diary entry, 23 May 1942, Schlemmer, *Letters and Diaries*, p. 400.

26. Diary entry, 1 April 1943, Schlemmer, *Letters and Diaries*, p. 411. Schlemmer is quoting from a letter written by Rilke to Baron Jakob Uexkull on 19 August 1909. See Rainer Maria Rilke, *Briefe*, ed. Rilke Archives, Weimar (Wiesbaden: Insel-Verlag, 1950), vol. 1, p. 263.

27. Diary entry, 2 September 1915, Schlemmer, *Letters and Diaries*, p. 29.

28. Diary entry, mid-March 1916, Schlemmer, *Letters and Diaries*, p. 34.

29. Schlemmer to Martha Luz, 9 June 1918, Schlemmer, *Letters and Diaries*, p. 53.

30. Diary entry, 18 March 1931, Schlemmer, *Letters and Diaries*, p. 277.

31. El Lissitzky, "K. und die Pangeometrie," *Europa-Almanach*, 1925, p. 112. In this almanac Schlemmer published his important essay, "Der theatralische Kostümtanz," pp. 189–191.

32. Diary entry, 9 April 1935, Schlemmer, *Letters and Diaries*, p. 337.

33. Diary entry, 27 April 1915, Schlemmer, *Letters and Diaries*, p. 27.

34. Autobiographical sketch, written around 1923, unpublished manuscript, one page, Oskar Schlemmer Archiv, Staatsgalerie Stuttgart.

35. Fritz Schneider, "Herbstschau Neuer Kunst," *Süddeutsche Zeitung*, 14 November 1919, and Konrad Düssel, "Neue Kunst im Kunstgebäude II," *Stuttgarter Neues Tagblatt*, 20 November 1919.

36. Alexander Archipenko, "Polychromatic Manifesto," *Archipenko: An International Visionary*, ed. Donald A. Karshan (Washington, D.C.: Smithsonian Institution, 1969), p. 23ff.

37. Diary entry, November 1919, Schlemmer, *Letters and Diaries*, pp. 73–74.

38. Diary entry, around 1922, in Maur, *Schlemmer Monographie*, p. 132.

39. "Gestaltungsprinzipien bei der malerisch-plastischen Ausgestaltung des Werkstattgebäudes des Staatlichen Bauhauses," in *Das Kunstblatt* 7, no. 11/12 (November–December 1923), p. 341. Also Schlemmer, *Letters and Diaries*, p. 142.

40. Schlemmer, *Letters and Diaries*, pp. 148–149, mistakenly described as a diary entry; in fact it is a separate manuscript entitled "Wesen der Plastik," dated 8 January 1924, two pages.

41. Diary entry, September 1922, Schlemmer, *Letters and Diaries*, p. 126.

42. Diary entry, 29 January 1928, Schlemmer, *Letters and Diaries*, p. 223.

43. Quoted from László Moholy-Nagy, *Von Material zu Architektur* (Munich: Langen Verlag, 1929), p. 162.

44. Schlemmer to Otto Meyer, 2 September 1930, Schlemmer, *Letters and Diaries*, pp. 266–267.

45. Schlemmer to Fritz Nemitz, 17 February 1937, Schlemmer, *Letters and Diaries*, p. 361.

46. Schlemmer to Willi Baumeister, 22 July 1931, Schlemmer, *Letters and Diaries*, p. 282.

47. Inaugural address at the Vereinigte Staatsschulen für Kunst in Berlin, "Perspektiven," delivered 9 November 1932, in Maur, *Schlemmer Monographie*, vol. 1, p. 337.

48. Moholy-Nagy, *Von Material zu Architektur*, pp. 162 and 113ff.

49. Schlemmer to Julius Bissier, 11 May 1942, Schlemmer, *Letters and Diaries*, p. 400.

50. Diary entry, 3 September 1942, Schlemmer, *Letters and Diaries*, p. 402 (translation amended).

51. Diary entry, 8 July 1941, Schlemmer, *Letters and Diaries*, p. 390. See also entries for 22 March 1942 and 23 May 1942, Schlemmer, *Letters and Diaries*, pp. 397 and 400.

52. Diary entry, mid-November 1922, Schlemmer, *Letters and Diaries*, p. 134; and manuscript, "Der Rückzug" (unpublished, about 1922), Oskar Schlemmer Archiv, Staatsgalerie Stuttgart.

53. Schlemmer to Fritz Nemitz, 17 February 1937, Schlemmer, *Letters and Diaries*, p. 361 (translation amended).

54. Franz Marc, "Geistige Güter," p. 3.

55. Paul Klee, "Über moderne Kunst," lecture delivered 26 January 1924 in Jena, in Paul Klee, *Das bildnerische Denken*, ed. Jörg Spiller (Basel and Stuttgart: B. Schwabe, 1956), p. 93.

56. Kasimir Edschmid, "Epochen des Expressionismus," *Frühe Manifeste* (Hamburg: C. Wegner, 1957), pp. 37–39.

57. Friedrich Schiller, "Über die ästhetische Erziehung des Menschen in einer Reihe von Briefen," in *Schillers sämmtliche Werke*, 12 vols. (Stuttgart and Tübingen: J. G. Cotta, 1838), vol. 12, p. 42.

58. Schiller, "Über Matthissons Gedichte," *Schillers sämmtliche Werke*, vol. 12, p. 387.

59. Schlemmer to Fritz Nemitz, 17 February 1937, Schlemmer, *Letters and Diaries*, p. 361 (translation amended).

60. Beckmann actually said, "One must place the debris of objects against the emptiness of space . . . "; quoted from Werner Haftmann, *Malerei im zwanzigsten Jahrhundert: Eine Bildenzyklopädie* (Munich: Prestel-Verlag, 1965), p. 272.

61. Manuscript of the lecture "Formale Elemente der Bühne," delivered 4 March 1933, p. 14, Oskar Schlemmer Archiv, Staatsgalerie Stuttgart.

62. "Perspektiven" address, Maur, *Schlemmer Monographie*, p. 343.

63. Friedrich Nietzsche, *Der Wille zur Macht*, bk. 3, sec. 4, "Der Wille zur Macht als Kunst," in *Nietzsches Werke*, pocket edition, ed. E. Foerster-Nietzsche and P. Gast (Leipzig: C. G. Naumann, 1906), vol. 10, pp. 87–88.

64. Diary entry, 18 January 1942, Schlemmer, *Letters and Diaries*, p. 394.

65. The present Maur essay is based in part on the text which appeared in Karin von Maur, *Oskar Schlemmer*, the catalogue accompanying the 1977 retrospective exhibition at the Staatsgalerie Stuttgart and Kunstverein Hamburg (published Württembergischen Kunstverein Stuttgart, 1977).

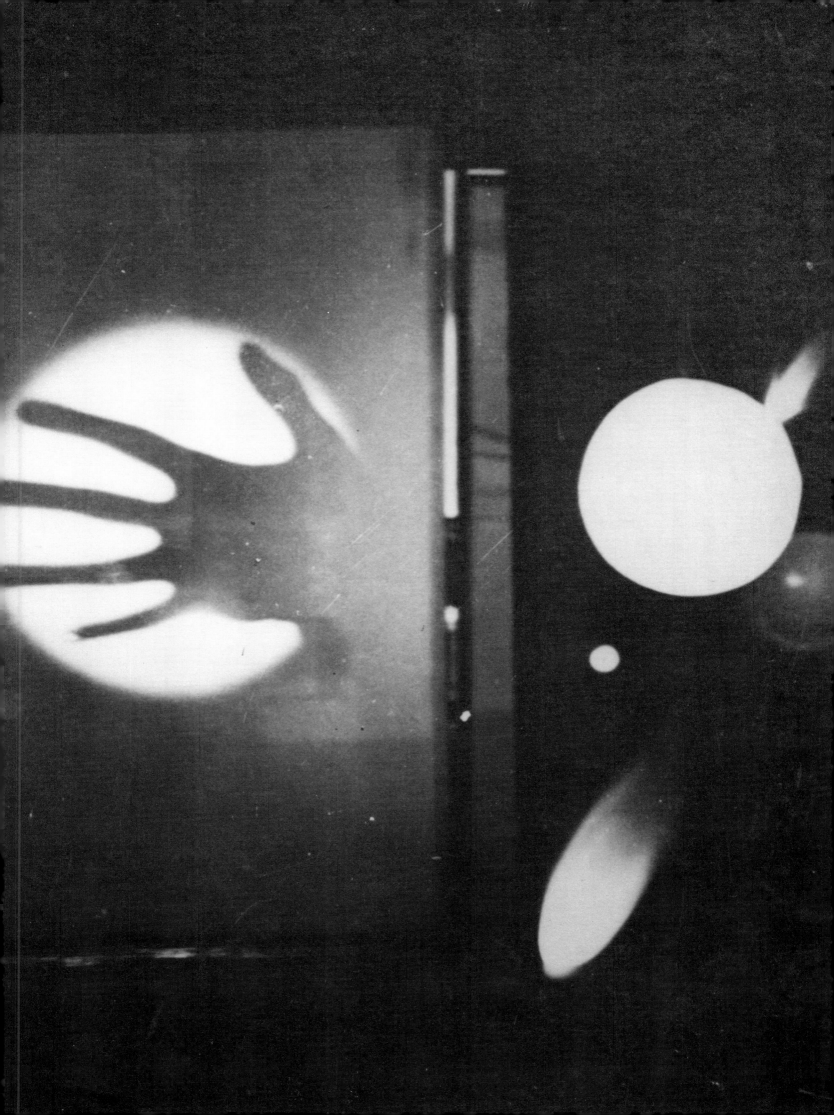

STELZENLÄUFER

Stilt-Runner. (1927). Watercolor. 17⅞ × 23⅞ in. Oskar Schlemmer
Theater Estate, Collection UJS. [Cat. no. 159].

The Art of Reconciliation:
Oskar Schlemmer's Work for the Theater

"Perhaps the ultimate wisdom is: compromise."[1] This observation, made by Oskar Schlemmer in a diary entry on November 12, 1924, provides a valuable key to understanding the essential character of the artist's entire oeuvre. For Schlemmer regarded his own artistic impulses in terms of an inner conflict between the fundamental principles of Dionysian intoxication and Apollonian restraint; the challenge he set for himself was to find an aesthetic form in which he could resolve these two opposing modes. "I vacillate between two styles, two worlds, two attitudes toward life," he wrote in September 1915. "If I could succeed in analyzing them, I think I would be able to shake off all these doubts."[2]

The problem presented itself first of all in the sphere of painting, where Schlemmer initially felt compelled to choose between the Romanticism he saw embodied in the work of Delacroix, van Gogh, and Böcklin on one hand, and, on the other, the Classicism he associated with Ingres, Cézanne, and Leibl. But rather than simply settling on a single approach, Schlemmer determined that "Everything should merge into one great current . . . all the elements must be drawn upon."[3] Accordingly, he sought a means of channeling the propensity for emotional expression that he recognized within himself: "I would like to present the most romantic idea in the most austere form."[4]

This dialectical attitude informs many of Schlemmer's statements, and it emerges as a prominent, if not indeed a determining element in all of his artistic work. One finds it repeatedly in his discussions of particular aesthetic issues—for example, his notion of "the painter's vision," which Schlemmer defined as "abstraction won of familiarity with nature." In fact, the reconciliation of opposites was central to his understanding of art itself: In response to the rhetorical question, "What does the artist do?"

Schlemmer answered, "He makes the unclear appear clear, the unconscious conscious, the impossible possible; plucks the One out of the Chaos, simplicity out of multiplicity."[5] Throughout the teens and twenties Schlemmer worked to forge out of these beliefs a unique painting style in which his fundamental respect for the integrity of the human figure, located in an essentially naturalistic space, was balanced by his commitment to simplification and geometric abstraction as a means of conveying the order that he felt was inherent in pictorial form. He thus achieved what he described in 1917 as "a felicitous combination by putting the most abstract depictive methods at the service of the visible world."[6] In doing so, Schlemmer approached nature and the real world not in objective, visual terms, but as "a source of strength . . . the basis of everything spiritual,"[7] whose metaphysical and emotive qualities he conveyed in generalized, abstracted forms.

Schlemmer's involvement with the theater and dance proceeded along a course that closely paralleled his evolution as a painter. The theater of types that he established at the Bauhaus in the 1920's was preceded by more than a decade of gestation during which Schlemmer struggled to harmonize the competing claims that self-expression and self-control placed on his conception of any work of art, including one that was destined for the theater. Thus, in order to grasp the full significance of his mature theatrical productions at the Bauhaus, it is helpful to explore their origins, beginning with *The Triadic Ballet*, Schlemmer's first project in the realm of the performing arts.

In the autumn of 1912, upon his return to Stuttgart after a year in Berlin, Schlemmer enrolled as a *Meisterschüler* in the painting class taught by Adolf Hölzel at the Stuttgart Akademie.[8] Hölzel was an influential teacher with a wide following that included not only his art students but also a number of young architects as well as the ballet dancer Albert Burger, whom Schlemmer met at this time. Although Burger was a soloist with the Royal Opera Ballet, he was passionately interested in modern dance. During the summer of 1912, he and his future wife, the dancer Else Hötzel, had visited Hellerau, near Dresden, where they saw a performance of scenes from Christoph Gluck's *Orpheus and Euridice* at a school headed by the Swiss composer Emile Jaques-Dalcroze. Burger was deeply impressed by the radically simplified staging designed by Adolphe Appia, and by the affective intensity of the dancers, whom Jaques-Dalcroze had trained as a group to convey the emotional content of Gluck's music through rhythmically orchestrated body movements liberated from the constraints of classical ballet. Upon his return to Stuttgart, determined to carry out a similarly unconventional dance production, Burger immediately enlisted Schlemmer to create the setting for a modern ballet which Burger entitled *The Courtship*. Within a matter of months, if not at the time of its conception, Schlemmer was also included among the projected ballet's dancers, performing the role of a demon opposite a pair of lovers who were to be danced by Burger and Hötzel. The theme, as described by Burger at the time, involved a progression from "unconscious purity to conscious purity"; as Helmut Günther has more recently explained, "Proceeding through [the opposite poles of] the ecstatic and the demonic, the pair [of lovers] find their way to purity and form."[9]

In a diary entry of December 1912, which constitutes his earliest recorded reference to the dance, Schlemmer noted that the sequence of scenes, in what is presumed to have been Burger's original conception of the ballet, traced the "Development from the old dance to the new." The performance was to begin with a gray, conventional set that was intended to provide an appropriate background for choreography and music that were "familiar, easy to absorb." The initial "old dance," represented by the forms of traditional ballet, which the audience would naturally approve of, was to be interrupted by a demon scurrying across the stage. Wearing a mask and costumed in a "provocative yellow-orange color," the demon embodied "the Dionysian element," from which the pair of conventional dancers would "shrink back, startled." Thereafter, a dark brown backdrop or veil that gradually grew "lighter, more reddish," would provide an atmosphere that "has something unclear, groping, about it, as of something just taking shape." The music would have the same "dark and confused" qualities, to which the dancer's erratic movements would now also correspond. When the demon returned, the brown veil would be lifted and a change of color from red to bright orange would

establish an intensified mood "full of passionate excitement—erotic delirium." At this point the color would shift gradually "from orange to lemon yellow, symbolizing morbid over-stimulation, ecstasy. The movements of the dancers and the music: shrill, high notes." Abruptly, a black backdrop would then descend to shroud the stage "like a sudden fall into darkest night." The dancers would be "wrapped in gray. The music deep, minor. Mourning." From upstage center, a violet dot would slowly grow into a circle and then become a blue square, eventually engulfing the entire space, as the dancers would make "measured, noble" movements to "majestic, solemn" music. In the last scene, as the color would change from dark blue to pure white, "an angel in silver, very airy, misty, delicate," would bring the two dancers together under the sign of a distant white star. Finally, the music would fade away and the demon would be dead.[10]

This scenario, with its emphasis on the expressive potential of an intimately related development of musical, coloristic, and formal themes, clearly reveals Schlemmer's debt to the ideas of Wassily Kandinsky. He knew Kandinsky's essay, *Concerning the Spiritual in Art*, which had been published in Munich early in 1912. In it, Kandinsky had described the new dance of the future as "the only medium in terms of time and space expressing the interior meaning of motion," and argued that "harmonious or contrapuntal composition" of musical, pictorial, and dance movements "will help to realize stage composition, the first form of a monumental art."[11] Kandinsky also made reference to Alexander Scriabin's theory of the correspondence between specific musical and coloristic tones, the combination of which leads to mutual intensification and hence to enhanced affect and spiritual resonance. Schlemmer read a more detailed consideration of these ideas in an article devoted to Scriabin by Leonid Sabaneiev that appeared in May 1912 in the *Almanach Der Blaue Reiter*, edited by Kandinsky together with Franz Marc. In addition, the *Almanach* contained an essay on abstraction and music by Arnold Schönberg, whom Kandinsky had also mentioned in *Concerning the Spiritual in Art*. Burger and Schlemmer were familiar with Schönberg's music, having attended a performance of *Pierrot Lunaire* in Stuttgart on November 11, 1912. As Schlemmer wrote to the Swiss artist, Otto Meyer, early in the following year, "First I must tell you the latest developments in my dance project. Some time ago, a friend and I heard a concert of Arnold Schönberg's melodramas; a lady wearing a modern Pierrot costume spoke to the accompaniment of dissonant, naturalistically illustrative, but very expressive music. We were much taken with the concert and wrote to Schönberg, asking him if he might be interested in composing music for

Pantomime. 1912. Ink. 8⅜ × 11⅛ in. Staatsgalerie Stuttgart: Schlemmer Family Estate Deposit. [Cat. no. 73].

mobilization in the summer of 1914, the project was temporarily put aside. However, Schlemmer managed to maintain contact with Burger during the next two years when, despite the adverse conditions of wartime, he was able to continue painting and eventually also to work on the ballet.

Toward the end of 1916, Schlemmer received permission to leave his military post in order to prepare for a performance of several scenes from the ballet that were presented as an interlude in the context of a charity event organized by his regiment in the Stuttgart Stadtgarten on

modern dance or if he could recommend a young composer to us. Schönberg wrote back: 'My music is completely lacking in dance rhythm, but if you think it suitable, then so do I.' ''[12] However, at the time, in late December 1912, Schönberg was committed to other projects, and nothing came of this potential collaboration. Instead, Burger and Schlemmer turned to a young student of Jaques-Dalcroze named Albert Jeanneret (the brother of Charles-Edouard Jeanneret, later to be known as Le Corbusier), with whom they corresponded about their ballet during the course of 1913.

There is no evidence that Jeanneret ever composed any music for the ballet, but his ideas were nevertheless important for the development of Schlemmer's attitude toward this particular work and toward the dance in general. Jeanneret objected to the radical opposition in the original scenario between the initial experience of the life force as pure sensuality, and the emphasis on metaphysical order and control that only emerges subsequently. He argued that a ''full rhythmic life'' is not achieved until these two elements are brought together; it was, he felt, not the overcoming of the body by the spirit, but the union of the one with the other that ''makes a higher life possible.'' Although Burger rejected his critique of the ballet as too philosophical in orientation, Jeanneret's belief that the resolution of opposing forces is the crucial formative experience of both art and life would undoubtedly have appealed to Schlemmer.[13]

The initial intensity with which Schlemmer and Burger developed their balletic ideas appears to have slackened after 1913, as Schlemmer focused his attention primarily on painting. With the declaration of war and Schlemmer's

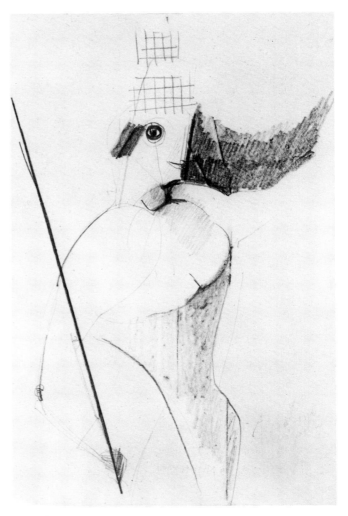

The Figurine ''Absalom.'' (1912). Pencil. 7⅝ × 4⅞ in. Staatsgalerie Stuttgart. [Cat. no. 71].

the evening of December 7, 1916. This first, fragmentary performance of no more than three pas de deux that would eventually be reincorporated into the full *Triadic Ballet* was carried out by Burger and Hötzel to music by the contemporary Italian composer Mario Enrico Bossi.[14] Schlemmer supervised the rehearsals, and it seems that he had by that time emerged as the dominant creative force behind what he was already referring to as "my ballet."

Little is known about this performance, but the remark of a newspaper correspondent that the dancers appeared as two "puppet figures" suggests its relationship to the work of Heinrich von Kleist, whom Schlemmer subsequently acknowledged as a major influence on his own ideas. Von Kleist's brief but provocative "Essay on the Puppet Theater"[15] has been widely and variously interpreted since it was first published in 1810, and it became the object of particularly intense interest on the part of virtually everyone involved with the theory of drama and dance in the early twentieth century. At that time, innovative dramatists were seeking to overcome what they considered to be the debased illusionism of the realist theater that had predominated in the second half of the nineteenth century, and they came to view the puppet as a vehicle of stylization and abstraction on the stage. In an influential article of 1908, Edward Gordon Craig modeled his notion of the ideal actor as the "Über-Marionette" on von Kleist's puppet, which despite its human shape, is neither capable of expressing physically a specific state of mind, nor subject to the limitations imposed by gravity and nature's other organic laws.[16] What Craig and a host of others throughout Europe found most attractive in von Kleist's discussion of the puppet was the argument that because it lacks consciousness, the puppet's movements cannot be determined by mental affect, and they are therefore exceedingly graceful.[17] Von Kleist valued the mechanical movements of the puppet above those of even the greatest human dancer, but he nevertheless left open the possibility of a future performance art that would transcend simple self-awareness or self-expression through the attainment of "an infinite consciousness," a state of "grace that returns after knowledge."[18]

This ideal of transcendence was precisely what Schlemmer sought to convey in *The Triadic Ballet*. As his ideas for its staging developed in the mid-teens, he thought increasingly in terms of abstracting the human body into regular geometric shapes that suggest the simplified form of a puppet or a marionette: "The square of the ribcage./the circle of the belly,/the cylinder of the neck,/the cylinders of the arms and lower thighs,/the circles of the elbow joints, elbows, knees, shoulders, knuckles,/the circles of the head, the eyes. . . ."[19] At the same time that he was developing this conception of geometric equivalents for parts of the human body, he continued to think in terms of an opposing expressive extreme that was also manifested in his interest in puppet-like forms. Its result, he wrote in 1917, was embodied in "my spirits, masks, dolls."[20]

Back at the front, in February 1918, Schlemmer was still thinking about the ballet performance that had taken place more than a year earlier, and the possibilities for future projects that it had opened up. "I myself took the first step," he wrote to Otto Meyer, "and now I am expected to follow up with more. In addition, this involves me directly, for I am planning on dancing my own inventions; after all, if the copy was effective, the original should be all the more so."[21] When the war ended, and he returned to Stuttgart, Schlemmer was once again united with Burger and Hötzel, with whom, by the end of 1919, he had begun rehearsing the ballet. As he did so, Schlemmer identified himself ever more closely with the dances, becoming convinced that "I am the key to them. What suits my body is determined by my kinesthetic sense and cannot be adequately reproduced by other bodies." He even thought of the dance in general in terms of his own psychic make-up, describing dance as "pure effect," the love of which he had inherited from his father, whereas his mother had given him what he called "my better part"—presumably referring to his regard for order and control. "I am very conscious of these two souls in my breast; they contain the germ of constant new conflict."[22] *The Triadic Ballet*, like all of Schlemmer's art, grew out of this sense of conflict, and the form it ultimately assumed was the result of his search for a meaningful resolution of the opposing Dionysian and Apollonian modes of expression.

In an effort to complete preparations for *The Triadic Ballet* as well as two other theatrical productions, in the spring of 1920 Schlemmer moved to the Stuttgart suburb of Cannstatt, where above his studio there was a large hall with a dance stage and the fabrication of costumes was in progress. When in July he was invited by Walter Gropius to join the faculty of the Bauhaus, he initially put off making a decision, citing his involvement with these projects as his excuse. Even in December, after he accepted the Bauhaus appointment, he continued to work intermittently in Cannstatt. He did not move permanently to Weimar until after the performance on June 4, 1921 of "two operatic one-acters, one in grand theatrical style, the other 'for Burmese marionettes,' with an idiotic text—comic, erotic, Indian."[23] The first of these was Oskar Kokoschka's expressionist tragedy, *Murderer, Hope of Women*, which concerns a symbolic battle between the

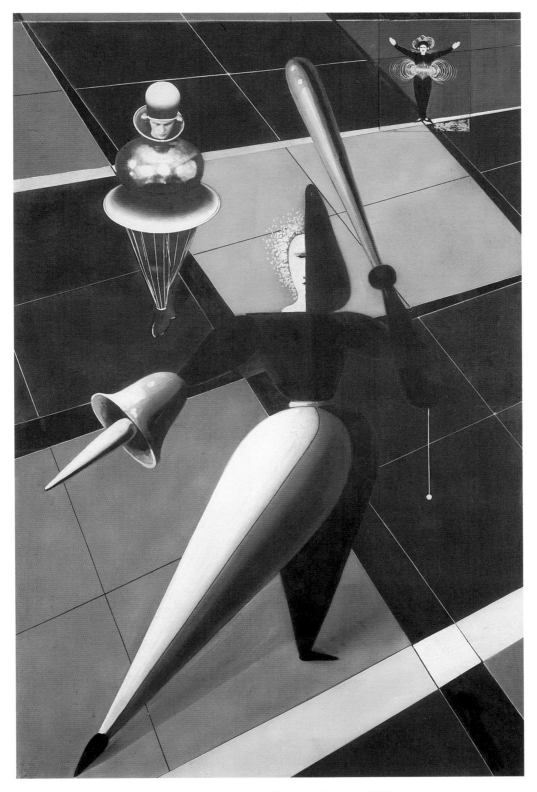

Figurines in Space: Study for The Triadic Ballet. (ca. 1924).
Gouache and photographs. 22⅝ × 14⅝ in. The Museum of Modern
Art, New York: Gift of Lily Auchincloss. [Cat. no. 90].

elemental sexual urges of man and woman. The second was Franz Blei's *Das Nusch-Nuschi (The Thingamajig)*, a much more frivolous and irreverent piece, for which Schlemmer designed not only the set and costumes but also the dance sequences for the actors who played the marionettes. These he described as being "far superior to the rest of the production."[24] As Karin von Maur has observed, the presentation of these two operas in one evening gave Schlemmer an opportunity to experience the juxtaposition of heroic monumentality and measured solemnity on one hand and, on the other, irony and grotesque distortion;[25] both of these modes were contained in *The Triadic Ballet*, which was finally given its premiere in Stuttgart on September 30, 1922.

As its title suggests, *The Triadic Ballet* was based on the principle of a trinity; it consisted of three acts, each of which was governed by a different color established by a backdrop curtain. The colors corresponded to a mood that was projected by the music as well as by the gestures and movements of the dancers: in the first act, yellow evoked the burlesque and comical; this was followed by rose and the opposed mood of solemnity and ceremoniousness that characterized the second act; finally, black provided for an atmosphere of heroic monumentality in which the conflict was resolved in the last sequences. Three dancers (Schlemmer, Burger, and Hötzel) performed solos, duets, or trios in a total of twelve different scenes, for which there were eighteen costumes in all.

The costumes were without doubt the most important component of *The Triadic Ballet*; Schlemmer conceived of them before any of the other elements, the character of which was in each case determined by the shapes of the costumes. Constructed of diverse materials, including wood, cardboard, glass, and metal, as well as stuffed or padded fabrics, the costumes developed in part out of Schlemmer's experiments in the Bauhaus sculpture workshop, which he directed. That he was seriously exploring the possibilities of combining such materials soon after his arrival at the Bauhaus is demonstrated by a diary entry of February 1922: "The New Series! White plaster plates as a basis, these hollowed out, shaped in relief, pierced—and on them—in them, glass, glass pipes, mirror glass, colored glass. Painting behind and in front of glass, several pieces lined up in succession, to be placed against the light; wire made of nickel, brass, copper, steel filaments. Polished, sculpted woods." Despite the technological associations evoked by many of these materials, Schlemmer was adamant about where his real interests lay, and he made this clear in his diary: "Not machine, not abstract—always man!"[26] In the costumes, the materials were formed into geometrical shapes, such as spheres, demi-spheres, cylinders, disks, spirals, and ellipses. Strapped

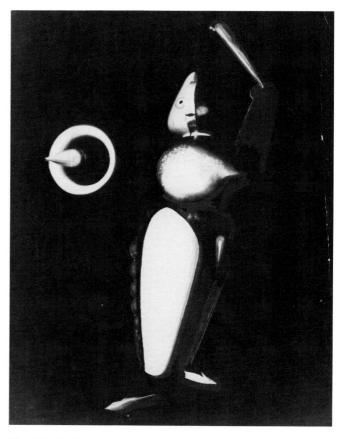

Fig. 1. Oskar Schlemmer as "The Abstract" in The Triadic Ballet, 1927.

into and constrained by these forms, the dancers were physically able to make only a limited number of movements. Schlemmer later described this aspect of *The Triadic Ballet* as "the first consequential demonstration of spatially-plastic costumery. Spatially plastic, for they are so to speak colored and metallic sculptures which, worn by dancers, move in space, whereby physical sensation is significantly influenced, in such a manner that the more the apparently violated body fuses with the costume, the more it attains new forms of dance expression manifestations."[27] What he had in mind was perhaps best embodied in *Der Abstrakte*, which Schlemmer himself performed in the first scene of the last act (fig. 1). The asymmetrical costume of "the abstract" was based on the principle of disequilibrium: the white right leg was very thickly padded and accented with red, while the left leg, in black tights, was hardly visible against the black backdrop. The arms were given similarly unbalanced emphases, and the mask that covered the entire head divided the face into two unequally weighted halves. The costume's asymmetrical features were echoed in the movements of "the abstract," for example by the dominant right leg, which took huge, lunging steps in directions that were diagonal to the front of the stage. Thus a lack of balance in the choreography was intended to express the specific character of the costume. In other cases, the dances were designed to demonstrate the trajectory of a geometric shape set into motion. For example, in the first scene of the ballet, the female dancer wore a round skirt made of cardboard in the shape of a shallow bowl turned upside down. On it and on her knob-like hat were painted numerous brightly-colored, concentric rings. The choreography called for the dancer to move in circles, which must have made her resemble a spinning top. Later, in the third act, the same female dancer was clothed in a spiral, and with her arms outstretched, the rotating movements of her body represented the three-dimensional form of her costume as it passed through space (fig. 2).[28]

Together with geometric abstraction, there was in both the costumes and the choreography of *The Triadic Ballet* a pronounced emphasis on mechanical qualities. Eric Michaud has convincingly argued that "Schlemmer does not want to create 'robots,' he is not seeking to reduce his actors to the status of automatons composed of

Fig. 2. "The Spiral" in The Triadic Ballet, 1927(?).

mechanical parts, like those of Depero or Ivo Pannaggi in Italy, of Exter or Kliun in the U.S.S.R. Rather, he wants to constrain the body with the costume. The precision of the machine is not to be mimicked in a more or less efficacious fashion, it is the very structure of the costume that requires 'precision.' "[29] Yet the fact remains that Schlemmer himself acknowledged the importance of the machine and technology, although in this as in every other realm he eschewed an extreme position. In *The Triadic Ballet*, the powerful influence of the mechanical, which resulted in the dancers appearing to act like puppets or marionettes, was offset not simply in the manner that Michaud suggests, but also by the expressionist aspects of what remained of the original scenario. These were reflected in the progression from the initial comic passages, through the ceremonial second act, to the transcendental and metaphysical mode that culminated in the last scene where, spotlighted on the darkened stage, the three dancers, in costumes made of wires and gold spheres, demonstrated in abstract terms the laws that govern movement in space. As Schlemmer wrote in his diary, "Both these modes of consciousness—the sense of man as a machine, and insight into the deepest wells of creativity—are symptoms of one and the same yearning," which he defined as a "yearning for synthesis." And he wrote of *The Triadic Ballet*: "Thus the dance, which is Dionysian and wholly emotional in origin, becomes strict and Apollonian in its final form, a symbol of the balancing of opposites."[30]

Having evolved slowly over a ten-year period, *The Triadic Ballet* was a very rich and complex work. Not only was its scenario a distilled version of Burger and Schlemmer's original conception of *The Courtship*, but, with several costumes adapted from those of the conventional ballerina and the *commedia dell'arte* (which had also inspired Schönberg's *Pierrot Lunaire*), it still contained references to the forms of the traditional dance and theater. By 1922, however, Schlemmer's interest in the issues of abstraction and mechanization had emerged as the salient features of his approach to the stage.

Among the Bauhaus faculty at this time Schlemmer was a vocal proponent of the need to repudiate the tendency toward escapist utopianism and "the medieval concept of craftsmanship" that prevailed at the institution during its early years: "We can and should concentrate only on what is most real, the realization of ideas. Instead of cathedrals, the 'Living-machine.' "[31] Moreover, he had already recognized that given the absence of opportunities for building due to the economic crisis in post-war Germany, the "illusionary world of the theater offers an outlet" for those who could only dream of creating modern architecture.[32] Gropius seemed to share this idea, when in the fall of 1921, he appointed Lothar Schreyer to direct a theater workshop at the Bauhaus. "So now," Schlemmer wrote at the time, "the Bauhaus has a commitment to theater, which makes me happy. Theatrical questions will henceforth play an important role among the subjects we treat."[33] Initially, Schreyer's religiously oriented symbolism probably appealed to Schlemmer, fresh as he was from his work several months earlier on Kokoschka's expressionist opera. But by the spring of 1922 he was already seeking to distinguish his approach from Schreyer's cultic notion of the theater as lived, spiritual experience. He wrote to Meyer on March 13, 1922: " . . . the theater is gradually being admitted to the Bauhaus. Schreyer was the opening wedge—he is both a poet and a painter, but in the realm of the 'holy.' That leaves me the dance and the comic element, which I gladly, i.e. unjealously, acknowledge to be my department."[34]

During the course of the following year, the interests of many faculty members, including Schlemmer, as well as of a majority of students at the Bauhaus, shifted decisively away from expressionism toward a more practically oriented, rationalist attitude. In this atmosphere, Schreyer's theater experiments were increasingly met with indifference or, on occasion, hostility; in the spring of 1923 he decided to resign. Several months later, the new orientation of the Bauhaus was symbolized by Gropius's proclamation of the motto, "Art and technology: a new unity," in the context of the Bauhaus exhibition that took place in August 1923. As part of the festivities surrounding the exhibition, *The Triadic Ballet* was performed in Weimar, where it was, Schlemmer reported, "a big success."[35]

One would expect to find that, as a result of these events, Schlemmer was able to consolidate his position with respect to the theater workshop at the Bauhaus, whose direction he assumed upon Schreyer's resignation. Yet his situation remained problematic for several reasons. First of all, as he wrote to Meyer at the beginning of June 1923, "The future development of the Bauhaus stage lies in darkness. The Bauhaus lacks the first prerequisite, a stage, and Gropius ignores all suggestions to this effect."[36] Second, Schlemmer found that he could exercise only a limited influence on the students in the theater workshop, who insisted on their independence: "They want to run things themselves," Schlemmer reported to Meyer in early October 1923.[37] Moreover, the students insisted on concentrating almost exclusively on the idea of mechanization, and Schlemmer felt compelled to urge restraint in that regard. In another letter to Meyer of October 1923, he described how the tables had suddenly turned at the Bauhaus, where the emphasis on the machine and technology was now being defended—even exalted—by precisely those people who had originally argued against it: "So much so that I found myself in the curious position of leaning over backwards to restore equilibrium."[38] In the *Figural Cabinet* (see figs. 3–6), his first Bauhaus theater project, which had been produced in the spring of 1922, Schlemmer had in fact already manifested a degree of skepticism about the almost romantic spirit of optimism and faith in the benefits of technological progress that were emerging at the Bauhaus. Inspired by the tales of Hoffmann, the Dadaistic *Figural Cabinet* was, according to Schlemmer, a "Medley, i.e., variety of sense and nonsense, methodized by Color, Form, Nature, and Art; Man and Machine, Acoustics and Mechanics." In it, a series of flat, painted wooden figures, half-man and half-machine, moved across the stage, while in their midst, "the Master, E. T. A. Hoffmann's Spalanzani, [was] spooking around, directing, gesticulating, telephoning, shooting himself in the head, and dying a thousand deaths from worry about the function of the functional."[39]

Determined to strike a balance between man and the machine as well as between figuration and abstraction, Schlemmer drew up a program of study for the Bauhaus theater workshop, probably in the fall of 1923. He described its "field of activity" as the "investigation of the basic elements of stage production and design: *space, form, color, sound, movement, light*," and the utilization of these elements in "*productions* (design of stage sets and figures) in *theaters* of every kind: opera, play, ballet, circus, variety theater, cinema."[40] Given the lack of a stage at the Bauhaus, and the fact that "literary theater is avoided almost on principle," it was necessary and understandable that he would concentrate on "formal matters": "Mobility, portable backdrops. Mechanical effects, lighting. At the very most dance, which naturally suits the craftsmanship-oriented Bauhaus students better than acting."[41] Schlemmer recognized the importance of exploring the elements of the theater in terms of scientific principles, basic forms and laws, but he also recognized the danger that, "when applied to the human figure, this scientific approach would yield what one might expect to see at a hygiene exhibit. . . ."[42] Instead, what he sought to develop in the theater, as in his paintings of the period, was the figural type: "Distillation of the type represents the final and ultimate task," he wrote at the time.[43]

During the course of 1924, Schlemmer had an opportunity to set out his ideas in an essay, "Man and Art Figure," which was published the following year in the fourth *Bauhausbuch*, devoted to the theater.[44] The essay provides a cogent statement of his concept of the modern theater and the central place in it that Schlemmer accorded to man. At the start Schlemmer described the history of the theater as "the history of the transfiguration of the

Fig. 3. *Figural Cabinet*. (1922). Watercolor, pencil, ink. 12¼ ×
17¾ in. The Museum of Modern Art, New York: The Joan and
Lester Avnet Collection. [Cat. no. 113].

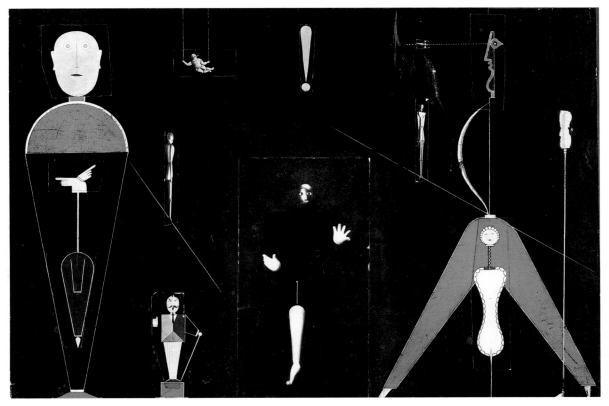

Fig. 4. *Figural Cabinet, Version II*. (1922). Gouache, collage, photo-
montage. 14¼ × 21 in. Oskar Schlemmer Theater Estate, Collection
UJS. [Cat. no. 114].

Fig. 5. *Figural Cabinet I*, photo-montage created for "Bauhausbuch" 4, (1922–1923).

Fig. 6. *Figural Cabinet*. (1922). Ink. 11¼ × 16⅞ in. Oskar Schlemmer Theater Estate, Collection UJS. [Cat. no. 112].

human form'' according to the painterly and sculptural materials of color and form in the arena of architecture. The contemporary theater is, he wrote, further conditioned by ''the emblems of our time'': abstraction, mechanization, and ''the new potentials of technology and invention.'' Although he acknowledged the possibility of a completely mechanized performance in which man would take part not as an actor on the stage but only as '' 'the perfect engineer' at the central switchboard, from where he would direct this feast for the eyes,'' Schlemmer argued that in order to have meaning, man's presence on the stage is required.

Having established the fundamental premise that ''Man, the human organism, stands in the cubical, abstract space of the stage,'' Schlemmer proceeded to describe how, in the modern theater, ''natural man, in deference to abstract space, is recast to fit its mold.'' He provided a diagram of the stage (fig. 7) as a five-sided box articulated by an ''invisible linear network of planimetric and stereometric relationships'' in which the human body ''creates its balance by means of movements, which by their very nature are determined *mechanically and rationally*.'' Thus, corresponding to the laws of cubical space are bodily movements that constitute a ''geometry of calisthenics, eurhythmics, and gymnastics.'' In addition, man is also governed by the organic laws of ''his inner self: heartbeat, circulation, respiration, the activities of the brain and nervous system.'' A second diagram (fig. 8) showed how movements determined by these factors, which Schlemmer referred to as ''the *psychical impulses*,'' radiate outward from the body to create an imaginary space on the stage. These, then, are the two fundamental principles with which ''*Man the Dancer*'' is involved. ''*He obeys the law of the body as well as the law of space; he follows his sense of himself as well as his sense of embracing space*.''

At this point in the essay Schlemmer turned to the function of the costume in establishing the relationship of the human body to the space of the stage through abstraction and metamorphosis. He articulated four basic sets of laws that determine how the costume carries out its transforming role. The first corresponds to the ''*laws of the surrounding cubical space*,'' which may be transferred to the body in the cubic forms of the costume so that the body becomes ''*ambulant architecture*'' (fig. 9). Conversely, the second set of laws derives from the functions of the body. When these are typified in the costume as ''the egg shape of the head, the vase shape of the torso, the club shape of the arms and legs, the ball shape of the joints,'' the result is ''*the marionette*'' (fig. 10). Third are the ''*laws of motion of the human body in space*,'' including ''rotation, direction, and intersection

Fig. 7. *Figure and Space-Delineation*. 1924. Ink. 8⅝ × 11 in. Staatsgalerie Stuttgart: Schlemmer Family Estate Deposit. [Not in exhibition].

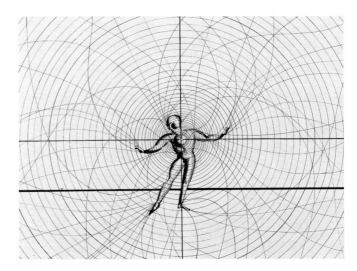

Fig. 8. *Egocentric Space-Delineation*. (1924). Ink. 8⅛ × 10⅝ in. Staatsgalerie Stuttgart: Schlemmer Family Estate Deposit. [Cat. no. 133].

of space.'' A costume generated according to these principles expresses the body as ''a technical *organism*'' (fig. 11). Finally, there are the ''*metaphysical forms of expression* symbolizing various members of the human body'' in abstract shapes, resulting in ''*dematerialization*'' (fig. 12). ''These,'' Schlemmer wrote, ''are the possibilities of Man as Dancer, transformed through costume and moving in space.'' The only physical restriction on the body is the law of gravity which, he noted, cannot be overcome unless the human organism is replaced by the

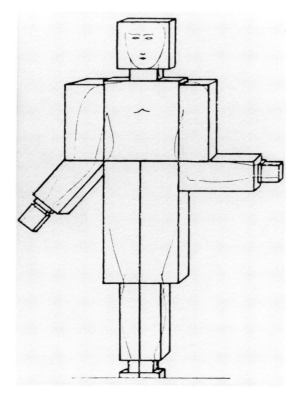

Fig. 9. *Ambulant Architecture*. (1924). Ink. Dimensions and whereabouts unknown.

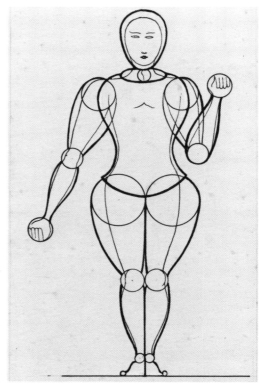

Fig. 10. *The Marionette*. 1924. Ink. 8¹³/₁₆ × 4⁹/₁₆ in. Staatsgalerie Stuttgart: Schlemmer Family Estate Deposit. [Not in exhibition].

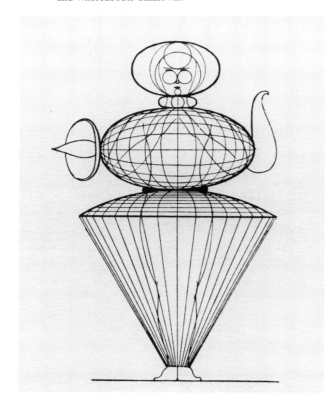

Fig. 11. *A Technical Organism*. (1924). Ink. Dimensions and whereabouts unknown.

Fig. 12. *The Symbol in Man (Dematerialization)*. (1924). Ink. 8¹³/₁₆ × 5⅜ in. Staatsgalerie Stuttgart: Schlemmer Family Estate Deposit. [Not in exhibition].

mechanical human figure in the form either of the automaton or of the marionette. ''E. T. A. Hoffmann extolled the first of these, Heinrich von Kleist the second.'' Schlemmer had been inspired by both of these authors, and he went on in his essay to describe the ''extraordinary'' possibilities that contemporary technological advances opened up for the mechanical human figure in the modern theater, all the while emphasizing that the ''*potentialities of constructive configuration are extraordinary on the metaphysical side as well.*'' He explicitly stated that technology in and of itself was not his goal, but only a means toward a higher end: ''This materialistic and practical age has in fact lost the genuine feeling for play and for the miraculous. Utilitarianism has gone a long way in killing it. Amazed at the flood of technological advance, we accept these wonders of utility as being already perfected art form, while actually they are only prerequisites for its creation.''

At the end of the essay Schlemmer stated his belief that there were three paths open to the artist who worked in the contemporary theater. ''*He may seek realization within the confines of the given situation*,'' in which case he would be subordinate to writers and actors, whose work he would be expected to give an ''appropriate optical form.'' ''*Or he may seek realization under conditions of the greatest possible freedom*,'' in productions dominated by ''visual display'' such as ''ballet, pantomime, musical theater, and the like.'' Finally, ''*he may isolate himself altogether from the existing theater*,'' and design projects without any immediate prospect of carrying them out. For the artist who chooses this path, the production itself is not a determining factor: ''His idea has been demonstrated, and its realization is a question of time, material, and technology. This realization will come with the construction of the new theater of glass, metal, and the inventions of tomorrow. *It depends as well*,'' Schlemmer wrote in closing, ''*upon the inner transformation of the spectator— Man as alpha and omega of every artistic creation which, even in its realization, is doomed to remain Utopia so long as it does not find intellectual and spiritual receptivity and response.*''

As one would expect, Schlemmer chose the middle road. He rejected the traditional theater, in which the literary element—hence the writer and actor, rather than the scenic designer—predominated, but he also refused to confine himself to projects that ''remain paper and model, materials for demonstration lectures and exhibitions of theater art.'' Instead, he accepted the basic conventions of the historical stage and suggested new ways of working within them. The ''cubical, abstract space'' he defined was essentially the same as the traditional perspectival stage that had been developed primarily in Italy between the late fifteenth and the early seventeenth centuries. Although in his drawing of man on the stage (see fig. 7) he did not include the proscenium arch that typically was used to distinguish between the representational space of the actor on the stage and the real space of the spectator in the auditorium, he did both acknowledge and accept that primordial condition of the theater, which resides in the ''confrontation of passive spectator and animate actor.'' This concept is important because it distinguishes Schlemmer from many other visual artists of the period whose work either involved the theater or in some other way directly engaged the issue of the spectator's relationship to the work of art.

In 1910, the Italian Futurists had been the first explicitly to reject the conventions of beholding, which had previously been determined by the requirements of perspectival illusionism in painting. Instead of an immobile spectator standing opposite a painted image, they aimed to ''put the spectator in the center of the picture.''[45] Three years later, Filippo Marinetti extended this idea to the Futurist Variety Theater which, he wrote, ''is alone in seeking the audience's collaboration. It [the audience] doesn't remain static like a stupid voyeur, but joins noisily in the action, in the singing, accompanying the orchestra, communicating with the actors in surprising actions and bizarre dialogues. . . . And because the audience cooperates in this way with the actors' fantasy,'' he continued, ''the action develops simultaneously on the stage, in the boxes, and in the orchestra.''[46]

Many painters subsequently took up similar notions of the spectator's active participation in the work of art, which they sought to bring about by locating their work outside the limits of easel painting, in an architectural setting that surrounded the viewer. As the Dutch artist, Theo van Doesburg, explained in 1918, the goal was ''to place man within (instead of opposite) the plastic arts and thereby enable him to participate in them.''[47] In 1923, van Doesburg's friend and colleague, the Russian artist El Lissitzky, expressed this conception of man's relationship to the work of art in his *Proun Space*, an exhibition interior articulated only by abstract forms projecting from the walls. The *Proun Space* was to be experienced not simply in visual terms but by moving through it, for, as Lissitzky argued, it is ''not there for the eyes alone, it is not a picture. . . . Therefore the room should be organized so that of itself it provides an inducement to walk around in it.''[48]

Schlemmer's exploration of the laws that govern the movement of man in space was obviously related to these ideas, but his concerns were restricted to the ''cubical, abstract space of the stage'' as a self-contained volume to which the audience has only visual access. His work was therefore very different from that of Constructivist artists, like Lissitzky, who in the aftermath of the Russian Revolution were concerned during the early 1920's with making their theatrical productions accessible to mass audiences. As Lissitzky explained in 1923, they felt it was necessary "to conquer the closed-in box of the theater design" and, in some cases, to move the drama out into the street. This was Lissitzky's aim in the *Electrical-Mechanical Spectacle*, for which he envisioned the construction of "a scaffolding in a public square, open and accessible on all sides."[49] The scaffolding was to be a vast complex of movable parts which, together with "all the play objects" were to be "activated by means of electrical-mechanical forces and devices, controlled from a central station by one man"—the "SHAPER OF SPECTACLES." Not surprisingly, Lissitzky never spelled out precisely how this fantastic display, involving loudspeakers and flashing beams of light, was to be carried out: "I leave to others the further development and practical application of ideas and forms presented here, and I myself go on to my next project." Ironically, Lissitzky's politically engaged theater for the masses led him into the utopian cul-de-sac that Schlemmer described in his 1924 essay. Schlemmer, on the other hand, was a staunch believer in the separation of art from politics, and consistently avoided the political arena.[50] He confined his theatrical projects to what could actually be achieved on the stage, "under conditions of the greatest possible freedom"—with emphasis on the word "possible."

Focusing on what he described as the visual stage of an optical event, Schlemmer did not seek the participation of the viewer, nor was he concerned with bridging the gap that separated the passive viewer from the action on the stage. However, Schlemmer's work needs to be distinguished from another tradition of the "visual stage" that is perhaps best exemplified by the Ballets Russes, for which numerous painters active in Paris designed sets and costumes during the teens and twenties. As Jean-Jacques Roubine has pointed out, the decors of the Ballets Russes were in most cases perceived as painted backdrops to which the dancers were assimilated by their costumes.[51] Thus the ballets were conceived in two-dimensional, stylized, but nonetheless painterly terms that were quite different from Schlemmer's emphasis on the three-dimensional movement of the human figure in relation to a fully articulated architectural setting.

The kind of pictorial theater exemplified by the Ballets Russes was forcefully attacked by Friedrich Kiesler in the catalogue of the "International Ausstellung neuer Theatertechnik" which he organized in Vienna in 1924.[52] Like Schlemmer, Kiesler accepted the basic structure of what he called the "peep-show stage," which he described as

"a box appended to an assembly room." Also like Schlemmer, he emphasized the importance of movement in space, arguing that if the spectator is to experience the vital action of contemporary theater, that action must be placed not before a decorative, frontal "picture-stage," but on a "space-stage, which is not merely a priori space but also appears as space." But unlike Schlemmer, Kiesler wanted to use machinery in order to put the stage itself into motion. He had in fact done this in Berlin in a 1923 production of *The Emperor Jones* in which the set was transformed continuously throughout the performance so that it developed in concert with the dramatic action, and motion was "converted into space." As Roger Held has described it, the setting for *The Emperor Jones* was "shaped like a funnel and began to move on a cue in the script and continued to change the shape and quality of the space in time with the action of the play, not coming to rest until it was reassembled in its funnel shape 45 minutes later."[53]

Closer to home, indeed in the same book where Schlemmer's essay appeared, his Bauhaus colleague László Moholy-Nagy evoked a completely abstract theater consisting only of space, form, motion, sound, and light; he also advocated the use of complex machinery in order to achieve "dynamic construction."[54] Moholy-Nagy wanted the audience to participate in and "fuse with the action on the stage," and he believed that a mechanically movable stage would help to bring this about. In addition, he suggested that theaters ought to be equipped with "SUSPENDED BRIDGES AND DRAWBRIDGES running horizontally, diagonally, and vertically" in order to join various parts of the theater that are ordinarily kept separate from one another. Many of Moholy-Nagy's ideas were incorporated into a design by Farkas Molnár for a "U-Theater" (so called for the shape of the auditorium, which surrounded the stage on three sides), which was also published in the fourth *Bauhausbuch*.

The uniqueness of Schlemmer's attitude to the theater emerges clearly in comparison with these other ideas. Although he condemned the conventional, literary theater, he also avoided total abstraction. He recognized the importance of the machine but refused to make it the central focus of his theatrical work. Instead of breaking down the confrontational relationship between actor and audience, Schlemmer accepted it as the essential condition of the theater. By the mid-1920's it was clear that what he required was a simple, conventional stage on which he could involve the human figure in an exploration of the most basic elements of the theater. He insisted on the human presence because it was through man's relationship to the architectural environment of the stage that he sought to establish the formal principles of space, movement, form, and color which were to become the crucial components of his theatrical and dance productions during the mid- and late 1920's.

Schlemmer was able to realize this vision of the theater after 1925, when the Bauhaus moved from Weimar to Dessau, where a rudimentary stage was included in the building complex that Gropius constructed to house the school. In November 1925, Schlemmer described how he had to argue with several students and at times also with Gropius in order to ensure that the Dessau theater would function as Schlemmer felt it must: "Schmidtchen keeps very busy in theater matters. Yesterday a grand debate with Gropius over the outfitting of the theater. Schmidtchen wants a purely mechanical theater. Out of the question, as I had foreseen; and besides, that is not what I have in mind. It would cost thousands, and Gropius must watch every penny. . . . Schmidtchen wants to do something with the Theater, Schawinsky also has ideas, but I am going to insist on my plan for a type stage."[55]

The Bauhaus stage in Dessau was ideally suited to Schlemmer's needs. Although it was small and intended to serve as a platform for lectures as well as for performances, it was equipped with four lateral overhead tracks from which curtains, screens, or other scenic elements could be suspended.[56] Located between the dining hall and the auditorium, it opened onto both rooms. However, Schlemmer does not appear to have exploited its potential for providing multiple points of view, which is not surprising, given his preference for a box-like stage enclosed on five sides. Photographs of his productions indicate that he consistently used a screen to block the view from the dining hall side and to create a back wall for the stage. Working within this context he conceived of the theater as "an orchestral complex" like the conception of building to which the Bauhaus as a whole was dedicated. Just as the other Bauhaus workshops were involved with an investigation of materials as elements of larger constructive complexes, so under Schlemmer's

Fig. 13. *Curtain- and Motion-Studies*, from "Bauhaus" 3, (1927).
Photograph by Ruth Hollos-Consemüller.

Oskar Schlemmer

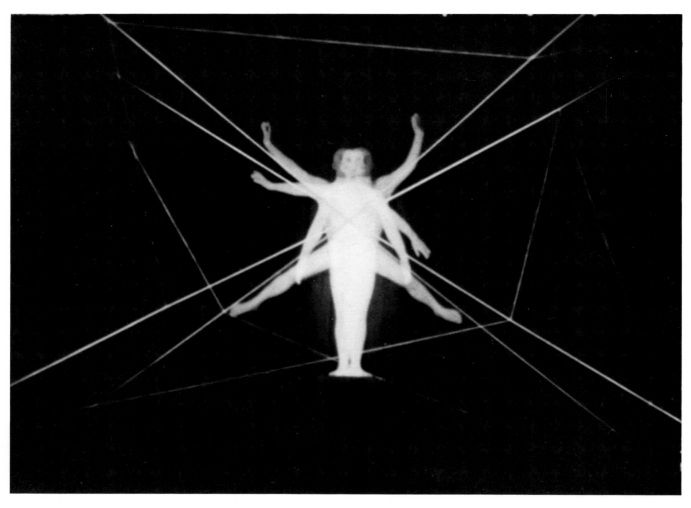

Fig. 14. *Figure and Space-Delineation*, (ca. 1924). Photograph by
T. Lux Feininger.

direction the Bauhaus theater was engaged in an analysis
of the fundamental properties of the stage. "It is because
of this endeavor," Schlemmer declared in a lecture in
March 1927, "that the stage here has become an organic
link in the total chain of Bauhaus activity."

Schlemmer described the stage as an "architectonic-
spatial organism" where every element and activity exist
"in a spatially conditioned relationship." He explained
that space is articulated by form, which can in turn be
broken down into color and light. The visual play comes
into being when all these elements are comprehended as
a totality. But first they must be understood completely
on their own terms. This was what Schlemmer set out to
do in the Dessau Bauhaus theater.

Before he embarked on the exploration of the stage's
spatial properties, Schlemmer first took up the curtain as
an even more immediate artistic problem: "Together with
the ramp, it separates the two worlds of auditorium and

stage into two hostile-friendly camps. It imposes a state
of excitement on both sides: Out there the audience's
excitement asks: What's going to happen? Back here our
question is: What's going to be the effect?" Moreover,
the curtain can "go up in any of a hundred different
ways," each of which might have a different expressive
effect. "We can imagine a curtain-play which would
evolve literally from its own 'material' and reveal in an
entertaining way the curtain's secret nature." When the
curtain is manipulated in various ways by actors (fig. 13),
"the possibilities of this sort of play are further multi-
plied."

With the curtain lifted, the empty stage presents itself
for spatial articulation. Schlemmer delineated the geometry
of the floor surface by dividing it into regular segments
circumscribed by a circle. Then the cubical space could
be divided stereometrically by taut wires stretching from
each corner to the one diagonally opposite it. "By adding

142

as many such aerials as we wish, we can create a spatial-linear web which will have a decisive influence on the man who moves about within it'' (fig. 14). This system amounted to a materialization of ''the invisible linear network of planimetric and stereometric relationships'' that Schlemmer had diagrammed in his earlier essay. The moment that man enters the stage, Schlemmer explained, he becomes ''a 'space-bewitched' creature,'' and all his movements are governed by the confrontational nature of the theater: ''This is the situation which any person creates who instinctively steps back from a group of two or more curious spectators in order to 'act out' something for them. It is the basic situation which produced the peep show. It might even be called the origin of all theatrics.''

Once this situation has been established, Schlemmer went on to explain, ''two fundamentally different creative paths are possible. Either that of psychic expression, heightened emotion, and pantomime; or that of mathematics in motion, the mechanics of joints and swivels, and the exactitudes of rhythmics and gymnastics.'' The essence of his earlier thinking about the transformative role of the costume was still operative, but in a much more simplified form. The costumes that were used in Dessau were very different from those for *The Triadic Ballet*. Made of padded tights and papier-mâché masks, they regularized ''the various and diffuse parts of the human body into a simple, unified form.'' But the actor, thus reduced to a type, could still be ''altered, transformed, or 'entranced' by the addition of some applied object'' or prop that would influence ''his habitual behavior and his physical and psychic structure.'' The *Form Dance* was created in precisely this way. Three figures in red, yellow,

Fig. 15. *Form Dance* (with dancers Oskar Schlemmer, Werner Sied-hoff, and Walter Kaminsky), as performed at the Dessau Bauhaus, (ca. 1927?). Photograph by Ruth Hollos-Consemüller.

Fig. 16. *Pole Dance* (with dancer Amanda von Kreibig), 1927.
Photograph by Albert Braum.

or blue tights were each given basic forms—balls, wands, or a pole—and encouraged to "let their gestures and movements instinctively follow what these shapes convey to them" (fig. 15).[57] Thus the genesis of the dances was often improvisational. Props were used not only to suggest various movements or gestures, but also to affect the mood of the piece. Xanti Schawinsky, one of the three principal dancers, later recalled that "there were scenes of playful action and reaction, sometimes utilizing objects and sometimes between each other. We used gestures, meaningless syllables, and sounds as if in a 'conversation.' The macabre and the witty counted of equal weight, and there was a whole scale of shadings between the two—pride, doubt, force, idea unity, deteriorization. . . ."[58] Not surprisingly, the colors of the costumes were also significant, as Eric Michaud has shown.[59] However, rather than the purely emotional qualities that, under Kandinsky's influence, Schlemmer had sought to convey in the original scenario of *The Triadic Ballet*, now he thought in terms

of the system of correspondences between the primary colors and certain simple geometric forms that Kandinsky tried to work out on a scientific basis during the 1920's.[60] Michaud has analyzed the movements, gestures, and positions assumed by the three figures in Schlemmer's *Gesture Dance* and demonstrated that they literally embodied Kandinsky's ideas about the affective properties of shapes and colors, here acted out on the stage. The figure in yellow, the active and intellectual type, entered the stage first, making very rapid movements. He then seated himself on an incline so that his body formed an acute triangle when seen in conjunction with the supporting elements of his chair. Entering next was the figure in red, a color that according to Kandinsky is both active and passive, hot and cold. The red figure represented the middle ground and, accordingly, he sat at the center of the stage in a position that emphasized balance through the right-angle relationships assumed by his limbs. Finally, there was a figure in blue, representing passivity and self-absorption. His movements were slow and heavy, and when he reclined on a bench, his upper torso rested on one arm so that his body formed an obtuse angle of 150 degrees.

Even the *Pole Dance* (fig. 16), Schlemmer's most daring and impressive attempt to articulate man's relationship to the space around him, was conceived with respect to the costume. As Schlemmer noted in 1929, the twelve poles fixed to the body of the dancer were part prop and part costume, "an intermediary state between that which the actor wears and that which he manipulates."[61] This manner of emphasizing the dancer's penetration of space is reminiscent of Rudolph Laban's use of the "icosahedron," an open-sided polyhedral form within which the three-dimensional movements of a dancer at any given moment could be located. Apparently Laban actually constructed a cage-like structure of wire and enclosed his students in it so that they could define exactly the limitations of any potential movement.[62] Although Schlemmer's *Pole Dance* might have looked somewhat similar, the effect was radically different because, instead of locating movement in a very well defined, centralized area, the poles transposed the mechanics of the body into what Schlemmer described as "astonishing figures in space."[63]

These and other similarly conceived dances that Schlemmer presented at the Bauhaus and elsewhere in Germany during the second half of the twenties marked the high point of his contribution to the stage. In them he staked out a unique position among the artists of his time, one that was simultaneously conservative in its respect for the conventions of the theater, yet radical in its reductive form. Whereas others might dream of creating complex machinery or new architectural settings in order to solve the problems of contemporary theater, Schlemmer believed that solutions could be found only by concentrating on the materials of the stage itself. His single-minded commitment to this endeavor led him to doubt the efficacy of Gropius's 1926 design for a Total Theater even though it included a conventional stage among its three possible configurations. Schlemmer not only feared that the spectator would be overwhelmed by the accumulation of visual effects for which Gropius provided, but he also lamented the fact that the Total Theater (commissioned by Erwin Piscator but never built) was destined to be used only for dramas of an overtly political nature. This should not automatically be taken to mean that Schlemmer refused to confront the issues of his day. Indeed, he explicitly rejected the contention that his approach to the theater was simply a matter of art for art's sake. Rather, he sought to engage "the philosophical, the metaphysical, the religious, and the entire spectrum from the comic to the pathetic" in the belief that these were "equally full of actuality and possibilities for renewal."[64]

Schlemmer was able to maintain this position so long as Gropius remained director of the Bauhaus and ensured that not only architecture and the crafts but also the performing and the fine arts had a place in its program. Even so, as political and economic pressures on the institution mounted after the mid-1920's, it became increasingly difficult to justify the activities of artists and workshops that did not produce a profit for the school. When Gropius resigned and Hannes Meyer assumed the directorship in February 1928, the theater workshop was allowed to continue only as an extracurricular activity. However, despite Meyer's insistence on reorienting the Bauhaus along a more actively engaged, leftist political course, Schlemmer was given a full-time appointment to teach a class on "Man," and he continued to manifest his commitment to a theater of types. He took the Bauhaus theater on several successful tours in 1928 and early 1929, but all the while he was becoming more and more frustrated by Meyer's opposition to his ideals. In early April 1929, he wrote to a friend that he was "fed up" with the Bauhaus: "Hannes [Meyer] a disappointment. Not only to me. Gropius was a man of the world, after all, capable of the grand gesture, of taking risks when it seemed worthwhile. The other fellow is petty-minded, a boor— and, most important, not up to the job. Toward the Theater, my special area, he is 'personally' negative; he wants a social and political slant, which rubs me the wrong way."[65] In July, Schlemmer accepted an appointment to the Staatliche Akademie für Kunst und Kunstgewerbe (State Academy for the Arts and Crafts) in Breslau where he believed he would be free to continue his work in the theater on his own terms: "I shall pick up our previous projects en bloc and take them to Breslau. (The Bauhaus people seem glad to give them to me, i.e. to get rid of them)."[66]

Schlemmer's initial optimism could not have lasted for long. Although in October 1929 he was able to begin teaching a course on the "Art of the Theater," within a matter of months he learned that financial constraints brought on by the Depression would preclude the possibility of initiating a full-fledged experimental theater at the Breslau Akademie, which was eventually closed in 1932. Thereafter Schlemmer's artistic activity was increasingly hampered by the climate of growing hostility to modernism that accompanied the rise to power of the National Socialists in Germany. By 1934, Schlemmer's active involvement with the theater had come to an end.

NANCY J. TROY

Notes

I am grateful to numerous friends and colleagues for their assistance in the preparation of this essay. In particular, at the Northwestern University Library, Russell Maylone, Curator of Special Collections, and Marjorie Carpenter and her staff in the Interlibrary Loan Office, went to great lengths to make source materials available to me. In Stuttgart, Dr. Karin von Maur generously put the fruits of her research in the Oskar Schlemmer Archiv at my disposal. In addition, Professor Larry Silver of the Department of Art History at Northwestern provided valuable editorial advice. My greatest debt is to my husband, Wim de Wit, who, in countless discussions of Schlemmer's work in the theater, both encouraged and contributed to the formulation of the ideas that are set out here.

1. Oskar Schlemmer, *The Letters and Diaries of Oskar Schlemmer*, selected and edited by Tut Schlemmer, trans. Krishna Winston (Middletown, Connecticut: Wesleyan University Press, 1972), p. 156.
2. Schlemmer, *Letters and Diaries*, p. 30.
3. Schlemmer, *Letters and Diaries*, p. 31.
4. Schlemmer, *Letters and Diaries*, p. 29.
5. Schlemmer, *Letters and Diaries*, p. 23.
6. Schlemmer, *Letters and Diaries*, p. 49.
7. Schlemmer, *Letters and Diaries*, p. 44.
8. The ensuing account of the genesis of *The Triadic Ballet* is indebted to Helmut Günther, "Vom dämonischen zum triadischen Ballett: Neues Material über Oskar Schlemmer," *Stuttgarter Zeitung*, 6 July 1963, p. 66.
9. Günther, p. 66.
10. Schlemmer, *Letters and Diaries*, pp. 7–8.
11. Wassily Kandinsky, *Concerning the Spiritual in Art and Painting in Particular*, trans. Michael Sadleir et al. The Documents of Modern Art, 5 (1947; reprint ed., New York: George Wittenborn, 1972), pp. 71 and 72.
12. Schlemmer, *Letters and Diaries*, p. 8.
13. See Helmut Günther's essay, cited in note 8 above.
14. Karin von Maur, *Oskar Schlemmer: Monographie und Oeuvrekatalog der Gemälde, Aquarelle, Pastelle und Plastiken* (Munich: Prestel-Verlag, 1979), vol. 1, p. 69. Von Maur's two-volume work on Schlemmer provides the necessary basis for understanding the artist's oeuvre as a whole; this essay is indebted throughout to von Maur's definitive contribution.
15. Heinrich von Kleist, "Über das Marionettentheater," ("Essay on the Puppet Theater"), trans. Eugene Jolas, *The Partisan Review* 14, no. 1, (January–February 1947), pp. 67–72.
16. Edward Gordon Craig, "The Actor and the Über-Marionette," *The Mask* 1, no. 2 (April 1908), pp. 3–15.
17. For a discussion of the puppet's simultaneously "primitive" and mechanistic implications for numerous avant-garde artists of the period, particularly those associated with the Dutch De Stijl group, see Nancy J. Troy, "Figures of the Dance in De Stijl," *The Art Bulletin* 66, no. 4 (December 1984), pp. 645–656.
18. Kleist, "Essay on the Puppet Theater," p. 72.
19. Schlemmer, *Letters and Diaries*, p. 32.
20. Schlemmer, *Letters and Diaries*, p. 49.
21. Schlemmer, *Letters and Diaries*, p. 49.
22. Schlemmer, *Letters and Diaries*, p. 77.
23. Schlemmer, *Letters and Diaries*, p. 105.
24. Schlemmer, *Letters and Diaries*, p. 105.
25. Maur, *Schlemmer Monographie*, pp. 115–116.
26. Schlemmer, *Letters and Diaries*, pp. 115–116.
27. Oskar Schlemmer, in "Stage Elements," a 1931 lecture
28. quoted in Karin von Maur, *Oskar Schlemmer: Sculpture*, trans. Anne Engel (New York: Abrams, 1972), p. 43.
28. The dances and costumes are described in detail in Dirk Scheper, *Oskar Schlemmer: Das Triadische Ballett* (Berlin: Akademie der Künste, 1977).
29. Eric Michaud, *Théâtre au Bauhaus (1919–1929)* (Lausanne: La Cité, L'Age d'Homme, 1978), p. 76.
30. Schlemmer, *Letters and Diaries*, pp. 127 and 128.
31. Schlemmer, *Letters and Diaries*, p. 124.
32. Schlemmer, *Letters and Diaries*, p. 107.
33. Schlemmer, *Letters and Diaries*, p. 107.
34. Schlemmer, *Letters and Diaries*, p. 116.
35. Schlemmer, *Letters and Diaries*, p. 144.
36. Schlemmer, *Letters and Diaries*, p. 140.
37. Schlemmer, *Letters and Diaries*, p. 145.
38. Schlemmer, *Letters and Diaries*, p. 146.
39. Program notes in Oskar Schlemmer, László Moholy-Nagy, and Farkas Molnár, *The Theater of the Bauhaus*, ed. Walter Gropius, trans. Arthur S. Wensinger (1961; reprint ed., Middletown, Connecticut: Wesleyan University Press, 1979), p. 40.
40. Oskar Schlemmer, "The Stage Workshop of the Bauhaus in Weimar," in Hans M. Wingler, *The Bauhaus: Weimar, Dessau, Berlin, Chicago*, trans. Wolfgang Jabs and Basil Gilbert (1969; reprint ed., Cambridge, Massachusetts: The MIT Press, 1981), p. 59.
41. Schlemmer, *Letters and Diaries*, p. 140.
42. Schlemmer, *Letters and Diaries*, p. 147.
43. Schlemmer, *Letters and Diaries*, p. 142.
44. Oskar Schlemmer, "Man and Art Figure," in *The Theater of the Bauhaus* (see note 39), pp. 16–32.
45. Umberto Boccioni et al., "Futurist Painting: Technical Manifesto," in *Futurist Manifestos*, ed. Umbro Apollonio, trans. Robert Brain et al., The Documents of 20th-Century Art (New York: The Viking Press, 1973), p. 28.
46. Filippo Tommaso Marinetti, "The Variety Theatre," trans. Victoria Nes Kirby, in Michael Kirby, *Futurist Performance* (New York: E. P. Dutton, 1971), p. 181.
47. Theo van Doesburg, "Notes on Monumental Art," trans. R. R. Symonds in *De Stijl*, ed. Hans L. C. Jaffé (1967; reprint ed., London: Thames and Hudson, 1970), p. 103.
48. El Lissitzky, "Proun Room, Great Berlin Art Exhibition," in Sophie Lissitzky-Kuppers, *El Lissitzky: Life, Letters, Texts*, trans. Helene Aldwinckle (London: Thames and Hudson, 1968), p. 365.
49. El Lissitzky, "The Electrical-Mechanical Spectacle," trans. Standish D. Lawder, *Form* 3 (15 December 1966), p. 12.
50. See Karin von Maur, *Oskar Schlemmer und die Stuttgarter Avantgarde 1919* (Stuttgart: Akademie der bildenden Künste Stuttgart Institut für Buchgestaltung, 1975), p. 22.
51. Jean-Jacques Roubine, *Théâtre et mise en scène 1880–1980* (Paris: Presses Universitaires de France, Litteratures Modernes, 1980), pp. 134–137.
52. Friedrich Kiesler, "Debacle des Theaters: Die Gesetze der G. K.-Buhne," in *International Ausstellung neuer Theater-technik* (1924; reprint ed., Vienna: Konzerthaus, 1975), pp. 43–58. A modified version of the essay was translated as "Debacle of the Modern Theater," in a special number of *The Little Review* 11, no. 2 (Winter 1926), pp. 61–72. The citations that follow have been taken from the English version.
53. Roger Held, "Endless Innovations: The Theories and Scenic

Designs of Frederick Kiesler," Ph.D. dissertation, Bowling Green State University, 1977, p. 40.

54. László Moholy-Nagy, "Theater, Circus, Variety," in *The Theater of the Bauhaus* (see note 39), pp 49–70.

55. Schlemmer, *Letters and Diaries*, p. 182.

56. See Ned A. Bowman, "Bauhaus Influences on an Evolving Theatre Architecture: Some Developmental Stages," *Theatre Survey* 6, no. 2 (November 1965), p. 120.

57. This and preceding citations are from Oskar Schlemmer, "Theater (Stage)," in *The Theater of the Bauhaus* (see note 39), pp. 81–101.

58. Xanti Schawinsky, "From the Bauhaus to Black Mountain," *The Drama Review* 15, no. 3a (Summer 1971), p. 41.

59. Michaud, *Théâtre au Bauhaus*, pp. 129–136.

60. For a discussion of Kandinsky's color theory during this period, see Clark V. Poling's essay in *Kandinsky: Russian and Bauhaus Years, 1915–1933* (New York: Solomon R. Guggenheim Museum, 1983), pp. 63–67.

61. Oskar Schlemmer, "Eléments scéniques," in Oskar Schlemmer, *Théâtre et abstraction (L'Espace du Bauhaus)*, ed. and trans. Eric Michaud (Lausanne: La Cité, L'Age d'Homme, 1978), p. 93.

62. See Annabelle Henkin Melzer, *Latest Rage the Big Drum: Dada and Surrealist Performance*. Studies in the Fine Arts: The Avant-Garde, no. 7. Michigan: UMI Research Press, 1980, p. 96.

63. Schlemmer, "Eléments scéniques," p. 93.

64. Oskar Schlemmer, "Piscator und das moderne Theater," *Das neue Frankfurt* 2, no. 2 (February 1928), p. 25.

65. Schlemmer, *Letters and Diaries*, p. 241.

66. Schlemmer, *Letters and Diaries*, p. 245.

Metal Dance (with dancer Brian Hanna), 1984. Reconstruction by Debra McCall of Schlemmer's 1926 "Bauhaus Dances" first performed at the Stage Workshop of the Dessau Bauhaus.

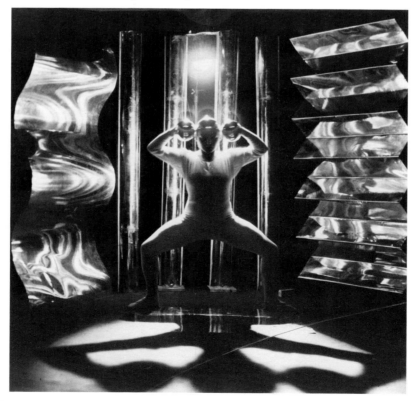

Metal Dance, from the 1926 "Bauhaus Dances." Specific date and location of the depicted performance unknown.

Reconstructing Schlemmer's Bauhaus Dances:
A Personal Narrative

Life has become so mechanized, thanks to machines and a technology which our senses cannot possibly ignore, that we are intensely aware of man as a machine and the body as a mechanism. In art, especially in painting, we are witnessing a search for the roots and sources of all creativity; this grows out of the bankruptcy brought on by excessive refinement. Modern artists long to recover the original, primordial impulses; on the one hand they woke up to the unconscious, unanalyzable elements in the art forms of . . . the Africans, peasants, children, and madmen; on the other hand, they have discovered the opposite extreme in the new mathematics of relativity. Both these modes of consciousness—the sense of man as a machine, and insight into the deepest wells of creativity—are symptoms of one and the same yearning. A yearning for synthesis dominates today's art and calls upon architecture to unite the disparate fields of endeavor. This yearning also reaches out for the theater, because the theater offers the promise of total art.

Oskar Schlemmer
Letters and Diaries
September 1922

Two films of fantastic sculptural choreography were screened in 1978 at a dance-film festival in New York. In the first were dancers in eighteen costumes, ranging from high-tech ballerinas surrounded by wire hoops and spirals, to medieval knights encircled by colored disks, metallic spheres, and geometric armor. This three-part abstract ballet was clearly an avant-garde conception, but of what period? The second film revealed an even more arresting and contemporary style. On a grid-patterned white floor, set against a blackened cubical space, were three figures in red, blue, and yellow. Their metallic masks and costumes recalled bulky, padded fencing uniforms. Using basic movements—walking and simple gesturing—and varying time, shape, space, and color, these three representative characters created a series of abstract geometric dances. In certain of the pieces, primary forms such as spheres, poles, and colored cubes were introduced. In one of the dances, a chair, stool, and bench were placed on stage, and glasses, mustaches, and coattails added to the costumes, heightening the sense of social context. In the last piece, a black figure was magically transformed when its limbs were elongated in space by twelve white poles.

The concern for geometry and clean line, the minimalist shapes and colors, the non-narrative structure, all defined the dances as contemporary. Yet something in their composition marked them as futuristic fantasies from the 1920's. The credits rose: they were reconstructions filmed in 1968–1970 of *The Triadic Ballet* and Bauhaus Dances.[1] Thus began a fascinating four-year involvement with the stage work of Oskar Schlemmer.

Integrating all the arts—painting, music, sculpture, design, dance—and working with the most basic elements of the stage—space, form, color, sound, movement, light—Schlemmer and his students created avant-garde precursors to modern and postmodern dance and performance art. The formal abstraction, non-narrative structure, chance composition, and collaboration with visual artists that mark Merce Cunningham's work, for example, can be traced back to Bauhaus explorations. (Cunningham was at Black Mountain College during the time that Josef and Anni Albers, both former Bauhaus faculty members, taught there, and where a former Schlemmer stage student presented a Bauhaus-like dance.) Bauhaus stage experiments comprise the historical roots of Alwin Nikolais's transformation of the figure through light, mask, costume, prop; of the minimal geometric floor patterning of Lucinda Childs and Laura Dean; and of the task-oriented, pedestrian style that emerged from The Judson Dance Theater. Schlemmer's seminal influence has also extended into such multimedia performance art as that of Laurie Anderson and Meredith Monk.

> Thus it is sensible and necessary for the art of a new age to make use of technology and of the newly invented materials of a new age in order to make art serviceable as form and as a vehicle for a substance which is spiritual, abstract, metaphysical, and ultimately religious in nature.[2]

Blending spontaneous play, abstraction and standardization, and new technology with conventional theatrical forms—opera, vaudeville, religious ritual, circus, ballet—Schlemmer developed powerful archetypes whose relationship with the surrounding space typified "The New Architecture," the new social order of Gropius's Bauhaus. A genius of paradox, Schlemmer sought to reconcile and harmonize the organic and emotional with the abstract and rational. Inspired by Heinrich von Kleist's essay on the "gravity-free" marionette,[3] Schlemmer transformed the *Tänzermensch* (Man the Dancer) into the *Kunstfigur*

(Art Figure) without sacrificing the human element. Performance stripped to its basics, artifice transformed into illusion, theatrical element altered by spontaneous play—Schlemmer was a "Master Magician" of the stage.

Schlemmer's work is characterized by humor, classicism, geometric relationships between body and space, and striking visual design. Viewing the film reconstructions of Schlemmer's ballets coincided with my study of the geometric dance theories of Rudolph Laban, the German dance pedagogue of the early twentieth century. Laban is best known for his dance notation systems, Labanotation and Laban Movement Analysis, and for his performances with the Dada group. Two of his famous pupils were Mary Wigman and Kurt Jooss, whose *Green Table* ballet, Schlemmer claimed, was inspired in part by the Bauhaus Dance Tour of the late 1920's. Laban and Schlemmer served together on the committee for the Magdeburg Dance Congress of 1927, and each was aware and respectful of the other's work.

Bauhaus Band, ca. 1926–1927. Photograph by Ruth Hollos or Erich Consemüller, courtesy Oskar Schlemmer Theater Estate, Collection UJS.

In the art world during the late 1970's and early 1980's, there was perceptibly increased interest in careful examination of the beginnings of abstract modern art. Concurrently, new enthusiasm was building for the apparent trend toward reemergence of the figure in painting after a virtual thirty-year absence. Schlemmer's conflict between the figurative and the abstract seemed especially topical at this moment. The time was ripe for resurrecting the Bauhaus Dances.

I began by studying the filmed reconstructions of Schlemmer's work and translating some of his published notes. Using the film and available photographs, I reconstructed the *Pole Dance*.[4] It was only in November 1979 that I learned that Andreas Weininger, a former Schlemmer student and Bauhaus performer, was then living in New York.

> The stage was there on the very day the Bauhaus opened, because enjoyment in designing was there on that first day. This enjoyment was first expressed in the celebrations (the lantern party and the kite-flying party), in the invention of masks, the making of costumes and the decoration of rooms. And it was expressed in *dancing, dancing, dancing!* The music evolved from the Bauhaus dance, which developed from the clown dance into the "Step"; from the concertina to the jazz band.[5]

Andreas Weininger was the clown in the "clown dance" and the leader of the jazz band. My first visit with Weininger and his wife Eva, both former Bauhaus students, was cordial but marked with the skepticism of fellow artists dedicated to protecting the integrity of Schlemmer's work. After three evenings of captivating Bauhaus anecdotes, Weininger examined the photographs of my *Pole Dance* reconstruction. He advised a trip to Germany to study, visit the Oskar Schlemmer Archiv, and meet the artist's widow Tut Schlemmer; he also suggested a talk with Ise Gropius, the widow of the late Walter Gropius. Having recently returned from Germany where she had visited the restored Bauhaus in Dessau, Mrs. Gropius suggested that in order to comprehend the Bauhaus Dances, it would be essential to experience the space in which they were created.[6]

Two weeks later in Stuttgart, I interviewed dance historians and scholars of the period, and studied the voluminous collection of materials at the Oskar Schlemmer Archiv of the Staatsgalerie Stuttgart. This body of work included the remaining original costumes, paintings, sculpture, drawings, and—most crucial for my purpose—documentation in many notes and sketches for the Bauhaus Dances. At the Berlin Akademie der Künste, Dirk Scheper was packing the costumes for a new production of *The Triadic Ballet*. These facsimiles were beautifully done, but of lighter weight than the originals. A new score and

new choreography made the reconstruction seem contemporary. Scheper showed me notes from the ballet and from the Bauhaus Dances, and described the difficulty in translating Schlemmer's often indecipherable notation, which made exact reconstruction almost impossible.

> I readily concede that I came to the dance from painting and sculpture; I appreciated its essential element, movement, all the more because the expressive range of the former two arts is restricted to the static, the rigid, to "movement captured in a fixed moment."
>
> Oskar Schlemmer
> *Letters and Diaries*
> 7 September 1931

The Triadic Ballet was Schlemmer's first exploration into dance; thus, its choreography was that of a painter/sculptor. He began the piece in 1917, but did not officially premiere it until 1922 in Stuttgart. First creating the sculptural figurines, Schlemmer then choreographed the "floor geometry" according to the shapes of the costumes.

> Why "triadic"? Because three is a supremely important, prominent number, within which egotistic one and dualistic contrast are transcended, giving way to the collective. . . . Derived from trias = triad, the ballet should be called a dance of the threesome. . . . One female and two male dancers: twelve dances and eighteen costumes . . . form, color, space; the three dimensions of space: height, depth, breadth; the basic forms: ball, cube, pyramid; the primary colors: red, blue, yellow . . . dance, costume, and music.
>
> Oskar Schlemmer
> *Letters and Diaries*
> 5 July 1926

The first yellow "scherzo" section of this abstract ballet was originally set to music by Bossi, Tharenghi(?), and Debussy; the second solemn rose section had music by Haydn and Mozart; and, finally, the black "Eroica" scene was set to music by Haydn, Paradies, Galuppi, and Handel. In 1926, Hindemith composed a new score for the ballet for player piano. Because of its imaginative costumes and appealing mood of fantasy, *The Triadic Ballet* is better known than the later Bauhaus creations.

Moving on to Dessau, I made my way through the streets of bombed-out Renaissance and postwar block buildings to the rebuilt Bauhaus, a handsome white-gray edifice with magnificent glass walls. Few buildings surpass its classical elegance and harmony. The theater door onto the stage was unlocked for me. The effect was magical. A black cube overlooked a slightly raked auditorium and the scale of the space exaggerated the presence of the figure on the proscenium, recalling Schlemmer's dictum, "Man . . . is the measure of all things. Well, then! Architecture is the noblest art of measuring: Let us unite."[7]

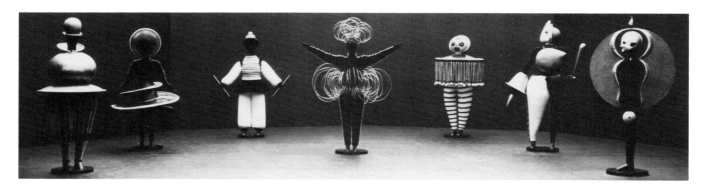

Figurines from ''The Triadic Ballet'': *Gold Sphere, Spiral, Turk, Wire Figure, Diver, The Abstract*, and *Disk Dancer*. (1922). Various materials; plexiglas armatures. Each approx. 79 in. high. Staatsgalerie Stuttgart. [Not in exhibition; see cat. nos. 60–63].

Performers from ''The Triadic Ballet,'' Berlin, 1926.

Standing silently on the stage for a long time, I felt, and understood, why his dances were architectonic.

After visits to see additional Schlemmer material in Essen and Cologne, I returned to New York to work with Weininger on the very exacting process of translating the rich material I had collected in Germany. Mrs. Weininger would translate the German into English, Weininger would define Schlemmer's context, and I would interpret the movement nuance. Some words that were untranslatable Weininger recognized as onomatopoeic inventions of Schlemmer's, devised to describe movement. It became clear that any authentic reconstruction of Schlemmer's work depended on someone who understood his unique, inventive vocabulary.

Translation of the dance notes permitted preliminary studio experimentation. The amount of notation varied for each dance; in many instances, choreographic judgments regarding timing, specific form, floor pattern, and transitions had to be made without benefit of original notation. In *Space Dance*, the quintessential Bauhaus piece, three dancers—blue, red, yellow—trace geometric patterns on the gridded floor, in the respective tempi of slow, medium, and quick. The dancers move continuously until synchronizing at the center of the grid. Each represents not only time and color but also character type. In his notes, Schlemmer states their final movements to be "8 *Ausfalls*" [lunges]. But only one pose in one position was indicated in the sketches. For the remaining seven, a rotating matrix was developed, in which the figures crossed over each other visually, always returning to their own starting positions. When notes and cues were unavailable, decisions were closely based on Schlemmer's aesthetic, as indicated in his sketches and writings. *Gesture Dance* was much surer, for Schlemmer was very specific in plotting the actions, timing, and music. In this piece, the dancers add coattails, mustaches, and glasses to their costumes while conversing in jibberish and gesturing abstractly. They parody social convention by whispering, plotting, jumping onto a bench, stool, or chair, and celebrate their camaraderie to the tune of a toy piano.

> [the Stage Workshop's] primary endeavor [which] is to approach all our materials from a basic and elementary standpoint . . . it is natural that the aims of the Bauhaus—to seek the union of the artistic-ideal with the craftsman-like-practical by thoroughly investigating the creative elements, and to understand in all its ramifications the essence of *der Bau*, creative construction—have valid application in the field of theater. For, like the concept of *Bau* itself, the stage is an orchestral complex which comes about only through the cooperation of many different forces. It is the union of the most heterogeneous assortment of creative elements. Not the least of its functions is to serve the metaphysical needs of man by constructing a world of illusion and by creating the transcendental on the basis of the rational.[8]

Although the dances were "translated," rehearsals could not proceed without the props and costumes so integral to the pieces. An exceptional group of architecture, design, and theater students from Pratt Institute volunteered to work on the project. To construct the wands, poles, and spheres of *Form Dance* and the cubes of *Block Play*, original photographs were used to scale the props to the proportions of the dancers' bodies and the size of the floor grid. The sculptural costumes could only be built layer by layer on the dancers' bodies, keeping the scale of the grid and props in mind. The masks were particularly problematic. Initial experiments with the papier-mâché and lacquer of the originals were unsuccessful. T. Lux Feininger described the masks as "neither spherical nor elliptical, but a most subtle combination of both shapes."[9] Heads were molded of plaster bandage, lacquered, appliquéd with gold, silver, and copper leaf, and then painted with features. They were very expressive, reminding one of wide-eyed children.

Minimal resources and limited access to machines and tools necessitated fundamental decisions regarding props and costume construction. Materials were selected to be as close as possible to the originals in design, weight, and proportion. This fidelity was imperative, for if the costumes were lighter or less bulky, the dancers would have greater freedom and quickness of movement, as opposed to the slower, more weighted movement inherent to Schlemmer's originals. By not replacing plaster with plastic, or gold leaf with paint, the rich resolution and luster of the original materials could be reproduced.

> Mechanistic cabaret, metaphysical eccentricity, spiritual tightrope walking, ironic *variété*. . . . The recipe the Bauhaus Theater follows is very simple: one should be as free of preconceptions as possible. . . . One should be simple, but not puritanical . . . one should start with the fundamentals . . . with space . . . . One should start with one's physical state, with the fact of one's own life, with standing and walking, leaving leaping and dancing for much later. For taking a step is a grave event, and no less so raising a hand, moving a finger. One should have deep respect and deference for any action performed by the human body, especially on the stage. . . .
>
> Oskar Schlemmer
> *Letters and Diaries*
> May 1929

It was important to permit the dancers the sense of discovery, play, and improvisation that characterized the Bauhaus stage workshop. Walking was the first exercise.

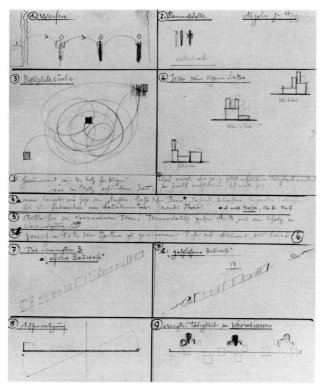

Schlemmer's Choreographic Notation for ''Block Play.'' (1926–1929). Pencil. 11 × 8¹/₁₆ in. Oskar Schlemmer Theater Estate, Collection UJS. [Not in exhibition].

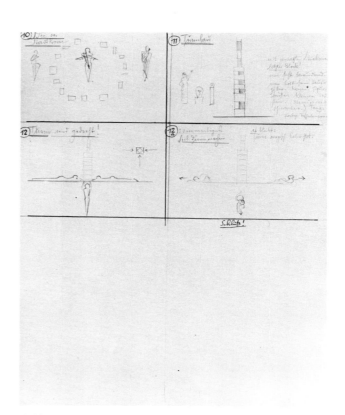

Schlemmer's Choreographic Notation for ''Block Play'' (sheet 2). (1926–1929). Pencil. 11 × 8¹/₁₆ in. Oskar Schlemmer Theater Estate, Collection UJS. [Not in exhibition].

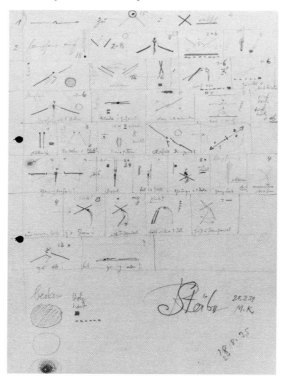

Schlemmer's Choreographic Notation for ''Pole Dance'' (sheet 1). (1929). Pencil. 11⅝ × 8¼ in. Oskar Schlemmer Theater Estate, Collection UJS. [Not in exhibition].

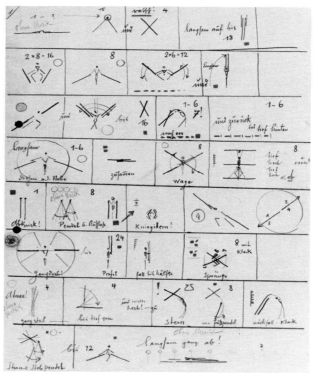

Schlemmer's Choreographic Notation for ''Pole Dance'' (sheet 2). (1929). Pencil. 11⅛ × 8⅞ in. Oskar Schlemmer Theater Estate, Collection UJS. [Not in exhibition].

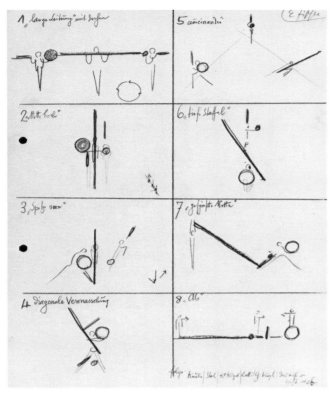

Schlemmer's Choreographic Notation for "Form Dance." (1926–1929). Pencil. 11¾₆ × 8¹⁵⁄₁₆ in. Oskar Schlemmer Theater Estate, Collection UJS. [Not in exhibition].

Three dancers observed and learned each other's walking "styles," and then varied the walk tempi. One dancer's forward inclination propelled him into space quickly, while another's balletic posture gave her a strong vertical line and an assured medium gait. Modern and postmodern performance experience was obvious in one dancer's strong connection to gravity, and she was most convincing as the slow blue dancer. Color and form were also improvised. Which primary form lent itself to which tempo and color?

Statements by famous contemporaries:

p o e l z i g : "the people needs bread and movies."
g r o p i u s : "we have to clean up around here."
k a n d i n s k y : "the circle is blue."
s c h l e m m e r : "the circle is red."
g r o p i u s : "art and technology—a new duality."
b r e u e r : "the chair gets sat on until it breaks."
m o h o l y : "v-o-n-d-e-r-f-u-l."

Oskar Schlemmer
Letters and Diaries
October 1923

The acute tension of the triangle seemed to be quick yellow; the solid square, a slow blue; and the circle, medium red. As color and form evolved from the dancers' styles, a variety of music and character types was tested to get at the essence of the roles. We improvised with the available geometry: the grid; the line, plane, and volume of the cubical stage; the shape and pathway of the body in space; and the human anatomy. Schlemmer continually posed questions: "Which prevails? The laws of the body or the laws of abstract space?" In other words, do the internal rhythms/physiology/impulses/feelings of the dancer determine the shape and form of the stage space, or does the network of line/plane/volume dictate the nature of the performer's movements? This dialectic was most evident in *Pole Dance*. As the dancer began rehearsals with the twelve white poles attached to his limbs and torso, he had difficulty breathing and fought the confinement. Gradually he came to feel less encumbered by imagining the poles as naturally exaggerating his movement. Next he sensed his body interacting with and defining the surrounding space. Only then did the dance become three-dimensional and sculpturally alive.

Schlemmer's notes for *Pole Dance* and *Hoop Dances I–IV* are similar. The drawings indicate the visual form of each pose in these black dances whose white props appear to be suspended in space. But the notes do not indicate the transitions between the poses or any of the qualities of tension, weight, or time. The dancers followed the Bauhaus adage—form follows function—and attempted to discover the most functional and economical route from one pose to the next. They learned to recognize what "felt" correct in their bodies and in relation to the relative ease or difficulty in manipulating the props.

It should be mentioned that man's innate sense of proportion can, when used creatively, constantly express itself in new ways and produce new phenomena. Granted: geometry, the Golden Section, the laws of proportion. They are lifeless and unproductive unless they are experienced, touched, and felt.

Oskar Schlemmer
Letters and Diaries
July/August 1923

The process was the same for *Form Dance* and *Block Play*. In *Form Dance*, Schlemmer asked how large geometric props would alter the dancers' movements and the shape of the stage space. His sketches show eight poses. One pose includes the directive "Diagonale Vermasselung" (the latter apparently a Schlemmer vocabulary invention to suggest "massing together"), a type of improvisation along the diagonal line created by the yellow dancer's long pole. If the role of the dancers is to improvise, the role of the choreographer is to choose and edit the emerging patterns, relying for reference on visual images of Bauhaus work by Schlemmer and others.

Another mystery arose around *Form Dance*. In each photograph, the costumes were slightly different. It became clear upon closer examination that Schlemmer had drawn accent lines on his dance photos, thus further altering the figures. The notes for *Block Play*, a parody on the architects at the Bauhaus, presented similar difficulties. With sets of multicolored cubes, each "player" creates his own construction. Schlemmer's notes on this piece are narrative and suggestive: " . . . notices his neighbor, visits him, gets interested . . . eventually quarreling." Two cajole a third into joining them in playful construction until they finally build the "crown" or "center of the city" (a metaphor for the "cathedral of socialism," as Schlemmer once referred to the Bauhaus ideal). How to interpret this? Using Weininger's suggestions and Hasting's film reconstructions as bases, we played until the piece was cohesive.

Hoop Dance (with dancer Juliet Neidish), 1984. Reconstruction by Debra McCall of Schlemmer's 1926 "Bauhaus Dances" first performed at the Stage Workshop of the Dessau Bauhaus.

The basic error of the translator is that he preserves the state in which his own language happens to be instead of allowing his language to be powerfully affected by the foreign tongue. Particularly when translating from a language very remote from his own he must go back to the primal elements of language itself and penetrate to the point where work, image, and tone converge.[10]

After viewing a rehearsal, Andreas Weininger commented that the form of the dances was correct, but the feeling was inappropriate in its somewhat "militaristic"— quick, sharp angles, strong and tense—interpretation of Schlemmer's precision and mechanical emphasis. The dances should be more like Schlemmer's paintings and drawings, with their figures buoyantly suspended in space. The dancers were to be like puppets—light, soft, and resisting gravity. Schlemmer's emphasis on the mechanical was not one of dehumanization wherein the dancers would be rigid automatons, but rather the mechanical as offering freedom of the expressive potential inherent in technology. The human element should always triumph on Schlemmer's stage. The dancers had to lift their weight, as though suspended from the ceiling. Suddenly the serious mood was transformed into one of playful fantasy. The figures and surrounding space breathed. The grave characters became comical.

Weininger worked closely with our musician, coaching him on the accompaniment and interpreting the instructions in Schlemmer's notes. *Gesture Dance* and *Space Dance* were relatively specific and easy to complete. But for *Form Dance*, *Hoop Dance*, and *Block Play*, where the accompaniment had often changed from performance to performance, music was restricted to accent and minimal sound, with the result that the scores supported the stylistic intent of the dances.

After months of rehearsing without mask and costume, the dancers had become accustomed to depending upon peripheral visual cues and freedom of movement in space. The first rehearsal in costume looked like Pac-Man gone awry. The dancers wandered all over the grid, disoriented, unable to see lines or each other because of the small arc of vision permitted by the masks. There was another surprising discovery that day: while the performers expected the costumes and masks to minimize individualistic expression, the result was just the opposite. The idiosyncratic style of each dancer was exaggerated, confirming Schlemmer's contention that despite the abstraction, it is ultimately the human element which predominates.

An appropriate "black box," with simple but effective lighting to create a "puppet show" ambience, was constructed. Only then could the dances be seen as originally intended, for stage set and lighting are as integral as props, costumes, and dancers for the total work of art.

Form Dance (with dancers Jan Hanvik, Juliet Neidish, and Nancy
Ellen Stotz), 1984. Reconstruction by Debra McCall of Schlemmer's
1926 ''Bauhaus Dances'' first performed at the Stage Workshop of
the Dessau Bauhaus.

The first performance, at New York's alternate space, The Kitchen, in October 1982, was sold out, and the audience completely involved. *Pole Dance* was transfixing. Body and space, the Golden Mean of harmonic proportion, the organic geometry of the figure, and the mathematics of the abstract stage coalesced—fundamental, yet transcendent.

Since that first series of performances in the fall of 1982, other pieces have been reconstructed: *Metal Dance*, *Hoop Dance IV*, and *Flats Dance*. As with *Block Play*, there were difficulties in interpretation. Schlemmer left limited visual notes but more narrative description. *Metal Dance*, with its pleated, curving, reflective set, evokes a mythical, medieval quality while simultaneously suggesting an illusion of the future technological human. A figure, who appears for less than a minute, enters from backstage through tall columns as the light brightens and the music eerily intensifies. His image spills onto the set, shattering it with shadow, while the increasing brightness dissipates his presence. Is the figure reality or illusion? *Flats Dance* is also a mystery: Behind which flat is the dancer? How big is the dancer? How many are there? And, finally, who is the victim?

When these new dances premiered at The Solomon R. Guggenheim Museum in New York in 1984, the dance critic Anna Kisselgoff wrote, "The Bauhaus Works Were Prophetic. . . . Schlemmer's ideas allowed him to foresee that dance would be the performing art most open to the new in the 20th century."[11]

The appeal of Schlemmer's dances lies in their timeless and universal symbolism, and their power to inspire. These adult puppets demonstrate the joy of play within a rational world, symbolized by the grid. Their quality of abstract fantasy has the metaphorical impact of fairy tales. To experience these pieces is to look through a window to the power and drama of one of the most significant periods in the history of twentieth-century art. Yet they are ever humble in their subtle jab at the paradox of the "modern" condition, silently transforming the most primitive movement into a metaphysical apparition of the future. Their simple yet profound message permits universal identification. They remind us of the poet Rainer Maria Rilke's words, transcribed by Schlemmer as his last diary entry in April 1943: " . . . to consider art not a piece plucked out of the world, but the complete and utter transformation of the world into pure glory. . . ."[12]

DEBRA McCALL

Notes

1. These films, by Margaret Hasting, are *Triadische Ballett* © 1970, and *Man and Mask* © 1968.

2. Oskar Schlemmer, "The Stage Workshop of the Bauhaus in Weimar," in Hans M. Wingler, *The Bauhaus: Weimar, Dessau, Berlin, Chicago*, trans. Wolfgang Jabs and Basil Gilbert (1969; reprint ed., Cambridge, Massachusetts: The MIT Press, 1981), pp. 118–119.

3. Heinrich von Kleist, "Über das Marionettentheater" (see "Essay on the Puppet Theater," trans. Eugene Jolas, *The Partisan Review* 14, no. 1 (January–February 1947), pp. 67–72.

4. Irmgard Bartenieff, a former Laban student and Director of The Laban Institute for Movement Studies, assisted me in the translation of Schlemmer dance notes; Paul Lessard, then an architecture student at Pratt Institute, collaborated on the reconstruction of *Pole Dance*.

5. Wingler, p. 117.

6. Interviews with Andreas and Eva Weininger, New York City, December 1979–January 1984; conversations with Ise Gropius, Lincoln, Massachusetts, 4 November 1979, 23 December 1979, and 29 July 1980.

7. Wingler, p. 64.

8. Oskar Schlemmer, László Moholy-Nagy, and Farkas Molnár, *The Theater of the Bauhaus*, ed. Walter Gropius, trans. Arthur S. Wensinger (1961; reprint ed., Middletown, Connecticut: Wesleyan University Press, 1979), p. 81.

9. Letter to McCall from T. Lux Feininger, Arlington, Massachusetts, January 1982.

10. Walter Benjamin, "The Task of the Translator," *Illuminations* (New York: Schocken Books, 1969), p. 81.

11. Anna Kisselgoff, "The Bauhaus Works Were Prophetic," *The New York Times*, 29 January 1984, section 2, p. 14.

12. The recreation of Schlemmer's Bauhaus Dances involved the support, cooperation, and assistance of individuals and institutions around the world. In addition to those named in the text or notes above, I especially wish to acknowledge the generosity of Andreas and Eva Weininger, Dr. Karin von Maur, Staatsgalerie Stuttgart curator and director of the Oskar Schlemmer Archiv there; Dr. Hans Harksen of Dessau, Bauhaus historian and collector; our company's dancers Juliet Neidish, Jan Hanvik, Nancy Ellen Stotz, Brian Hanna, and Marsha Blank, musician Craig Gordon, technical director Jeffrey McRoberts, costume, mask, prop, set, and graphic design artists Paul Mantell, Laura Williams, Penny Howell, Suellen Epstein, Elliot Schwartz, Robert Russ, Peter Stathis, Paula Sloan, and Michael Rock; and Jamie Avins, dance curator at The Kitchen in New York City. I am particularly indebted to all those Bauhauslers who shared with me their expertise and memories, contributing substantially to the integrity of our effort, and to the artist's widow Tut Schlemmer, daughter U. Jaïna Schlemmer, and grandson C. Raman Schlemmer. Our company has now completed notating the Schlemmer dances, a project funded by the National Endowment for the Humanities. Support from the National Endowment for the Arts, The New York State Council on the Arts, the New York Foundation for the Arts, and Göethe House, New York, has been invaluable. A film of the dances is underway, and the company has completed successful tours of the United States and Europe.

Oskar Schlemmer as ''The Turk'' in ''The Triadic Ballet,'' 1922.

The Nimbus of Magic:
An Album of Schlemmer's Stage Work

Theater! Music! My passion! But also: the scope of this particular field. Theoretical possibilities that suit my disposition, because this is natural to me. Free run for the imagination. Here I can be new, abstract, everything. Here I can be traditional successfully. Here I need not stumble into the dilemma of painting, relapsing into an artistic genre in which I secretly no longer believe. Here my desires coincide with my temperament and with the contemporary mood. Here I am myself, and yet a new person. The only one in the field, without competition [Schlemmer diary, July 13, 1925].

Oskar Schlemmer's creative impulses found consistently advanced expression in his original stage work. In addition to "The Triadic Ballet," developed between 1912 and 1922, and the "Figural Cabinet" of 1922, the most experimental of these theater activities grew out of Schlemmer's direction of the Theater Workshop at the Dessau Bauhaus from 1925 to 1929. Many Schlemmer stagings were the informal products of instructional activities in the Theater Workshop, forged in collaboration with faculty colleagues and students. Photographs document Bauhaus productions which cannot be identified as among any of Schlemmer's known theater pieces for formal stage performance. Even more common, to judge from Schlemmer's letters and diaries, were those performances staged in conjunction with Bauhaus parties and impromptu revels. The annual Shrovetide (*Fasching*) festival at the Dessau Bauhaus was a particularly welcome occasion for theatrical entertainments, when Schlemmer and his friends indulged in every form of inspired, madcap stage frolic at this "carnival" season. For that matter, almost any event within the Bauhaus family was cause for celebration, whether birthday, Christmas or New Year's, a new faculty appointment, or a farewell—all occasions marked with ambitious theme parties featuring "amateur" theatricals. These parties introduced to the Bauhaus a form of artistic

invention which in the 1960's would be dubbed "happenings" or in the 1970's "performance art."

"Human beings," Schlemmer wrote, "will always love bright games, disguises, masquerades, dissimulation, artificiality, as they will always love any festive, eye-catching, colorful reflection of life. This speechless theatrical dance, this non-committal Muse who says nothing yet means everything, contains possibility for expression and articulation which an opera or a play could not offer in such purity. . ." [Schlemmer diary, July 5, 1926]. Schlemmer apparently conceived most of the party themes himself and outlined the basic motifs around which participants could improvise:

"The White Festival," the 1926 *Fasching* party: "Four-fifths white and one-fifth color. This will be: 'dappled, splotched, and striped' " [Schlemmer letter to Tut, February 5, 1926];

"Fête of Slogans," December 4, 1927 (first anniversary of the Bauhaus building and Kandinsky's birthday), in which current Weimar events were satirized and communication was via visual pun [see Schlemmer letters to Tut, December 1 and 5, 1927];

"Silent Night," the 1927 Christmas celebration: " . . . no one is allowed to speak a word. But flash cards will be available, for one word (one pfennig), ten words, one hundred words. Communication only by gesture, enforced by the Wopo (Word Police)" [Schlemmer letter to Tut, December 8, 1927];

"Beards and Noses," the 1928 *Fasching* party: " . . . it was good, with many fine masks. . . . Kandinsky had a Sudermann-style beard; Klee had muttonchops; Hannes Meyer a big nose. We had set up a barbershop, where Clabi went to work dressing hair and perfuming. On the stage: first a serious dance by the Kreibig girl, white-stockinged feet, rose-colored hand holding a silver head (and black head cap so that her face disappeared completely).

161

Then movements using these three things, illusionistic, against a black backdrop'' [Schlemmer letter to Tut, February 22, 1928];

"The Metallic Festival,'' the 1929 *Fasching* party on ''the theme of the metallic in general'': ''The unfettered imagination now wrought miracles. A children's slide covered in white sheet metal led one past innumerable gleaming silver balls, lined up and sparkling under spotlights . . . a tinsmith's shop. . . . wrenches, tincutters, can openers! . . . . steel chairs, nickel bowls, aluminum lamps. . . . walls of silvered masks and their grotesque shadows, ceilings studded with gleaming brass fruit bowls, everywhere colored metallic paper and the ever-beautiful Christmas-tree balls, some of enormous size'' [Schlemmer diary, February 1929].

In these informal performance contexts, Schlemmer had both absolute freedom and absolute control as a director. He was free of the constraints necessarily imposed on more public events: professional dancers and technicians, lighting and music, automated stage equipment, promotion, press, and public. Many of the Workshop activities, created in the absence of any audience other than the immediate participants, permitted Schlemmer the necessary latitude to develop what he called ''theatrical dance'' or ''pantomimic dance.'' Schlemmer described almost all of his original stage works as ''dance,'' though ordinarily with the qualifying adjective ''theatrical,'' despite the fact that the medium as he invented it had very little to do with conventional definitions of dance. Instructional exercises in the Workshop included experimental systems of structuring movement in space. The stage floor was geometrically gridded and dancers moved in mathematically prescribed sequences; dancers were clad in primary-color leotards and their movements defined by predetermined, symbolic color relationships; the center of the three-dimensional stage space would be demarcated by stretched ropes or wires, and the dancers moved within the restrictions imposed by those measured tensile lines. (It would be another forty years before Schlemmer's definition of dance conformed to that of other moderns, in the stagings of Robert Rauschenberg and John Cage, for example, or in the objectively structured motion patterns of Laura Dean or Twyla Tharp.) It was in this context that Schlemmer evolved his theories of abstraction in their purest form, and these Bauhaus stage works are as abstract as Schlemmer's work in any medium.

For me, abstract simply means style, and style, as we know, means polished form, the greatest possible degree of perfection. Attaining it necessitates overcoming naturalism, rejecting all unnecessary flourishes, moving toward greater and greater conceptual precision [Schlemmer diary, September 7, 1931].

It is ironic that Schlemmer's most abstract work should be in the medium of dance, since dance is by definition structured around the human form (the dancer). It is nonetheless true that the human figure seems somehow more present, more palpable, more essential, in most of Schlemmer's painting and sculpture than it ever seems in his stage work, where the ''conceptual precision'' of form and color in literal motion through real space reads (at least as conveyed in its photographic documentation) as extremely stylized, non-figurative abstraction. This effect was purposefully enhanced by Schlemmer's consistent use of face or head masks to obliterate individual human features, and by the fact that the artist's original stage works were silent (without narration, voiced dialogue between characters, or, occasionally, even musical accompaniment):

Now theatrical dance can provide the starting point for the renewal. Not burdened with tradition like the opera and the drama, not committed to word, tone, and gesture, it is a free form, destined to impress innovation gently upon our senses: masked, and—especially important—silent [Schlemmer diary, September 1922].

Though Schlemmer adored opera, ballet, theater (his letters and diaries are filled with enthusiasms and critiques of various performances he attended over the years), the startling innovation of his own stage work derived from his admiration of simpler, improvisational ''folk'' entertainments—circus, music-hall or vaudeville (*variété*), commedia dell'arte, pantomime, puppetry, films (especially Chaplin), masquerades, magic, jazz. His achievement was rooted in his understanding that incisive artistic structure could be etched in what was essentially comic, extemporaneous form, without sacrificing the integral properties of either. Schlemmer intuited the human significance of drama and humor, and often focused on the tensions and pleasures of a company of individuals working together to forge the ''personality'' of a performance:

. . . I am confused again, no longer sure which is my true calling—painting or the theater; I always succumb to the theater's wealth of figures and the fascination of dance, music, color, personality. Also the stretch for a climax, performance with its joys and sorrows. Joys and sorrows, and that in the company of others, upon whose ability, enjoyment, love, loyalty, etc. success depends [Schlemmer letter to Otto Meyer, December 1928].

While discretionary improvisation and the vagaries of casting defined Schlemmer's stage works as ultimately variable and non-duplicative, their creator had a clear vision of how they should be performed. In Paris in 1932 for a performance of ''The Triadic Ballet,'' Schlemmer wrote his wife Tut, ''Yesterday I performed the whole ballet for everyone, to general amazement and hilarity; I was in excellent form, and it is fortunate I can demonstrate how everything should be done, which, as Wagner says, is the simplest, surest, and quickest method'' [Schlemmer letter to Tut, June 7, 1932]. (In the Paris staging, Schlemmer danced ''The Abstract,'' a role he originated in the 1922 premiere performance.) Schlemmer's sophisticated selection of musical accompaniment for his stage works comprised a major component in establishing structural resonance to what might otherwise seem erratic dance movements: he opted for assertive, formal music, whether classical or contemporary, Handel or Hindemith.

Schlemmer was not a choreographer, though he choreographed many works. His dance notations are sheets of conceptual, impressionistic images with poetically opaque descriptions of movements, not performance scores. He was not a dancer, though he danced many roles. Photographs suggest an affecting delicacy to his stage presence as a performer, a quality not evident in photographs of the artist offstage. He was not a costume designer, though he designed many costumes. Most of the costumes for Schlemmer's stage works were created from found materials by performer-participants, based on Schlemmer sketches or ad hoc instructions. Tut hand-sewed some of the costumes for ''The Triadic Ballet'' (there were eighteen altogether), with Schlemmer encouraging her in correspondence to ''keep on sewing'' or to be ''careful with the measurements.'' (Costumes were either newly made or altered to fit the proportions of specific dancers. Schlemmer's warning to Tut about measurements was because the casting of the ''Spiral'' for the 1932 Paris performance was not yet definite and the costume could not be tailored to the lady's dimensions until the hiring was final.) Eric Michaud has suggested that Schlemmer ''wants to constrain the body with the costume. . . . [that] it is the very structure of the costume that requires 'precision' '' [see Troy, note 29]. Debra McCall discovered in her reconstructions the extraordinary constraints of Schlemmer's costumes in restricting and determining dance movements. At the same time, however, Schlemmer conceived the abstract visual effects of the costumes *in motion*; kinetic potential and expressive carriage could only be exploited if costume and performer were in physical harmony. Of the 1922 Stuttgart staging of ''The Triadic Ballet,'' Schlemmer reported, '' . . . the performance was the first chance I had to try out some costumes which so interfered with movement that they had to be completely revised. Who was my supervisor and helper? My imagination or the mirror'' [Schlemmer letter to Otto Meyer, October 25, 1922]. Schlemmer recognized the creative possibilities of minimal performance equipment (and, equally, the limitations and frustrations—aesthetic and mechanical—in the complex technical equipment found in professional theaters). In 1925 he wrote Tut that with

only a curtain, leotards, and some fabric he could ''theatricalize'' the Bauhaus. Neither choreographer, dancer, nor costume designer, Schlemmer was, clearly and with genius, a director: ''I realized that I should direct dances but not be a dancer myself. I can say what has to be said and keep an eye on everything if I am not participating; I can control the smallest detail'' [Schlemmer letter to Otto Meyer, October 25, 1922].

Masks, costumes, and characters often appeared interchangeably in various stagings. Although certain masks, for instance, were used exclusively as components of ''The Triadic Ballet,'' others were occasionally used as well for stagings of the ''Figural Cabinet,'' which in turn had certain masks and props unique to its stagings. Variants of Schlemmer's character, the ''Musical Clown,'' for instance, appeared as independent characters in several Bauhaus productions (including both the 1928 and 1929 *Fasching* parties). That Schlemmer conceived masks, costumes, and props as objects independent of the performer's body—that is, as color and shape in space—is clear from the fact that he almost always staged his pieces against a black backdrop, with a black dance carpet, and with performers' exposed body parts camouflaged in black, so that the ''costume'' elements assumed objective sculptural reality. In May of 1930 Schlemmer installed three of his ''Triadic Ballet'' figurines in Paris at the Grand Palais as his contribution to the Werkbund exhibition there, evidence that he saw the figurines—that is, masks/costumes/props mounted on armatures—as viable art works independent of any performance context.

It is difficult to substantiate the sources of Schlemmer's theater imagery. The forms he invented for his stage works are original, unique, and without obvious formal precedent, so that they seem indigenous only to Schlemmer's vivid imagination. While the improvisational wit of this work relates it to Dadaist performance of a slightly earlier era, both structure and visual effects are notably more defined in Schlemmer. While certain of Schlemmer's masks recall the sculpted heads of Brancusi, there is always in Schlemmer an immediacy of materials and something of the elemental that distinguish his forms from the elegantly-wrought, classical refinement of the older Rumanian-born sculptor's. If there is ''primitivism'' in Schlemmer's masks and props (where one might reasonably look for such an influence, given the hypothetical parallels in both form and content between costumed tribal dance ritual and the ''theatrical dance'' of Schlemmer), it appears visually to be that of the Eskimo or Northwest Coast Indians, rather than that of the African arts popular in Europe between the wars and so evident as an influence in the art of Picasso, which was much admired by Schlemmer. In the ''Figural Cabinet,'' which featured masks and flat, cut-out forms half-abstract, half-figural in feeling, there is something of tribal sensibility. In general, however, Schlemmer's masks and costumes, and the movements he choreographed, seem eerily extraterrestrial rather than tribal, a theatrical vision seemingly inspired by futuristic fantasies of space imagery. Neither mechanistic nor robotic, his figurines nonetheless are fundamentally extracorporeal. Schlemmer was committed to "theatrical innovation" in form and to "metaphysical theater" in content [see Schlemmer letters to Otto Meyer, February 17, 1925, and to Tut, July 14, 1925]. He did not see form and content in his stage works as either distinct or complementary, but rather as congruent. "An optical conception can develop out of a dramatic one" [Schlemmer letter to Otto Meyer, March 30, 1923], but the inverse could also occur as a product of the improvisational conjunction of costumes, props, and personalities.

"The Triadic Ballet" was internationally acclaimed for its extraordinary modernism, originality, and conceptual complexity, and new productions of the ballet were staged throughout the 1920's. As Schlemmer toured Germany with the Bauhaus Theater, he had occasion to stage the "Figural Cabinet" and "Bauhaus Dances" for appreciative audiences. Throughout his career he also staged performances of the work of other artists, writers, and composers, both avant-garde and traditional. In 1921 he designed the scenery and costumes and influenced the choreography for the Stuttgart premieres of Oskar Kokoschka's *Murderer, Hope of Women* and Franz Blei's *The Thingamagig*. In 1923–1925 he staged several productions for Berlin's Volksbühne, a theater he found particularly sympathetic to experimental forms. In 1928 he staged ballets in Hagen and at the Dresden Opera (where he designed the sets for "The Nutcracker"), and in 1928–1929 he created several Stravinsky productions in Breslau, including "Le Renard," "Le Chant de Rossignol," and "Les Noces." In 1930 he staged Schönberg's *Lucky Hand* at Berlin's Kroll Opera. Watercolor stage designs for some of these productions reveal unusual charm and intensity of color, with sets of severe geometric abstraction and stylized architectural forms. Schlemmer's commissioned productions (as opposed to his original stage works) seem tamed by the logistical constraints of the commercial theater and by the imposition of the narrative structure of an independent script or score. They stand in almost stately contrast with the improvisational inventions of Schlemmer's Bauhaus stage productions. At the Bauhaus, whether in the context of a party or the Theater Workshop, given free rein to experiment, Schlemmer forged a new theatrical medium in which slapstick, unconventional materials, and tragicomedy merged to convey the artist's essential message that metaphysical gravity and import reside in human gesture, that Man the Dancer (*Tänzermensch*) is a medium of spiritual communication:

One should start with one's physical state, with the fact of one's own life, with standing and walking, leaving leaping and dancing for much later. For taking a step is a grave event, and no less so raising a hand, moving a finger. One should have deep respect and deference for any action performed by the human body, especially on the stage, that special realm of life and illusion, that second reality in which everything is surrounded with the nimbus of magic. . . . [Schlemmer diary, May 1929].

BRENDA RICHARDSON

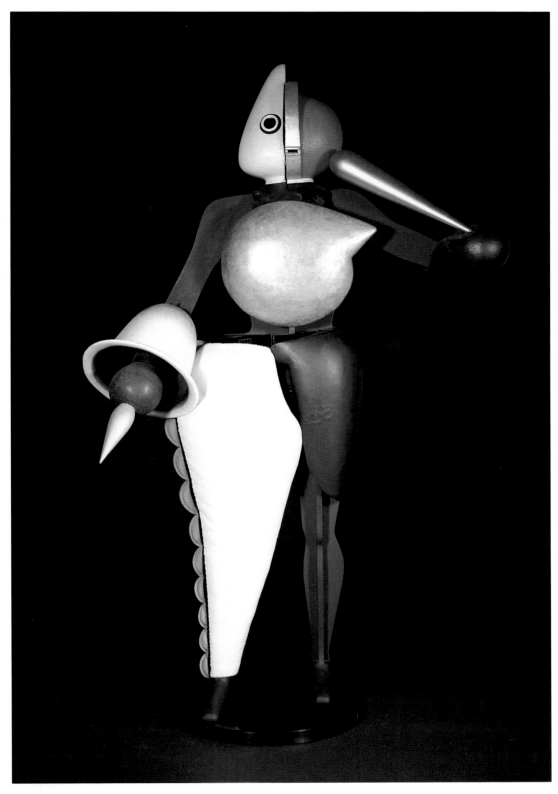

The Abstract (from "The Triadic Ballet"). (1922). Various materials, mounted on plexiglas armature. 79½ in. high. Staatsgalerie Stuttgart. [Not in exhibition; see cat. no. 60].

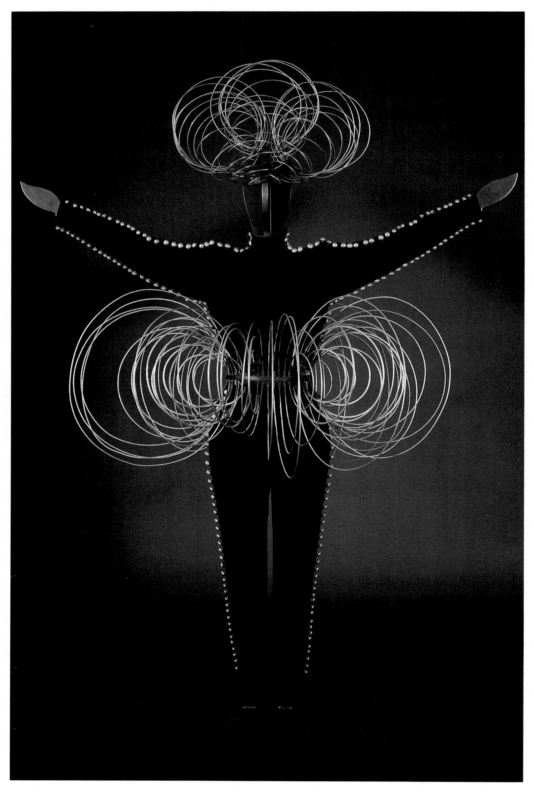

Wire Figure (from ''The Triadic Ballet''). (1922). Various materials, mounted on plexiglas armature. 80¾ in. high. Staatsgalerie Stuttgart. [Not in exhibition; see cat. no. 63].

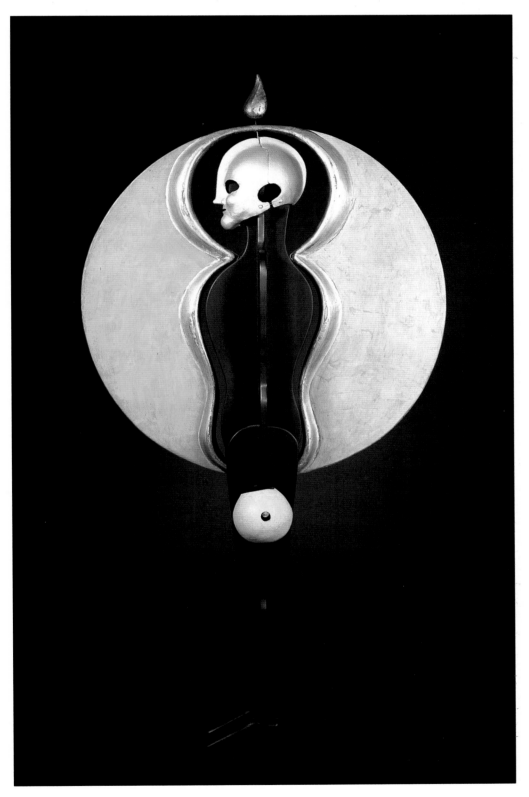

Disk Dancer (from ''The Triadic Ballet''). (1922). Various materials, mounted on plexiglas armature. 76⅜ in. high. Staatsgalerie Stuttgart. [Not in exhibition; see cat. no. 61].

Gold Sphere (from ''The Triadic Ballet''). (1922). Various materials, mounted on plexiglas armature. 76¾ in. high. Staatsgalerie Stuttgart. [Not in exhibition; see cat. no. 62].

The Gold Sphere (Study for ''The Triadic Ballet''). (ca. 1924).
Watercolor and gouache. 23⅝ × 15½ in. Oskar Schlemmer Theater
Estate, Collection UJS. [Cat. no. 91].

The Abstract (with Outstretched Arms) [Study for ''The Triadic Ballet'']. (ca. 1919). Watercolor. 10⅝ × 7⅞ in. Oskar Schlemmer Theater Estate, Collection UJS. [Cat. no. 86].

The Abstract (Study for "The Triadic Ballet"). (1919). Pencil, ink, and watercolor. 11 × 8¾ in. Oskar Schlemmer Theater Estate, Collection UJS. [Cat. no. 85].

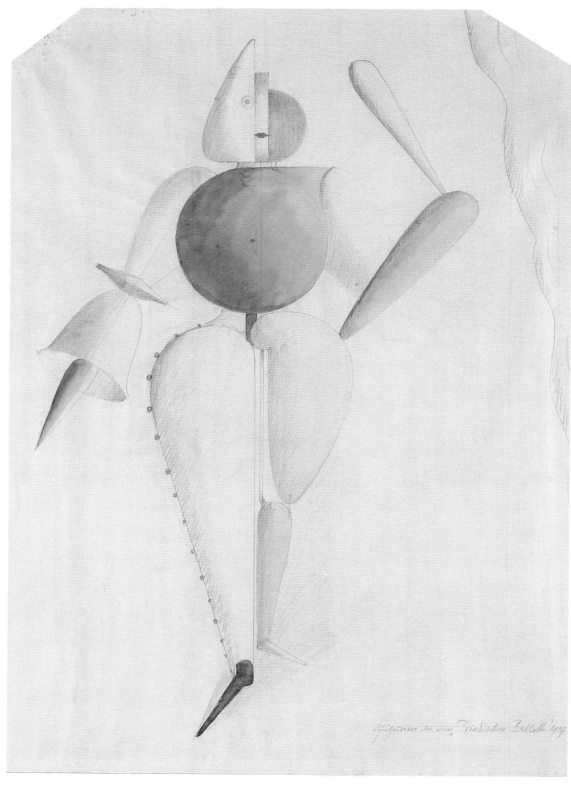

Abstract in White (Study for ''The Triadic Ballet''). (ca. 1924).
Pencil and watercolor. 21¾ × 15⅞ in. Oskar Schlemmer Theater
Estate, Collection UJS. [Cat. no. 89].

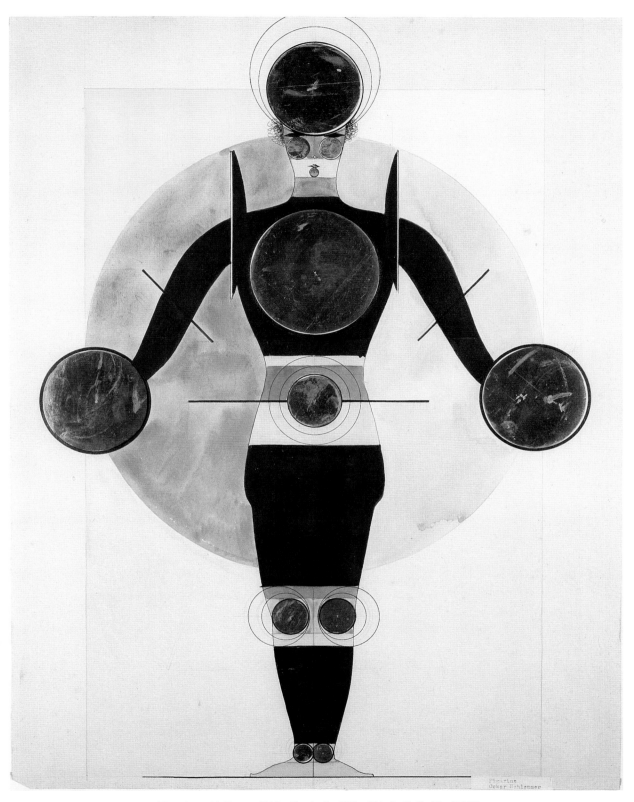

Figurine with Bronze Disks (Study for "The Triadic Ballet"). (1926).
Colored inks and collage. 23 × 17⅝ in. Oskar Schlemmer Theater
Estate, Collection UJS. [Cat. no. 93].

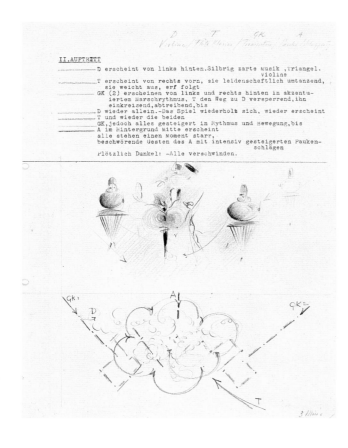

II.AUFTRITT

D erscheint von links hinten.Silbrig zarte Musik ,Triangel.
                                                    Violine
T erscheint von rechts vorn, sie leidenschaftlich umtanzend,
    sie weicht aus, erf folgt
GK (2) erscheinen von links und rechts hinten in akzentu-
    iertem Marschrythmus, T den Weg zu D versperrend,ihn
    einkreisend,abtreibend,bis
D wieder allein.-Das Spiel wiederholt sich, wieder erscheint
T und wieder die beiden
GK,jedoch alles gesteigert in Rythmus und Bewegung,bis
A im Hintergrund Mitte erscheint
alle stehen einen Moment starr,
beschwörende Gesten des A mit intensiv gesteigerten Pauken-
                                                    schlägen
Plötzlich Dunkel: -Alle verschwinden.

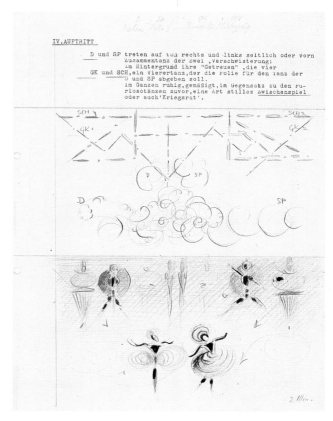

IV.AUFTRITT

D und SP treten auf von rechts und links seitlich oder vorn
    Zusammentanz der Zwei ,Verschwisterung;
    im Hintergrund ihre "Getreuen" ,die vier
GK und SCH,ein Viererttanz,der die Folie für den Tanz der
    D und SP abgeben soll.
    im Ganzen ruhig,gemäßigt,im Gegensatz zu den Fu-
    riosotänzen zuvor,eine Art stilles Zwischenspiel
    oder auch'Kriegsrat'.

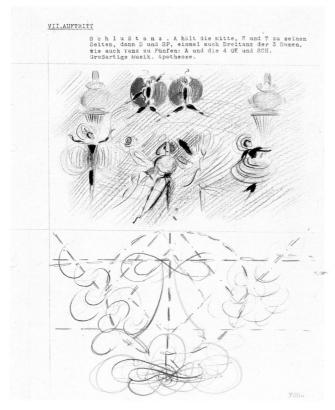

VII.AUFTRITT

S c h l u ß t a n z . A hält die Mitte, W und T zu seinen
    Seiten, dann D und SP, einmal auch Dreitanz der 3 Damen,
    wie auch Tanz zu Fünfen: A und die 4 GK und SCH.
    Großartige Musik. Apotheose.

Manuscript Pages, with Sketches, for the New Version of "The Triadic Ballet." (1936). Pencil and colored pencil. Three sheets, each 11 × 8¼ in. Oskar Schlemmer Theater Estate, Collection UJS. [Cat. no. 94-a-b-c].

Poster for "The Triadic Ballet" (Leibniz-Akademie). (1924). Lithograph, colored with tempera. 31⅞ × 22 in. Oskar Schlemmer Theater Estate, Collection UJS. [Cat. no. 223].

Tall Head Mask (from ''The Triadic Ballet''). (1922). Papier-mâché, painted and gilded. 18⅞ × 7⅞ × 9 in. Staatsgalerie Stuttgart: Oskar Schlemmer Theater Estate, Collection UJS Deposit. [Cat. no. 66].

Flat Mask (from ''Figural Cabinet''). (1922). Papier-mâché, painted and gilded. 16¹³⁄₁₆ × 11¼ × 3⅜ in. Oskar Schlemmer Theater Estate, Collection UJS. [Cat. no. 67].

Mask in Yellow/Black (from ''The Triadic Ballet''). (1922). Painted papier-mâché. 11 × 7½ × 10¼ in. Staatsgalerie Stuttgart: Oskar Schlemmer Theater Estate, Collection UJS Deposit. [Cat. no. 64].

Blue Mask (from ''Bauhaus Dances''). (1926). Painted papier-mâché. 8⅝ × 6⅛ × 3¹⁵⁄₁₆ in. Oskar Schlemmer Theater Estate, Collection UJS. [Cat. no. 69].

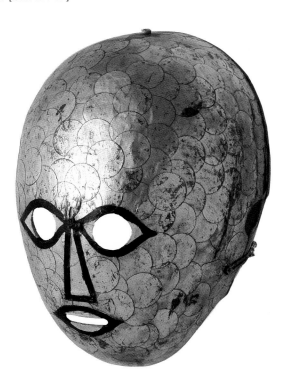

Small Gold Mask (from ''The Triadic Ballet''). (1922). Papier-mâché, painted and gilded. 5½ × 5¾ × 3⅞ in. Staatsgalerie Stuttgart: Oskar Schlemmer Theater Estate, Collection UJS Deposit. [Cat. no. 65].

Mask with Silver Dots (from ''Bauhaus Dances''). (1926). Papier-mâché, painted and gilded. 11 × 7⅞ × 9¹⁄₁₆ in. Oskar Schlemmer Theater Estate, Collection UJS. [Cat. no. 70].

Mask Variations. (ca. 1926). Watercolor over pencil. 18 1/16 × 24 1/8 in. Oskar Schlemmer Theater Estate, Collection UJS. [Cat. no. 156].

Figure Types and Coat Costume Types. (ca. 1926). Pen and watercolor over pencil. 18 1/4 × 24 1/8 in. Oskar Schlemmer Theater Estate, Collection UJS. [Cat. no. 155].

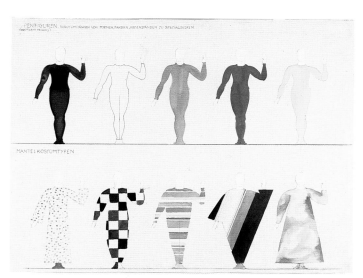

Examples of Costume Forms. (ca. 1926). Watercolor. 17 1/4 × 22 7/8 in. Oskar Schlemmer Theater Estate, Collection UJS. [Cat. no. 154].

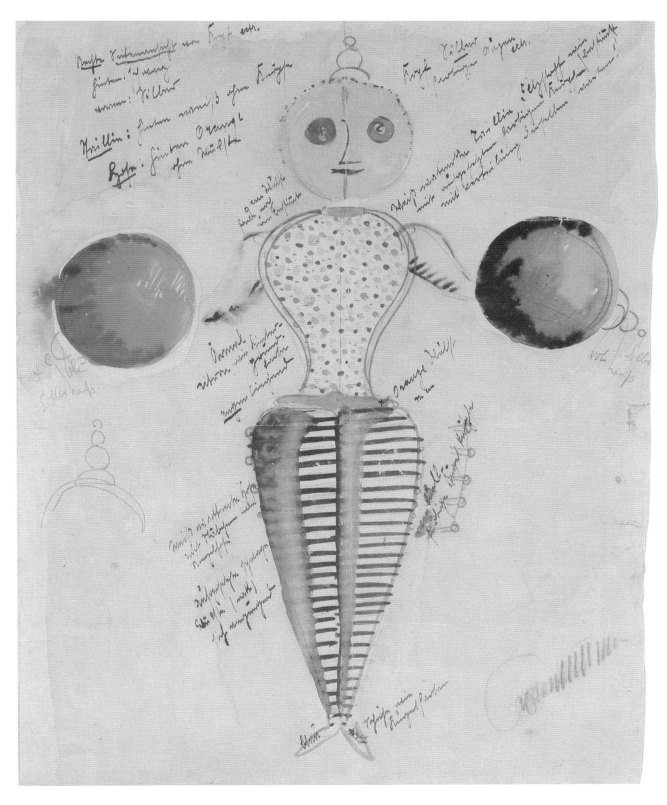

Figurine with Sphere Hands (Study for "The Triadic Ballet").
(1919). Watercolor. 12¼ × 9½ in. Oskar Schlemmer Theater Estate,
Collection UJS. [Cat. no. 88].

Many of Oskar Schlemmer's experimental stage works at the Theater Workshop of the Dessau Bauhaus, 1925–1929, were documented by Bauhaus artist-photographers T. Lux Feininger, László Moholy-Nagy, Ruth Hollos, and Erich Consemüller. Except as noted, the photographs reproduced here are archival documents printed from original glass negatives, believed to be by Ruth Hollos and her husband Erich Consemüller. The original negatives are from the personal archives of the Oskar Schlemmer Family Estate. Prints were provided by the Schlemmer Family and by the Bauhaus-Archiv, with all rights reserved by the Estate.

The Building as Stage, 1929: "The most outstanding of these [special occasions at the Dessau Bauhaus] was the grand enactment of Oskar Schlemmer's cherished dream of using the total Bauhaus architecture—roofs, balconies, terrace—for the outdoor staging of his *Mensch im Raum* idea, his humanistic symbol of the mission of art. Everybody able to point a camera and press a shutter showed up for this demonstration" [T. Lux Feininger, notes for an exhibition catalogue, Prakapas Gallery, New York, November 1980].

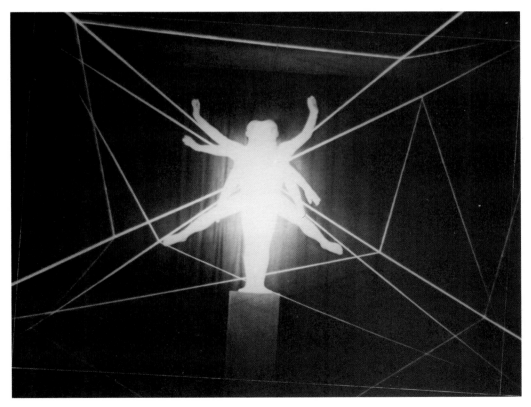

Space Delineations, 1926: " . . . we determined the center of the space by stretching ropes, and the 'tensions' radiating out from them resulted in entirely new configurations of space and movement" [Schlemmer diary, September 7, 1931].

Box Play, with dancer Werner Siedhoff, 1926. Photograph by Ruth Hollos.

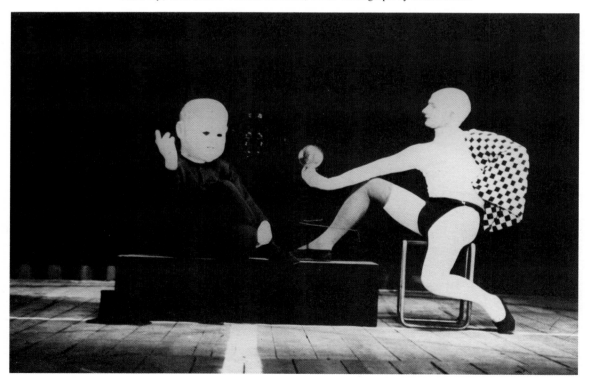

Improvisation, with dancers Lou Scheper and Werner Siedhoff, 1926.
Photograph by T. Lux Feininger.

A scene from the 1928 *Fasching* party, "Beards and Noses," at Dessau Bauhaus: " . . . *Fasching* . . . was good, with many fine masks . . . . Kandinsky had a Sudermann-style beard; Klee had muttonchops; Hannes Meyer a big nose . . ." [Schlemmer letter to Tut, February 22, 1928].

Backstairs Joke, 1929: The "metal stairway" set, from the *Fasching* "Metallic Festival": "A stairway, of which every step gave out a different tone, a true 'backstairs joke,' (in the course of the evening there emerged virtuosos of stair-climbing) . . ." [Schlemmer diary, February 1929]. Schlemmer appears here as a "Musical Clown" at the right.

Two views of the ''Musical Clown,'' with dancer Andreas
Weininger, ca. 1926.

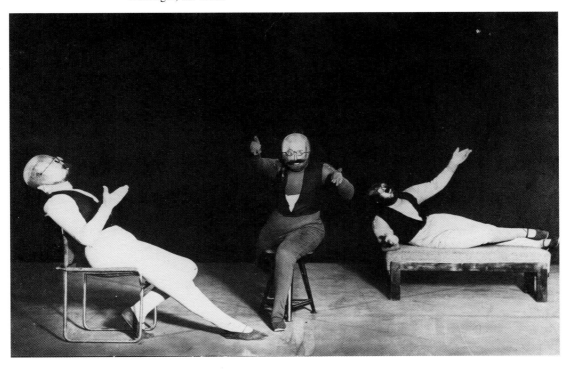

Gesture Dance, with dancers Oskar Schlemmer, Walter Kaminsky,
and Werner Siedhoff, 1927.

Unidentified dancer with hoops and spirals.

Unidentified dancers with hoops and spirals.

Unidentified dancer with hoops and a cane.

Shadow Play, 1926.

Space Dance, 1926.

Form Dance, 1926.

Composite Group on Stage: Pure Black and White, ca. 1926–1929.
Photograph by T. Lux Feininger, courtesy Prakapas Gallery, New
York.

Glass Dance, 1929.

Vorhang-Entwurf (Application,

„Triadischen Ballett" 1919

Oskar Schlemmer, ca. 1935. Photograph by Hugo Erfurth, Dresden.

Oskar Schlemmer: A Chronology

1888–1905

Oskar Schlemmer was born in Stuttgart on September 4, the youngest of six children, to Carl Schlemmer, a businessman who achieved some success as a writer of comedy, and Wilhelmine Neuhaus Schlemmer, the daughter of a Heidenheim goldsmith. Schlemmer attended secondary school in Göppingen while living with a married sister after the death of his parents. Because of the family's financial hardships, Schlemmer left school at fifteen to enter the building trade. By 1905 he had served a two-year apprenticeship as a design craftsman in a Stuttgart wood-inlay factory.

1906–1910

After resuming his education at the Kunstgewerbeschule (School of Arts and Crafts), Schlemmer received a scholarship to the Akademie der bildenden Künste (Stuttgart Academy of Fine Arts), where he studied painting with Landenberger and composition with von Keller. There he met two artists who became lifelong friends: Willi Baumeister and the Swiss, Otto Meyer-Amden. In the fall of 1910 Schlemmer took a leave of absence from the Akademie to work independently in Berlin.

1911–1913

In the spring of 1911, with Meyer-Amden's assistance, Schlemmer painted his first mural, an Annunciation (not extant), in the Catholic chapel built for an exhibition of religious art in Swabia. While in Berlin, he met Russian emigré avant-garde artists and artists of Herwarth Walden's Der Sturm gallery circle. Upon returning to the Stuttgart Akademie in 1912, he

Seated Male Nude. (1906). Pencil. 11⅞ × 10¹⁵⁄₁₆ in. Family Estate of Oskar Schlemmer. [Not in exhibition].

Schlemmer studio, Stuttgart, 1914.

became a master pupil of Adolf Hölzel. During this period he also experimented with dance and recorded in his diaries many notes on the subject. In 1913 Schlemmer and his brother Wilhelm opened a modern art gallery in Stuttgart, where they exhibited such avant-garde artists as Georges Braque, Albert Gleizes, Wassily Kandinsky, Paul Klee, Oskar Kokoschka, and Otto Meyer-Amden, among others.

1914–1918   Under Hölzel's direction, Schlemmer, Baumeister, and Herman Stenner painted murals (not extant) for the main pavilion of the Cologne *Werkbund* exhibition. The three students then traveled to Amsterdam, London, and Paris. Schlemmer volunteered for military service at the outbreak of war, and was almost immediately injured. Upon recovering, he was sent to the eastern front in June 1915, and wounded again. Granted a year's leave to continue his studies, he resumed painting, producing decidedly abstract compositions such as *Painting K*, *Homo*, and *Composition on Pink Ground—Relationship of Three Figures*. In the autumn of 1916, the young artist exhibited recent work in an exhibition "Hölzel and his Circle," shown in Freiburg and Frankfurt. He was also assigned to a surveying and aerial photography unit for the duration of the war. In the winter he worked with the dancers Albert Burger and Elsa Hotzel on ballet scenes that developed into *The Triadic Ballet*. In November 1918, while in Berlin for officer training, he witnessed the end of the war and a short-lived revolution before returning to the Stuttgart Akademie to work again with Hölzel.

1919   At the Akademie, Schlemmer was elected a student representative and delegate to the newly-founded Rat geistiger Arbeiter (Council of Intellectual Workers). When Hölzel resigned from the Akademie, Schlemmer and Baumeister campaigned unsuccessfully for major reforms in the instructional system and for Paul Klee's appointment as Hölzel's successor. In May Schlemmer received the manifesto of the Staatliche Bauhaus, recently established in Weimar by Walter Gropius. With Bau-

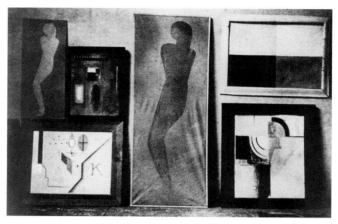
Schlemmer studio, Stuttgart, 1916.

Oskar Schlemmer as a World War I soldier, 1918–1919.

Schlemmer studio, Stuttgart, 1919.

meister he organized an October exhibition at the Württemberg Künstlerbund which included a notable selection of their own work as well as avant-garde works by Berlin's Der Sturm artists and by Klee.

1920 In the spring Schlemmer left the Akademie for nearby Cannstatt to work with his brother Carl on the figurines for the evolving *Triadic Ballet*, and he met the composer Paul Hindemith who was to provide the music for the ballet. During the year Schlemmer exhibited with Baumeister and Walter Dexel at Der Sturm in Berlin as well as with Baumeister and Kurt Schwitters in Dresden. Upon the invitation of Gropius, he visited the Bauhaus to discuss the offer of a faculty position. He married Helena Tutein ("Tut") of Mannheim in October.

1921 Until June, Schlemmer alternated between Weimar and Stuttgart, continuing his work on *The Triadic Ballet*. He also designed scenery and costumes for the first production of two one-act operas: Kokoschka's *Murderer, Hope of Women* with music by Hindemith, and Franz Blei's *The Thingamajig*. At the Bauhaus, Schlemmer's duties included directing the sculpture workshop, instructing classes in life drawing, and, in alternation with Johannes Itten, teaching mural painting. His teaching colleagues included Lyonel Feininger, Gropius, Itten, Klee, Gerhard Marcks, and Georg Muche. During this year the Schlemmers' first daughter, Karin, was born, and the first monographic article on Schlemmer, written by Paul Ferdinand Schmidt, was published in the *Yearbook of Recent Art*.

1922 Under Theo van Doesburg's influence, a new emphasis on industrial production rather than on handicrafts and painting caused conflicts within the Bauhaus. With Kandinsky's appointment as director of mural painting, Schlemmer taught sculpture, life drawing, and woodworking. He designed a Bauhaus logo, produced many pen and ink drawings, and concentrated on his painting, introducing in works such as *The Gesture (Dancer)* a new sculptural concept of form. In August he returned to

Curtain for The Triadic Ballet. (1922). Cotton sateen, in three panels, with appliqué. 149⅝ × 133⅞ in. Oskar Schlemmer Theater Estate, Collection UJS. [Not in exhibition].

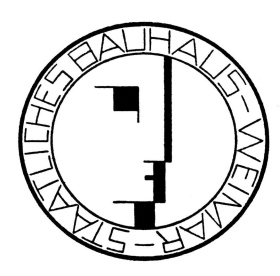

Bauhaus Logo. (1922). Lithograph. 9⅞ × 11⅞ in. Bauhaus-Archiv, Berlin. [Cat. no. 222].

Stuttgart to prepare the fully realized *Triadic Ballet* for its September 30 premiere at the Landestheater. Another daughter, Jaïna, was born.

1923   Upon the resignation of Lothar Schreyer, Schlemmer became director of theater activities at the Bauhaus. For Bauhaus Week, during which time all the school's accomplishments were highlighted, Schlemmer made important contributions with his murals and wall reliefs, painting, printmaking, and theatrical experiments. Following a well-received August production of *The Triadic Ballet* in Weimar, he staged Carl Hauptmann's *The Renegade Czar* at Erwin Piscator's Volksbühne (Popular Theater) in Berlin.

1924   As inflation and political unrest in Germany increased, severe budget cuts sanctioned by the right-wing Ministry of Education forced a radical reduction in the Bauhaus programs. When no compromise could be achieved, Gropius sought a new home for the school. Schlemmer executed two fresco murals for the Weimar house of Gropius's partner, Adolf Meyer. Schlemmer's theatrical success in Berlin brought subsequent commissions for stage designs at the Volksbühne, and his passionate interest in the stage was expressed in his essay ''Man and Art Figure,'' published in *The Theater of the Bauhaus* in 1925. Exhibitions of his work were held in Berlin, Jena, and Stuttgart during the year.

1925   When the Bauhaus relocated in Dessau, Schlemmer considered other employment, including a post at the Staatliche Bauhochschule (State Architecture School) at Weimar. Ultimately, however, he accepted Gropius's proposal that he develop an experimental theater at the Bauhaus. Working with such promising students as Xanti Schawinsky, Andreas Weininger, and Werner Siedhoff (a trained actor and dancer who became a congenial interpreter of Schlemmer's ideas), Schlemmer directed the theater workshop for the Dessau stage designed by Gropius. However, before moving to Dessau in September, he painted his ''gallery pictures,'' among

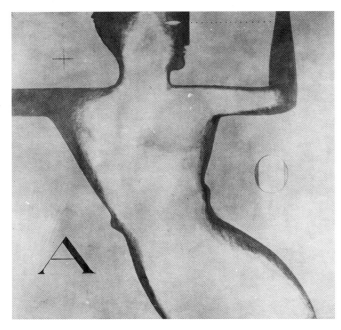

Mural Figure in Square Between A and O. (1924). Fresco for the house of Adolf Meyer, Weimar. No longer extant.

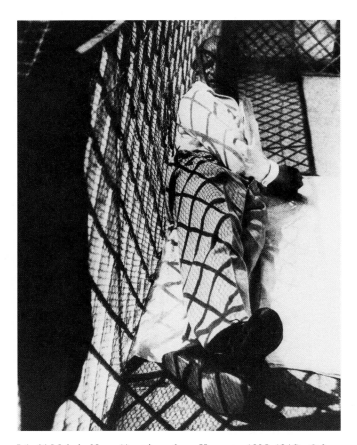

László Moholy-Nagy (American, born Hungary, 1895–1946). *Oskar Schlemmer*. (1926). Photograph. Staatsgalerie Stuttgart: Oskar Schlemmer Archiv.

Faculty of the Dessau Bauhaus, 1926: left to right, Hinnerk Scheper, Georg Muche, László Moholy-Nagy, Herbert Bayer, Joost Schmidt, Walter Gropius, Marcel Breuer, Wassily Kandinsky, Paul Klee, Lyonel Feininger, Gunta Stölzl, Oskar Schlemmer.

The Theater Group at the Dessau Bauhaus, 1928, with Oskar Schlemmer at center, holding a mask in his left hand.

Design for a Pantomime at the Stage of the Bauhaus. (1927). Pencil, watercolor, gouache, ink. 14¾₁₆ × 21⅝₁₆ in. Oskar Schlemmer Theater Estate, Collection UJS. [Cat. no. 157].

them *Five Figures in a Room (Classical Style)* and *Concentric Group*. The Schlemmers' son, Tilman, was born in April.

1926   At the Dessau Bauhaus, László Moholy-Nagy increasingly determined the direction of the school, and emphasized photography and film over painting. In July a new production of *The Triadic Ballet* premiered at the Donaueschingen music festival, while a shorter version was performed in Frankfurt and Berlin. At the formal dedication of the Dessau Bauhaus building in December, Schlemmer inaugurated the new stage with the first production of the Bauhaus Dances.

1927   Schlemmer played a major role in organizing the "Deutsche Theater-Ausstellung" in Magdeburg, where he presented the Bauhaus Dances, staged two other ballets, and lectured on theater at the Bauhaus. He also edited the third issue of the Bauhaus journal devoted to the goals and methods of the school's theater. He considered collaborative stage projects with the conductor Hermann Scherchen and Piscator, for whom Gropius had designed a Total Theater.

1928   Under pressure from various groups within the Bauhaus, Gropius resigned. For his farewell Schlemmer wrote and produced a pageant chronicling "The Nine Years of the Bauhaus." A new director, Hannes Meyer, reorganized the school to focus on the workshops and an active architecture department. During the academic year Schlemmer developed and taught a comprehensive required course on "Man." His proposed mural designs for Henri Van de Velde's rotunda at the Museum Folkwang in Essen won that competition. During the fall Schlemmer had a one-man show at the Nierendorf Gallery in Berlin as well as in Düsseldorf, where he was awarded the Gold Medal of the "Deutsche Kunst" exhibition. *Blue Painting*, *Four Figures and a Cube*, and *Fallen Figure with Column* exemplify Schlemmer's work of the period. He continued to stage ballets, in Hagen and at the Dresden Opera.

Murals (Cycle I) for the Fountain Room of the Museum Folkwang Essen, 1928 (with the Georg Minne fountain at center).

Installation of Schlemmer's work at the Bauhaus Exhibition, Berlin, 1931.

Schlemmer's "wire sculpture" installation at the house of Dr. Rabe, 1931.

1929 Schlemmer's *Metal Dance* was performed at the Bauhaus Mardi Gras Metallic Party. The school's theater troupe successfully toured Berlin, Breslau, Frankfurt, Stuttgart, and Basel. However, the demands of Hannes Meyer and some students that the theater become more political increasingly clouded the atmosphere. Schlemmer was unwilling to meet their demands since his conception was of a theater of universal types, neither political nor literary. Having accepted a professorship at the Staatliche Akademie für Kunst und Kunstgewerbe (State Academy for the Arts and Crafts) in Breslau, where he would teach a course on "Man and Space" and direct the theater class, he left the Bauhaus. Meanwhile his paintings created a stir at a Basel exhibition and earned prizes in Cologne and Darmstadt. Shortly before Christmas, he made his Breslau theatrical debut with set designs for two one-act operas by Igor Stravinsky.

1930 Schlemmer devoted himself to painting and to his "Man and Space" course. In Paris in May he mounted three of his *Triadic* figurines in the Gropius-designed section of the German *Werkbund* exhibition. While there he visited Gropius, Herbert Bayer, and other former Bauhaus colleagues, met Piet Mondrian and Jean Arp, and saw recent works by Braque, Laurencin, Léger, and Picasso. For the Kroll Opera in Berlin, he staged Arnold Schönberg's musical drama *The Lucky Hand*, a highly praised production that was to be Schlemmer's final theater piece. In his painting, he entered a self-described "baroque" phase with stronger colors and a greater sense of movement predominating. Throughout the year he exhibited designs for the Folkwang rotunda wall panels. In October came alarming news from Weimar that his 1923 murals and reliefs in the Bauhaus workshop building had been destroyed. Thus Schlemmer became one of the earliest victims of Nazi vandalism.

1931 Schlemmer worked on several wall designs for Breslau architects and the Berlin architect, Erich Mendelsohn, although only

Tut and Oskar Schlemmer, ca. 1930.

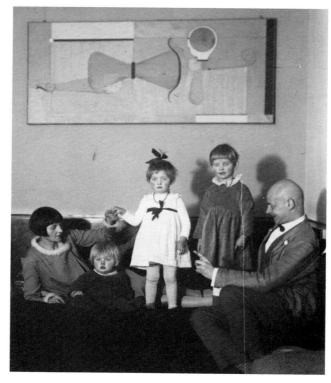

The Schlemmer family, ca. 1927: left to right, Tut (born 1890), Tilman (1925–1944), Jaïna (born 1922), Karin (1921–1981), Oskar (1888–1943), with *Mythical Figure*, 1923, in the background.

one was commissioned: the wire sculpture for a house near Leipzig designed by Adolf Rading for Dr. Rabe. In May Schlemmer participated in the Berlin Bauhaus exhibition and in one-man exhibitions in Berlin, Krefeld, and Zurich. At the end of the year the official order to close three Prussian art academies, including Breslau, was announced.

Schlemmer studio, Breslau, 1932.

1932   As chairman of the Silesian Künstlerbund, Schlemmer organized a comprehensive exhibition in Breslau of art in the eastern region of Germany. In his opening address and in the preface to the exhibition catalogue, he protested the closing of the academies, albeit futilely. In July Schlemmer staged *The Triadic Ballet* for an international dance competition in Paris where it received a prize and special laudatory recognition from Léger. During the summer, Schlemmer painted his last Breslau pictures including the major series of ''banister pictures'' and large watercolors. His well-received lecture on ''The Elements of Theater'' at the Berlin Kunstbibliothek in March was followed by an appointment in June to a post at the Vereinigte Staatsschulen für Kunst (United State Schools for Art) in the capital. After moving to Berlin in the fall, he delivered his inaugural address on ''Perspectives,'' in which he outlined his artistic credo.

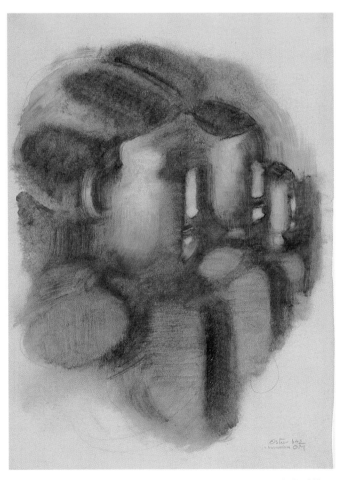

In Memoriam O.M. [Otto Meyer-Amden]: Three Heads. 1942. Oil on oiled paper. 18 × 12⅜ in. Family Estate of Oskar Schlemmer. [Cat. no. 45].

1933–1934   In January Otto Meyer-Amden, Schlemmer's closest friend and intellectual companion, died. Adolf Hitler was appointed Chancellor and Joseph Goebbels the Reich's propaganda minister. Schlemmer's first major retrospective exhibition scheduled to open in Stuttgart was closed through Nazi intervention. While confusion reigned at the Staatsschulen, Schlemmer and several colleagues were denounced by a Nazi poster as ''destructive, Marxist-Jewish elements.'' His teaching appointment was summarily terminated in August. Without means to support his family, Schlemmer sent them to live with relatives in Mannheim. Acting as artistic executor for Meyer-Amden, in December he traveled to Berne to arrange a memorial exhibition of his friend's work. His monograph on the life and work of Meyer-Amden was published in 1934. In Davos, Ernst Ludwig Kirchner encouraged him to paint landscapes. He found a farmhouse in South Baden where the family could be reunited. There was also the distressing news that the wall paintings at the Museum Folkwang in Essen had been removed, and there would be a new competition for its decoration. A more positive response to Schlemmer's art was the inclusion of an important group of his paintings in the Zurich Museum's "Neue Deutsche Malerei" exhibition. Perhaps encouraged by this, Schlemmer entered the competition for decoration of the Congress Hall in the Deutsches Museum in Munich. The jury rejected his designs as unsuitable.

1935–1937 In the spring of 1935 Schlemmer began to paint again: landscapes, reworkings of earlier paintings in darker tones, and works using oilstick on heavy paper. For diversion, he gardened and raised sheep. During the summers of 1936 and 1937 he was a guest at the Lausanne castle of Madame de Mandrot, an art patron. Here he spent several stimulating weeks in the company of writers and artists, among them Max Ernst, Herbert Read, Xanti Schawinsky, and others. He and former Bauhaus colleagues discussed emigrating. Schlemmer prepared a shortened version of *The Triadic Ballet* with new choreography, but this and other theater projects failed to materialize. Early in 1937 Schlemmer exhibited several works in Berlin, Stuttgart, and later in a retrospective in London. He was heartened by a mural commission for the landscape architect Hermann Mattern's house in Bornim. With a small inheritance, Schlemmer planned to build his own house and studio in Sehringen, not far from the Swiss border. A Bauhaus architect, Hans Fischli from Zurich, designed a simple wood building but by the fall, when the house was ready, Schlemmer learned that some of his finest paintings, confiscated from German museums, were being shown in the "Entartete Kunst" ("Degenerate Art") exhibition in Munich. His diary documents his despair: "What a summer!

The Schlemmer family, ca. 1930: clockwise, Oskar, Karin, Jaïna, Tut, Tilman.

Oskar Schlemmer, 1942.

A house-building! Munich and 'Degenerate Art.' A big, beautiful studio—useless and pointless.'' Any possibility of making a living as a practicing artist was now precluded.

1938–1939   With Baumeister's assistance, Schlemmer was employed by a contractor, painting exterior murals in and around Stuttgart. Because of the demands of clients and minor officials, as well as the pressure of deadlines, Schlemmer became physically exhausted and mentally depressed. With the coming war in September 1939, he worked full time at camouflaging barracks, factories, gasworks, and public buildings. Meanwhile, architect friends in Stuttgart arranged mural commissions that both lifted his spirits and helped his finances. Schlemmer feared that sanctions against him would be intensified for, without his knowledge, three of his paintings were included in a London exhibition of ''Twentieth Century German Art'' that had enraged Hitler.

1940–1942   The sheer number of his assignments and the strain of commuting took a heavy toll on Schlemmer's psychic and physical energy, so he welcomed an offer from Kurt Herberts to join other refugee artists at a paint experimentation laboratory in Wuppertal. Among those employed by Dr. Herberts were Baumeister, the architects Heinz Rasch and Franz Krause, the art historian Hans Hildebrandt, and the sculptors Alfred Lörchner, Gerhard Marcks, Edwin Scharff, and the Bauhaus artist, Georg Muche. In the spring of 1942 Schlemmer painted the ''window pictures'' and produced some plaster reliefs, both forms in small format. In the fall he returned to Stuttgart to do more camouflage painting but was soon hospitalized with diabetes and hepatitis.

1943   On January 4, Schlemmer fell into a coma in his Sehringen studio and was taken to the Universitätsklinik in Freiburg. He died of heart failure on April 13, at the age of fifty-five, while taking a cure at Baden-Baden.

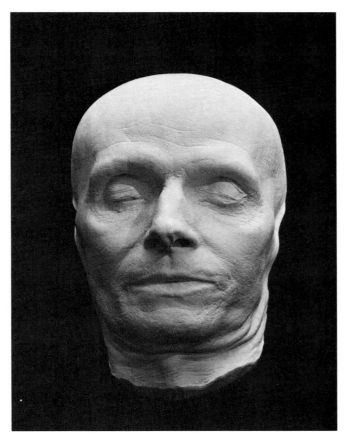

Death mask of Oskar Schlemmer, April 13, 1943.

Entrance to the Stadium. 1930/1936. Oil on canvas. 63½ × 38⅝ in.
Galerie der Stadt Stuttgart. [Cat. no. 33].

Works are catalogued in chronological order and, within each year, alphabetically by English-language title. Chronology or alphabetical order is broken in instances of paired or serial works, or in instances in which reconstructions are cited with originals, in order to retain a logical relationship between associated works.

Titles are cited in English translation, followed by bracketed citation of German titles. Dates that appear on works are cited without parentheses; dates ascribed on either documentary or stylistic bases are cited in parentheses. Mediums are cited with as much specificity as documentation and literate translation permitted. Dimensions are cited in inches and centimeters, height preceding width preceding depth, except as noted. Except as otherwise noted, German cities and states are in the Federal Republic of Germany (West Germany).

When known, museum accession or inventory numbers are cited in parentheses following the ownership credit. For accuracy of identification, catalogue raisonné numbers are cited, as follows:

Maur = Karin von Maur, *Oskar Schlemmer: Oeuvrekatalog der Gemälde, Aquarelle, Pastelle und Plastiken* (Munich: Prestel-Verlag, 1979), vol. II.

Grohmann-Schlemmer = Will Grohmann [and Tut Schlemmer], *Oskar Schlemmer Zeichnungen und Graphik: Oeuvrekatalog* (Stuttgart: Verlag Gerd Hatje), 1965.

S = Karin von Maur, *Oskar Schlemmer*, exhibition catalogue (Staatsgalerie Stuttgart), 1977.

When a Maur 1979 catalogue raisonné reference exists, that number is cited in the entry as "Maur [letter/numeral]"; G-numbers refer to works in oil on canvas or paper, A-numbers refer to watercolors, K-numbers refer to crayon or pastel mediums, and P-numbers refer to sculpture. If no Maur reference exists, a Grohmann-Schlemmer catalogue raisonné number is cited as "Grohmann-Schlemmer [letters/numeral]"; ZT-numbers refer to works in ink on paper, ZB-numbers refer to works in pencil, ZF-numbers refer to works in crayon or charcoal, and GL-numbers refer to lithographs. If neither a Maur nor a Grohmann-Schlemmer reference exists, then reference is given, as "S[numeral]," to the catalogue number of the Staatsgalerie Stuttgart exhibition of 1977. The absence of Maur, Grohmann-Schlemmer, or S-number references indicates that the work has not been published in any of these sources.

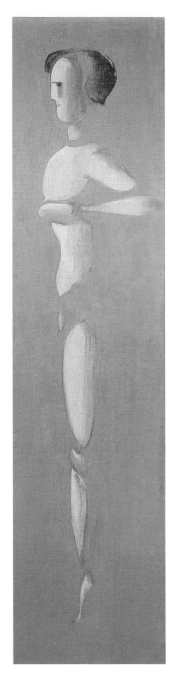

Cat. no. 26.

Paintings (oil or enamel on canvas or paper)

1. HUNTING LODGE IN GRUNEWALD
[Jagdschloss in Grunewald]
(1911)
Oil on canvas
25 × 19½ in. (63.5 × 49.5 cm.)
Maur G49
Staatsgalerie Stuttgart (2813)
Ill. p. 40

2. FEMALE HEAD IN GRAY
[Weiblicher Kopf in Grau]
(1912)
Oil on canvas
22⅝ × 15⅜ in. (57.5 × 39 cm.)
Maur G79
Private Collection
Ill. p. 41

3. MALE HEAD I (SELF-PORTRAIT)
[Männlicher Kopf I, Selbstbildnis]
1912
Oil on canvas
17⅞ × 13⁵⁄₁₆ in. (45.4 × 33.8 cm.)
Maur G77
Staatsgalerie Stuttgart: Hugo Borst Collection (2812)
Ill. p. 42

4. GIRL'S HEAD WITH SILVER
[Mädchenkopf mit Silber]
1913
Oil on brown paper, mounted on board
23 × 18¾ in. (58.5 × 47.5 cm.)
Maur G84
Staatsgalerie Stuttgart (2479)
Ill. p. 208

5. BROWN HOUSES
[Braune Häuser]
(1913–1914)
Oil on canvas
23¼ × 17½ in. (59 × 44.5 cm.)
Maur G65
Family Estate of Oskar Schlemmer
Ill. p. 44

6. STOVE AND ARM CHAIR III
[Ofen und Lehnstuhl III]
(1914)
Oil on yellowish parchment paper
13⅛ × 10⅜ in. (33.2 × 26.4 cm.)
Maur G74
Ulmer Museum: on indefinite loan from the State of
Baden-Württemberg (BW1974.62)
Ill. p. 43

Cat. no. 4.

7. STOVE AND ARM CHAIR IV
[Ofen und Lehnstuhl IV]
(1914)
Oil on yellowish transparent paper, mounted on board
17¾ × 10⅞ in. (45 × 27.7 cm.)
Maur G75
Staatsgalerie Stuttgart (C67/1506)
Ill. p. 43

8. COMPOSITION ON PINK GROUND—RELATIONSHIP
OF THREE FIGURES
[Komposition auf Rosa—Verhältnis dreier Figuren]
(1915 or 1916)
Oil and silver-bronze on canvas, with overpainted collage
element
51⅜ × 36⁷⁄₁₆ in. (130.5 × 92.5 cm.)
Maur G110
Private Collection
Ill. p. 45

9. COMPOSITION ON PINK GROUND
(SECOND VERSION)
[Komposition auf Rosa]
1930
Enamel and metallic paint on canvas mounted on plywood,
with wood relief
51⅛ × 38 in. (129.8 × 96.6 cm.)
Maur G111
Museum moderner Kunst, Vienna: Schlemmer Family
Estate Deposit
Ill. p. 46

10. PAINTING K
[Bild K]
(1915 or 1916)
Oil on canvas
23⅜ × 29⅞ in. (59.5 × 76 cm.)
Maur G112
Private Collection
Ill. p. 47

11. DIVIDED FIGURE
[Geteilte Figur]
(1915–1918)
Oil on canvas
38⁹⁄₁₆ × 28¹⁵⁄₁₆ in. (98 × 73.5 cm.)
Maur G107
Staatliche Kunstsammlungen Kassel: Private Collection
Deposit
Ill. p. 96

12. HOMO
[Homo]
1916
Oil on canvas, mounted on board
17⅞ × 18⅞ in. (45.5 × 48 cm.)
Maur G114
Private Collection
Ill. p. 114

13. MAN WITH FISH
[Mann mit Fisch]
1916 (1918?)
Oil on canvas, mounted on board
36⅛ × 15¾ in. (91.8 × 40.1 cm.)
Maur G115
Museum moderner Kunst, Vienna: Private Collection
Deposit
Ill. p. 98

14. SCHEME WITH FIGURES
[Plan mit Figuren]
(1919)
Oil and collage (metal foil) on canvas
36⅝ × 51⅛ in. (93 × 130 cm.)
Maur G116
Staatsgalerie Stuttgart (LK648)
Ill. p. 48

15. THE DANCER
[Der Tänzer]
1923
Oil and enamel on canvas
69 × 27¾ in. (175.2 × 70.5 cm.)
Maur G119
Staatsgalerie Stuttgart (2490)
Ill. p. 49

16. HEAD WITH CUP
[Kopf mit Tasse]
1923
Oil and enamel on paper glued to plywood
22⁷⁄₁₆ × 15 in. (57 × 38 cm.)
Maur G123
Daimler-Benz A.G., Stuttgart
Ill. p. 53

17. PARACELSUS (THE LAW-GIVER)
[Paracelsus, Der Gesetzgeber]
1923
Oil and enamel on canvas
39 × 29⅛ in. (99 × 74 cm.)
Maur G120
Staatsgalerie Stuttgart (2694)
Ill. p. 52

18. CONCENTRIC GROUP
[Konzentrische Gruppe]
1925
Oil on canvas
38⅜ × 24⅜ in. (97.5 × 62 cm.)
Maur G139
Staatsgalerie Stuttgart (2365)
Ill. p. 58

19. LOUNGE
[Ruheraum]
1925
Oil on canvas
43⁵⁄₁₆ × 35⁷⁄₁₆ in. (110 × 90 cm.)
Maur G134
Staatsgalerie Stuttgart (3238)
Ill. p. 56

20. NUDE, WOMAN, AND APPROACHING FIGURE
[Akt, Frau und Kommender]
1925
Oil on canvas
50⅜ × 25¼ in. (128 × 64.2 cm.)
Maur G138
Staatliche Museen Preussischer Kulturbesitz,
Nationalgalerie Berlin, Galerie des 20. Jahrhunderts (B196)
Ill. p. 20

Cat. no. 27.

21. SEATED YOUTH
[Sitzender Junge]
1925
Oil on canvas
24 × 18½ in. (61 × 47 cm.)
Maur G131
Private Collection
Ill. p. 46

22. BLUE PAINTING
[Blaues Bild]
1928
Oil and tempera on canvas
49⅜ × 46¼ in. (125.5 × 117.5 cm.)
Maur G175
Öffentliche Kunstsammlung Basel: Private Collection
Deposit
Ill. p. 65

23. BROWN-RED, MURAL STUDY I
[Braun-Rot, Wandbildstudie I]
(1928)
Oil on muslin, mounted on plywood
39½ × 9½ in. (100.5 × 24 cm.)
Maur G188
Staatliche Kunstsammlungen Kassel: Schlemmer Family
Estate Deposit (L47)
Ill. p. 31

24. YELLOW-RED, MURAL STUDY II
[Gelb-Rot, Wandbildstudie II]
(1928)
Oil and tempera on muslin, mounted on plywood
39¾ × 8¹⁄₁₆ in. (100.8 × 25.5 cm.)
Maur G189
Staatliche Kunstsammlungen Kassel: Schlemmer Family
Estate Deposit (L46)
Ill. p. 31

25. FOUR FIGURES AND A CUBE
[Vier Figuren und Kubus]
(1928)
Oil and tempera on canvas
96⅝ × 63 in. (245.5 × 160 cm.)
Maur G153
Staatsgalerie Stuttgart (2422)
Ill. p. 62

26. SOLITARY FIGURE (FIGURE ON GRAY GROUND)
[Einzelfigur, Figur auf grauem Grund]
1928
Oil and tempera on canvas
68⁵⁄₁₆ × 15¹⁵⁄₁₆ in. (173.5 × 40.5 cm.)
Maur G173
Staatsgalerie Stuttgart (2525)
Ill. p. 207

27. YOUTHS FORMING A GROUP
[Gruppenbildende Jünglinge]
1928
Oil and tempera on canvas
46⅞ × 35¼ in. (119 × 89.5 cm.)
Maur G154
Museum Folkwang Essen: Private Collection Deposit
Ill. p. 210

28. FALLEN FIGURE WITH COLUMN
[Gestürzter mit Säule]
(1928/1929)
Oil and tempera on canvas
94⅛ × 61 in. (239 × 155 cm.)
Maur G182
Staatsgalerie Stuttgart (2427)
Ill. p. 64

29. FIVE NUDES
[Fünf Akte]
1929
Oil on canvas
35½ × 23¾ in. (90.2 × 60.3 cm.)
Maur G194
Private Collection, New York
Ill. p. 211

30. GROUP OF FIFTEEN
[Fünfzehnergruppe]
1929
Oil and tempera on canvas
70⅛ × 39⅜ in. (178 × 100 cm.)
Maur G196
Wilhelm-Lehmbruck-Museum der Stadt Duisburg (612701)
Ill. p. 69

Cat. no. 29.

31. THREE FIGURES WITH FURNITURE FORMS
[Drei Figuren mit Möbelformen]
1929
Oil on canvas
35¾ × 23¾ in. (90.9 × 60.3 cm.)
Maur G192
Harvard University Art Museums (Busch-Reisinger Museum): Gift of G. David Thompson
Ill. p. 212

32. TWO WOMEN AT TABLE III (VARIATION)
[Zwei Frauen am Tisch III, Variante]
1930
Oil on canvas
23⅝ × 17¾ in. (60 × 45 cm.)
Maur G200
Collection of U. Jaïna Schlemmer
Ill. p. 212

33. ENTRANCE TO THE STADIUM
[Eingang zum Stadion]
1930/1936
Oil on canvas
63½ × 38⅝ in. (162 × 98 cm.)
Maur G221
Galerie der Stadt Stuttgart (0-1427)
Ill. p. 206

34. BEFORE THE MIRROR
[Vor dem Spiegel]
1931
Oil on canvas
26 × 15¾ in. (66 × 40 cm.)
Maur G228
The Saint Louis Art Museum: Bequest of Morton D. May
Ill. p. 213

35. GROUP WITH ECSTATIC FIGURE IN BLUE
[Gruppe mit blauem Ekstatiker]
1931
Oil on muslin, mounted on board
47⅞ × 26 in. (121.5 × 66 cm.)
Maur G226
Hamburger Kunsthalle (5124)
Ill. p. 70
[Baltimore and New York showings only]

36. ASCENDING THE STAIRS
[Treppensteigende]
(1932)
Oil on canvas
39 × 34⅝ in. (99 × 88 cm.)
Maur G263
Collection of Leonard and Evelyn Lauder, New York
Ill. p. 8

Cat. no. 31.

Cat. no. 32.

37. BANISTER SCENE
[Geländerszene]
(1932)
Oil on canvas
42½ × 27¾ in. (105.5 × 70.5 cm.)
Maur G268
Staatsgalerie Stuttgart (LK988)
Ill. p. 74

38. BAUHAUS STAIRWAY
[Bauhaustreppe]
(1932)
Oil on canvas
63⅜ × 44½ in. (161 × 113 cm.)
Maur G267
The Museum of Modern Art, New York:
Gift of Philip Johnson
Ill. p. 75

39. COMPANY AT TABLE
[Tischgesellschaft]
(1935)
Oil on canvas
23⅝ × 35⁷⁄₁₆ in. (60 × 90 cm.)
Maur G287
Private Collection
Ill. p. 214

40. CONVERSATION
[Unterhaltung]
(1935)
Oil on oiled paper, mounted on board
16⅝ × 23 ⅛ in. (42.2 × 58.7 cm.)
Maur G296
Daimler-Benz A.G., Stuttgart
Ill. p. 77

41. TRIO WITH SEATED FIGURES
[Dreiergruppe mit Sitzenden]
(1935)
Oil on paper
25¾ × 16½ in. (65.3 × 42 cm.)
Maur G312
Staatsgalerie Stuttgart (C67/1520)
Ill. p. 213

42. ARABESQUE (WITH CIRCLE AND RECTANGLE)
[Arabeske (mit Kreis und Rechteck)]
(1936)
Oil on oiled paper
25⅜ × 18⅞ in. (64.4 × 48 cm.)
Maur G355
Family Estate of Oskar Schlemmer
Ill. p. 79

43. GRAY WOMEN
[Graue Frauen]
(1936)
Oil on oiled paper
26½ × 19¾ in. (67.2 × 50 cm.)
Maur G331
Collection of U. Jaïna Schlemmer
Ill. p. 78

44. DIAGONAL TORSO
[Halbfigur diagonal]
(1941)
Oil over pencil on oiled paper, mounted on board
23⅞ × 16 in. (60.5 × 40.5 cm.)
Maur G434
Collection of C. Raman Schlemmer
Ill. p. 216

Cat. no. 34.

Cat. no. 41.

Cat. no. 39.

Cat. no. 121.

45. IN MEMORIAM O.M.: THREE HEADS
[In memoriam OM: Drei Köpfe]
1942
Oil on oiled paper, mounted on board
18 × 12⅜ in. (45.7 × 31.5 cm.)
Maur G466
Family Estate of Oskar Schlemmer
Ill. p. 203

46. NIGHTWATCH AND THE OLD MAN I
[Nachtwache und der Alte I]
1942
Pencil and oil color on white board
13¼ × 10¼ in. (33.5 × 26.2 cm.)
Maur G540
Staatsgalerie Stuttgart: Schlemmer Family Estate Deposit
Ill. p. 215

Cat. no. 47.

Cat. no. 46.

47. NIGHTWATCH AND THE OLD MAN II
[Nachtwache und der Alte II]
1942
Pencil and thinned oil color on white board
13¼ × 8⅜ in. (33.8 × 21.4 cm.)
Maur G541
Family Estate of Oskar Schlemmer
Ill. p. 215

48. TWO HEADS
[Zwei Köpfe]
1942
Oil on oiled paper, mounted on white board
19⅜ × 13½ in. (49.2 × 34.4 cm.)
Maur G504
Staatsgalerie Stuttgart (C67/1508)
Ill. p. 216

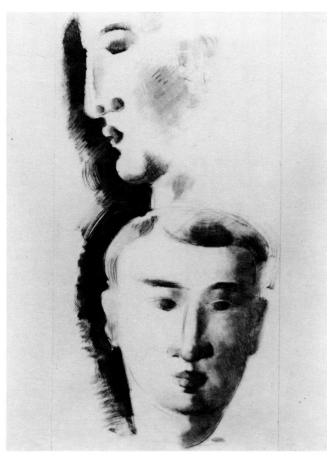

Cat. no. 48.

49. WINDOW PICTURE III: LIVING ROOM WITH STANDING WOMAN
[Fensterbild III, Wohnraum mit stehender Frau]
(1942)
Oil over pencil and colored pencil on laminated board
12⅞ × 9 in. (32.6 × 22.8 cm.)
Maur G484
Öffentliche Kunstsammlung Basel: Schlemmer Family Estate Deposit
Ill. p. 81

50. WINDOW PICTURE XII: ROOM WITH SEATED WOMAN IN VIOLET SHADOW
[Fensterbild XII, Raum mit sitzender Frau in violettem Schatten]
1942
Oil over pencil on laminated board
12 × 8⅛ in. (30.6 × 20.7 cm.)
Maur G478
Öffentliche Kunstsammlung Basel: Schlemmer Family Estate Deposit
Ill. p. 81

Cat. no. 44.

Sculpture

51. CONSTRUCTED SCULPTURE R
[Bauplastik R]
(1919)
Plaster
39⅜ × 9⅞ × 3⅞ in. (100 × 25 × 10 cm.)
Maur P10
Städtische Kunsthalle Mannheim: Schlemmer Family Estate
Deposit
Ill. p. 101

52. ORNAMENTAL SCULPTURE
[Ornamentale Plastik]
(1919)
Plaster
18⅞ × 8¼ × 3½ in. (48 × 21 × 9 cm.)
Maur P3
Städtische Kunsthalle Mannheim: Schlemmer Family Estate
Deposit
Ill. p. 10

53. RELIEF H
[Relief H]
(1919)
Plaster, with polished white finish
26⅜ × 11⅛ × 1⅛ in. (67 × 28.2 × 2.8 cm.)
Maur P6
Galerie Beyeler, Basel
Ill. p. 100

54. RELIEF H, BRONZED
[Relief H bronziert]
(1919)
Plaster, with bronze finish
26½ × 11 × 1¼ in. (67.2 × 28 × 3.3 cm.)
Maur P5
Sammlung und Archiv für Künstler der Breslauer
Akademie, Kassel
Ill. p. 100

55. RELIEF JG IN BRONZE
[Relief JG in Bronzen]
(1919)
Plaster, with bronzed and painted wood elements, and
original frame
26⁹⁄₁₆ × 12¹³⁄₁₆ in. (67.5 × 32.5 cm.), without frame
Maur P8
Staatsgalerie Stuttgart (P318)
Ill. p. 97

56. GROTESQUE II
[Groteske II]
(1923)
Walnut and ivory, with metal shaft
22 × 9¼ × 4⅛ in. (56 × 23.5 × 10 cm.)
Maur P14.II
Staatsgalerie Stuttgart (P245)
Ill. p. 104

57. ABSTRACT FIGURE
[Abstrakte Figur]
(Cast in 1961, in edition of 11, from the 1921/1923
plaster)
Nickel-plated bronze
41½ × 24⅝ × 8⅜ in. (105.5 × 62.5 × 21.4 cm.)
Maur P13a
The Baltimore Museum of Art: Alan and Janet
Wurtzburger Collection (BMA 1966.55.28)
Ill. p. 105

58. ABSTRACT HEAD (RECONSTRUCTION)
[Abstrakter Kopf—Rekonstruktion]
(1973 reconstruction, based on a 1923 working drawing
[see cat. no. 119])
Copper wire and nickel-plated chromium wire
16½ in. (42 cm.) high
Maur P21a
Collection of C. Raman Schlemmer, courtesy Nicholas
Wilder, New York
Ill. p. 112

59. HOMO WIRE FIGURE WITH BACK-VIEW FIGURE
ON ITS HAND
[Drahtfigur Homo mit Rückenfigur auf der Hand]
(1968 reconstruction, in edition of 10, from the left-hand
wire and metal section of the original installation in the
home of Dr. Rabe, Zwenkau, 1930–1931)
Steel wire and silver-plated zinc cast, mounted on wooden
support
121⅞ in. (309.5 cm.) high
Maur P25a
The Museum of Modern Art, New York: The Riklis
Collection of McCrory Corporation (fractional gift)
Ill. p. 115

Figurines and Masks

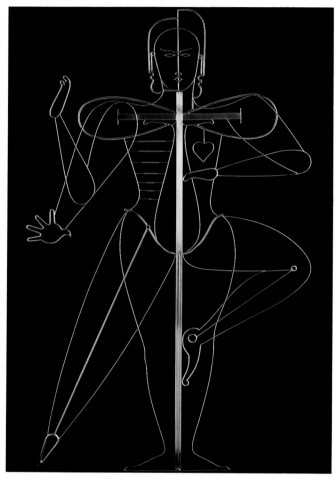

Figurine Armature. (1985). Stainless steel. 72⅝ × 43½ × 1⅜ in. (184.5 × 110.5 × 2.9 cm.). Oskar Schlemmer Theater Estate, Collection UJS.

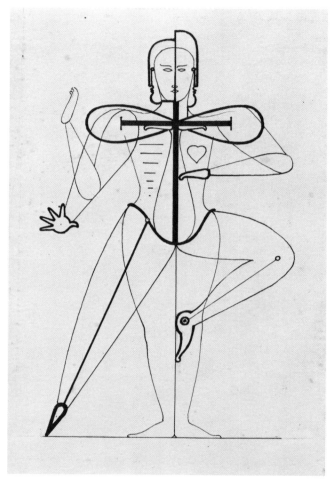

The Symbol in Man (Dematerialization). (1924). Ink. 8¹³⁄₁₆ × 5⅜ in. Staatsgalerie Stuttgart: Schlemmer Family Estate Deposit. [Not in exhibition].

As conceived by Schlemmer, his "Triadic Ballet" figurines were comprised of dancer, mask, costume, and props. Outside a performance context, the "costume" elements are mounted on display armatures which represent the dancer. Early versions of the costumes are displayed in the collection of the Staatsgalerie Stuttgart on plexiglas armatures. For the Baltimore exhibition, U. Jaïna Schlemmer conceived and designed new figurine armatures based on the 1924 ink drawing by Oskar Schlemmer, *The Symbol in Man (Dematerialization)* [see p. 259 for complete data]. The prototype of the 1985 reconstruction is in stainless steel and served as the basis for an edition of five black-painted stainless steel figurine modules (each a slight variant specific to one of the "Triadic Ballet" figurine postures) designed as display armatures. The 1985 figurine armatures were fabricated by Herbert Geiger, Kunstgewerbliche Metallwerkstätte, Stuttgart.

The Triadic Ballet

60. THE ABSTRACT
[Der Abstrakte]
(1967 costume reconstruction by Hans Warneke, based on
the 1922 original)
Papier-mâché, wood, and fabric on stainless steel figurine
Oskar Schlemmer Theater Estate, Collection UJS
Cf. ill. p. 165

61. DISK DANCER
[Scheibentänzer]
(1985 costume reconstruction by U. Jaïna Schlemmer,
based on the 1922 original)
Papier-mâché, wood, and fabric on stainless steel figurine
Collection of C. Raman Schlemmer, courtesy of
The Baltimore Museum of Art
Cf. ill. p. 167

62. GOLD SPHERE
[Goldkugel]
(1967 costume reconstruction by Hans Warneke, based on
the 1922 original)
Papier-mâché, wood, and fabric on stainless steel figurine
Oskar Schlemmer Theater Estate, Collection UJS
Cf. ill. p. 168

63. WIRE FIGURE
[Drahtfigur]
(1985 costume reconstruction by U. Jaïna Schlemmer,
based on the 1922 original)
Stainless steel wire on stainless steel figurine
Collection of C. Raman Schlemmer, courtesy of
The Baltimore Museum of Art
Cf. ill. p. 166

64. MASK IN YELLOW/BLACK
[Maske Gelbe/Schwarz]
(1922)
Painted papier-mâché
11 × 7½ × 10¼ in. (28 × 19 × 26 cm.)
Staatsgalerie Stuttgart: Oskar Schlemmer Theater Estate,
Collection UJS Deposit
Ill. p. 177

65. SMALL GOLD MASK
[Kleine Maske Gold]
(1922)
Papier-mâché, painted and gilded
5½ × 5¾ × 3⅞ in. (14 × 14.5 × 10 cm.)
Staatsgalerie Stuttgart: Oskar Schlemmer Theater Estate,
Collection UJS Deposit
Ill. p. 177

66. TALL HEAD MASK
[Hohe Kopfmaske]
(1922)
Gilded papier-mâché, with painted highlights on eyebrows
nose, and lips
18⅞ × 7⅞ × 9 in. (48 × 20 × 23 cm.)
Staatsgalerie Stuttgart: Oskar Schlemmer Theater Estate,
Collection UJS Deposit
Ill. p. 176

Figural Cabinet

67. FLAT MASK
[Flache Vorhaltemaske]
(1922)
Papier-mâché, painted and gilded
16¹³⁄₁₆ × 11¼ × 3⁵⁄₁₆ in. (42.7 × 28.6 × 8.5 cm.)
Oskar Schlemmer Theater Estate, Collection UJS
Ill. p. 176

68. PROFILE IN YELLOW
[Profil in Gelb]
(1922)
Tempera on canvas, stretched over wire and wood
framework
58¾ × 16½ in. (149 × 42 cm.)
Staatsgalerie Stuttgart: Oskar Schlemmer Theater Estate,
Collection UJS Deposit
Ill. p. 11

Bauhaus Dances

69. BLUE MASK
[Maske Blau]
(1926)
Painted papier-mâché
8⅝ × 6⅛ × 3¹⁵⁄₁₆ in. (22 × 15.5 × 10 cm.)
Oskar Schlemmer Theater Estate, Collection UJS
Ill. p. 177

70. MASK WITH SILVER DOTS
[Maske mit Silberplättchen]
(1926)
Papier-mâché, painted and gilded
11 × 7⅞ × 9¹⁄₁₆ in. (28 × 20 × 23 cm.)
Oskar Schlemmer Theater Estate, Collection UJS
Ill. p. 177

Works on Paper
(Watercolors, Pastels, Drawings, and Prints)

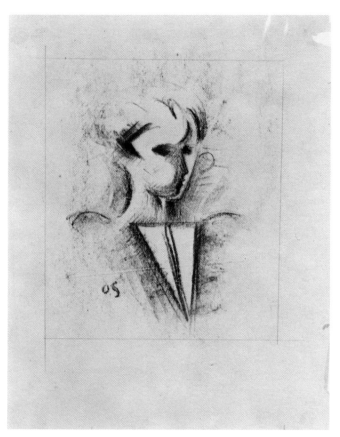

Cat. no. 74.

71. THE FIGURINE ''ABSALOM''
[Figurine ''Absalom'']
(1912)
Pencil on paper
7⅝ × 4⅞ in. (19.5 × 12.5 cm.)
Grohmann-Schlemmer ZB9
Staatsgalerie Stuttgart (C1951/366)
Ill. p. 129

72. HOUSES (CLOISTER GARDEN)
[Häuser (Klostergarten)]
1912
Pencil, touched with brownish watercolor, on whitish
paper, mounted on board and outlined in pencil
7½ × 5⅛ in. (19 × 13 cm.)
Maur A24
Staatsgalerie Stuttgart: Schlemmer Family Estate Deposit
Ill. p. 40

73. PANTOMIME
[Pantomime]
1912
Pen and ink on paper
8⅜ × 11⅛ in. (21.4 × 28.3 cm.)
Grohmann-Schlemmer ZT5
Staatsgalerie Stuttgart: Schlemmer Family Estate Deposit
Ill. p. 129

Cat. no. 75.

74. HEAD FACING RIGHT
[Kopf nach rechts]
(1913)
Colored pencil and oilstick on transparent paper
10⅝ × 8 in. (27 × 20.4 cm.)
Grohmann-Schlemmer ZF1
Staatsgalerie Stuttgart: Schlemmer Family Estate Deposit
Ill. p. 220

75. INCLINED FIGURE
[Geneigte Figur]
(ca. 1913)
Sepia-toned ink on thin paper, mounted on board
9 × 6¼ in. (22.9 × 15.9 cm.)
Maur A27
Staatsgalerie Stuttgart: Schlemmer Family Estate Deposit
Ill. p. 220

76. NUDE IN DARKNESS
[Akt im Dunkel]
(1913)
Pen and brush in sepia ink wash on thin yellowish paper,
mounted on board
12¾ × 7½ in. (32.3 × 19 cm.)
Maur A31
Family Estate of Oskar Schlemmer
Ill. p. 221

77. ABSTRACTION WITH FIGURE 5 AND HEAD
[Abstrakt mit 5 und Kopf]
(ca. 1915)
Watercolor on light brown paper, mounted on board
11 × 8⅜ in. (28 × 21.4 cm.)
Maur A47
Family Estate of Oskar Schlemmer
Ill. p. 83

78. FIGURE AND ATTRIBUTES
[Figur und Attribute]
(ca. 1915)
Watercolor on light brown board
9⅝ × 8½ in. (24.3 × 21.5 cm.)
Maur A48
Family Estate of Oskar Schlemmer
Ill. p. 239

79. FOUR FRONTAL FIGURES
[Vier Figuren von vorne]
(1915–1916)
Pen and ink on paper
8⅜ × 6⅜ in. (21.4 × 16.2 cm.)
Grohmann-Schlemmer ZT67
Staatsgalerie Stuttgart (C1951/367)
Ill. p. 222

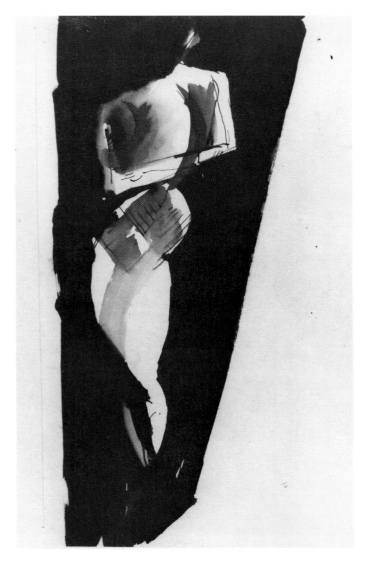

Cat. no. 76.

80. STUDY FOR ''PAINTING K''
[Studie zu ''Bild K'']
(ca. 1915–1916)
Pencil, touched in places with India ink wash, on verti-
cally-lined notepaper, lined in red at top and bottom
15¾ × 6⅞ in. (14.6 × 17.6 cm.)
Maur A50
Family Estate of Oskar Schlemmer
Ill. p. 222

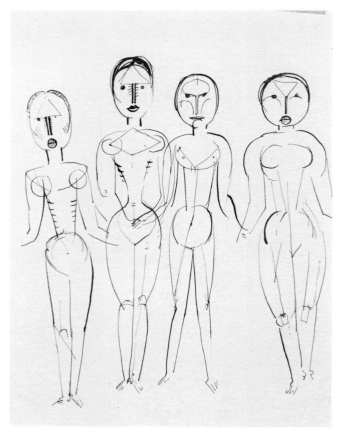

Cat. no. 79.

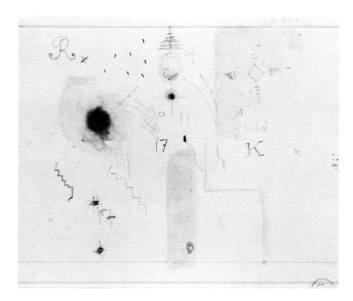

Cat. no. 80.

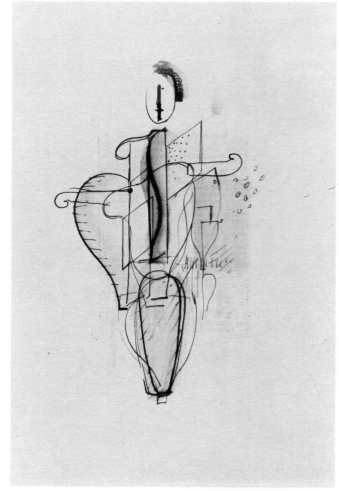

Cat. no. 81.

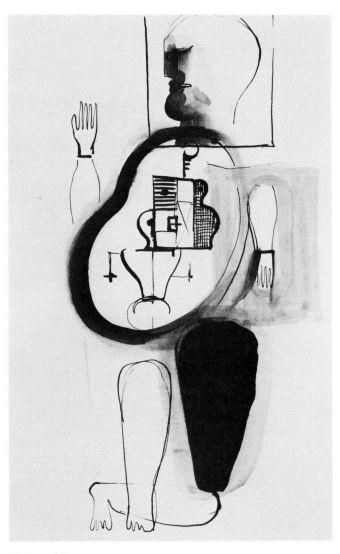

Cat. no. 82.

83. FEMALE FIGURE
[Weibliche Figur]
(1916–1919)
Pen and ink on paper
17⅜ × 12 in. (45.3 × 30.6 cm.)
Grohmann-Schlemmer ZT113
Staatsgalerie Stuttgart: Schlemmer Family Estate Deposit
Ill. p. 223

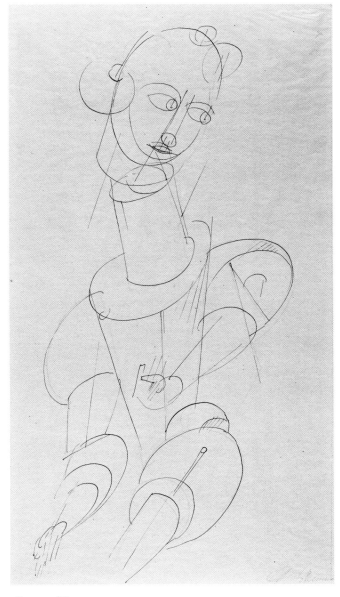

Cat. no. 83.

81. FIGURATION
[Figurisation]
(1916)
Pen and India ink wash on gray-white glossy paper
9 × 5¾ in. (22.8 × 14.7 cm.)
Maur A52
Staatsgalerie Stuttgart: Collection Karin and U. Jaïna
Schlemmer Deposit
Ill. p. 222

82. MAN IN SECTIONED FORMS
[Mann in aufgeteilten Formen]
(ca. 1916)
Pen and brush in black India ink wash on graph paper
7⅝ × 4⅜ in. (19.3 × 11.2 cm.)
Maur A51
Staatsgalerie Stuttgart: Schlemmer Family Estate Deposit
Ill. p. 223

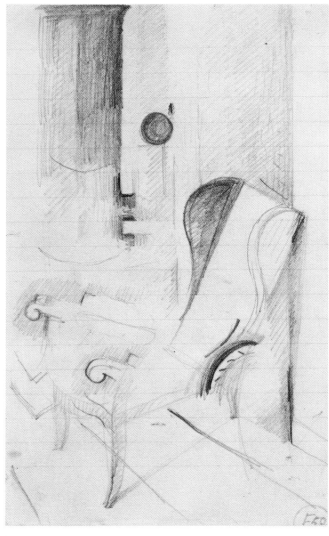

Cat. no. 84.

Studies for The Triadic Ballet, 1919–1936.
(Cat. nos. 85–94).

---

85. THE ABSTRACT
[Der Abstrakte]
(1919)
Pencil, black ink, and watercolor on blue-toned notepaper, mounted on brown board
11 × 8¾ in. (28.1 × 22.1 cm.)
Maur A71
Oskar Schlemmer Theater Estate, Collection UJS
Ill. p. 171

86. THE ABSTRACT (WITH OUTSTRETCHED ARMS)
[Der Abstrakte (mit ausgebreiteten Armen)]
(ca. 1919)
Watercolor and gold-bronze on yellowish tissue paper, mounted on board
10⅝ × 7⅞ in. (27.1 × 20 cm.)
Maur A69
Oskar Schlemmer Theater Estate, Collection UJS
Ill. p. 170

87. CURTAIN DESIGN
[Vorhangentwurf]
1919
Watercolor on thin white paper, mounted on white board
11⅜ × 17¼ in. (29 × 43.8 cm.)
Maur A60
Oskar Schlemmer Theater Estate, Collection UJS
Ill. pp. 192–193

88. FIGURINE WITH SPHERE HANDS
[Figurine mit Kugelhänden]
(1919)
Watercolor and silver-bronze on thin whitish paper, mounted on paper and board
12¼ × 9½ in. (30.1 × 24.2 cm.)
Maur A61
Oskar Schlemmer Theater Estate, Collection UJS
Ill. p. 179

89. ABSTRACT IN WHITE
[Abstrakt in Weiss]
(ca. 1924)
Pencil and watercolor on chamois-colored paper, mounted on board
21¾ × 15⅞ in. (55.3 × 40.2 cm.)
Maur A152
Oskar Schlemmer Theater Estate, Collection UJS
Ill. p. 172

84. STOVE WITH ARM CHAIR
[Ofen mit Lehnstuhl]
(1917)
Pencil on lined paper
6¾ × 4⅛ in. (17.1 × 10.6 cm.)
Grohmann-Schlemmer ZB34
Staatsgalerie Stuttgart: Schlemmer Family Estate Deposit
Ill. p. 224

90. FIGURINES IN SPACE: STUDY FOR THE TRIADIC
BALLET
[Figurinen im Raum]
(ca. 1924)
Gouache, brush and ink, incised enamel, and pasted photo-
graphs on board
22⅝ × 14⅝ in. (57.5 × 37.1 cm.)
Maur A150
The Museum of Modern Art, New York: Gift of Lily
Auchincloss (24.56)
Ill. p. 131

91. THE GOLD SPHERE
[Die Goldkugel]
(ca. 1924)
Watercolor and gouache on board
23⅝ × 15½ in. (59.9 × 39.3 cm.)
Maur A151
Oskar Schlemmer Theater Estate, Collection UJS
Ill. p. 169

92. FIGURINE PLAN FOR THE TRIADIC BALLET I
[Figurinen-Plan zum Triadischen Ballett I]
(1924–1926)
Pen and ink (outlines), watercolor, poster paint, ink and
bronze on brownish paper
15 × 21 in. (38.1 × 53.3 cm.)
Maur A153
Harvard University Art Museums (Busch-Reisinger
Museum), Museum Purchase
Ill. p. 13
[Baltimore and New York showings only]

93. FIGURINE WITH BRONZE DISKS
[Figurine mit bronzierten Scheiben]
(1926)
Colored inks and collage of bronze-toned metallic paper on
light, yellowish board
23 × 17⅝ in. (58.4 × 44.7 cm.)
Maur A247
Oskar Schlemmer Theater Estate, Collection UJS
Ill. p. 173

94. MANUSCRIPT PAGES, WITH SKETCHES, FOR THE
NEW VERSION OF ''THE TRIADIC BALLET''
[Manuskript mit Skizzen zur Neufassung des ''Triadischen
Ballett'']
(1936)
Manuscript with detailed notes on choreography, scenery,
and costume sketches in pencil and colored pencil, on
white paper
Ten pages, each 11 × 8¼ in. (28 × 21 cm.)
Oskar Schlemmer Theater Estate, Collection UJS

94-a. SHEET 5	94-b. SHEET 7	94-c. SHEET 10
[Blatt 5]	[Blatt 7]	[Blatt 10]
S600/5	S600/7	S600/10
Ill. p. 174	Ill. p. 174	Ill. p. 174

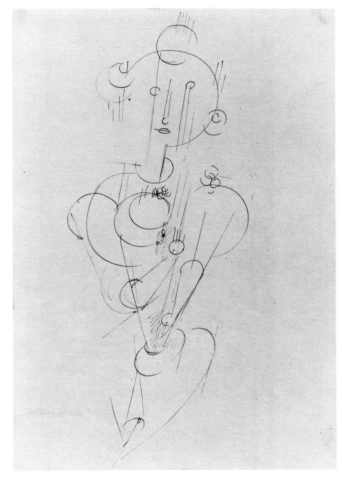

Cat. no. 95.

95. FEMALE FIGURE
[Weibliche Figur]
(1919)
Pen and ink on brownish transparent paper
18⅛ × 11⅞ in. (45.9 × 30.3 cm.)
Grohmann-Schlemmer ZT112
Staatsgalerie Stuttgart: Schlemmer Family Estate Deposit
Ill. p. 225

96. FIGURE WITH INFINITY SIGN
[Figur mit Unendlichkeitszeichen]
(1919)
Pen and ink on brown paper
20¼ × 13¼ in. (51.5 × 33.8 cm.)
Grohmann-Schlemmer ZT136
Staatsgalerie Stuttgart: Collection Karin and U. Jaïna
Schlemmer Deposit
Ill. p. 226

Cat. no. 96.

97. NUMEROLOGY WITH 5
[Zahlenmystik mit 5]
(1919)
Pen and ink over pencil on light transparent paper
13¼ × 12⅝ in. (33.6 × 32 cm.)
Grohmann-Schlemmer ZT132
Staatsgalerie Stuttgart: Schlemmer Family Estate Deposit
Ill. p. 83

98. NUMEROLOGY WITH 8
[Zahlenmystik mit 8]
(1919)
Pencil and pen and ink on light transparent paper
13⅜ × 12¾ in. (33.9 × 32.5 cm.)
Grohmann-Schlemmer ZT135
Staatsgalerie Stuttgart: Schlemmer Family Estate Deposit
Ill. p. 83

99. RENAISSANCE FRANCE
[Renaissance France]
(1919)
Pencil and pen and ink on brown parchment paper
20⅝ × 12⅝ in. (52.5 × 32.1 cm.)
Grohmann-Schlemmer ZT125
Staatsgalerie Stuttgart: Collection Karin and U. Jaïna
Schlemmer Deposit
Ill. p. 226

100. SEATED MALE FIGURE FACING LEFT
[Sitzender nach links]
(ca. 1920)
Pen and ink on yellowish transparent paper, mounted on
white board
15½ × 10⅝ in. (39.3 × 26.9 cm.)
S287
Staatsgalerie Stuttgart (C67/1505)
Ill. p. 227

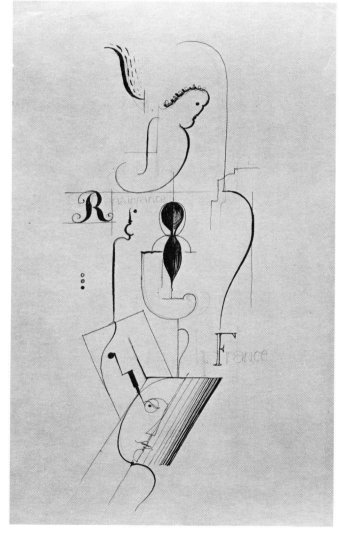

Cat. no. 99.

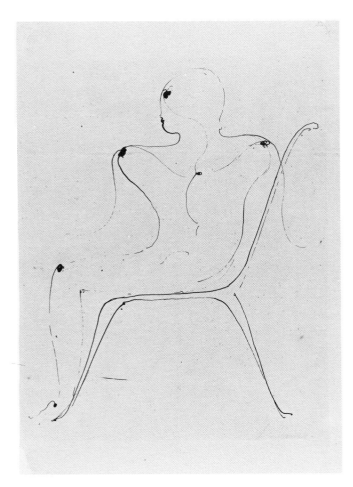

Cat. no. 100.

101. HOMO, FIGURE T
[Homo, Figur T]
(ca. 1920–1921)
Pen and ink on brownish parchment paper
16¼ × 11⅜ in. (41.2 × 29 cm.)
Grohmann-Schlemmer ZT147
Staatsgalerie Stuttgart: Schlemmer Family Estate Deposit
Ill. p. 82

102. ABSTRACT FIGURE, FRONTAL
[Abstrakte Figur, frontal]
(ca. 1921)
Pen and ink on brownish transparent paper
20¾ × 12½ in. (52.8 × 31.7 cm.)
Grohmann-Schlemmer ZT137
Staatsgalerie Stuttgart: Collection Karin and U. Jaïna
Schlemmer Deposit
Ill. p. 109

103. ABSTRACT FIGURE (WITH CROSSED LEGS)
[Abstrakte Figur (mit untergeschlagenen Beinen)]
1921
Pen and ink on gray-brown parchment paper
12⅝ × 9⅛ in. (32 × 23.1 cm.)
Grohmann-Schlemmer ZT156
Staatsgalerie Stuttgart: Collection Karin and U. Jaïna
Schlemmer Deposit
Ill. p. 227

104. DANCER (DESIGN FOR A SCULPTURE)
[Tänzerin (Entwurf für eine Plastik)]
(1921)
Pencil and pen and ink on brownish paper
23¼ × 12⅝ in. (59.2 × 31.9 cm.)
Grohmann-Schlemmer ZT162
Staatsgalerie Stuttgart: Collection Karin and U. Jaïna
Schlemmer Deposit
Ill. p. 228

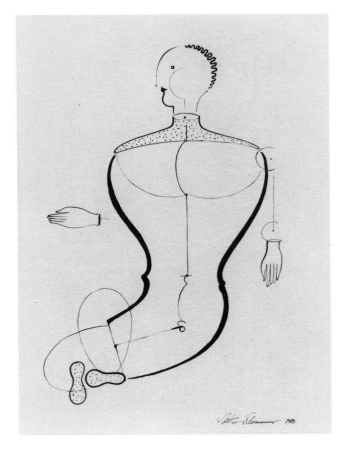

Cat. no. 103.

Cat. no. 104.

105. STAGE DESIGNS FOR "MURDERER, HOPE OF WOMEN"
(a one-act play by Oskar Kokoschka, 1907; opera by Paul Hindemith; for performance in Stuttgart, 4 June 1921)
(1921)
Oskar Schlemmer Theater Estate, Collection UJS

105-a. SCENE WITH CONVERTIBLE ARCHITECTURE, TOWER
[Szene mit verwandelbarer Architektur, Turm]
Watercolor on thin paper, mounted on white board
8½ × 11½ in (21.5 × 29.3 cm.)
Maur A75
Ill. p. 29

105-b. STAGE DESIGN WITH CONVERTIBLE ARCHITECTURE
[Bühnenbild mit wandelbarer Architektur]
Pen and black ink on whitish paper
11⅝ × 16⅞ in. (29.6 × 42.8 cm.)
S618
Ill. p. 29

105-c. SET DESIGN FOR FINALE
[Schlussbild]
Pen and black ink on thin paper, mounted on board
12⅜ × 17¹⁵⁄₁₆ in. (31.4 × 45.5 cm.)
S619
Ill. p. 29

106. ABSTRACT FIGURE: WORKING DRAWING 3
[Abstrakte Figur, Werkzeichnung 3]
(1921–1922)
Pencil and pen and ink on brown parchment paper
14¼ × 10⅝ in. (36.2 × 27 cm.)
Grohmann-Schlemmer ZT174
Staatsgalerie Stuttgart: Schlemmer Family Estate Deposit
Ill. p. 228

Cat. no. 106.

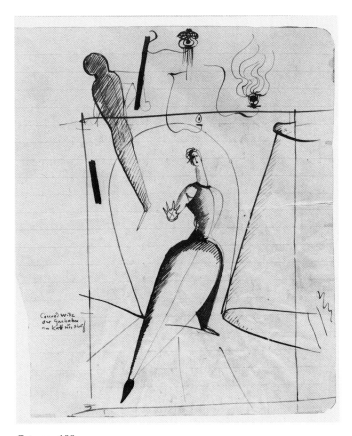

Cat. no. 109.

107. TWO CONSTRUCTIONAL HEADS: DESIGN FOR A METAL SCULPTURE
[Zwei konstruktive Köpfe, Entwurf für eine Metallplastik]
(1921–1922)
Pencil, pen and black ink, touched with black watercolor, on thin whitish paper
12 × 9⅜ in. (30.4 × 23.7 cm.)
Grohmann-Schlemmer ZT178
Staatsgalerie Stuttgart (C51/363)
Ill. p. 112

108. WIRE FIGURE
[Drahtfigur]
(1921–1922)
Pencil and colored pencil on thin whitish paper
12 × 9⅜ in. (30.4 × 23.7 cm.)
S262
Staatsgalerie Stuttgart (C51/390)
Ill. p. 112

109. DANCER AND OTHER MOTIFS
[Tänzerin und andere Motive]
(1922)
Pen and blue-black ink on yellowish lined notepaper
8¼ × 6⅞ in. (21 × 17.5 cm.)
Grohmann-Schlemmer ZT188
Staatsgalerie Stuttgart (C51/421)
Ill. p. 229

110. DANCER (THE GESTURE)
[Tänzerin (Die Geste)]
(ca. 1922)
Pen and black India ink, over pencil and watercolor on yellowish paper, mounted on white board
5⅞ × 4⅜ in. (15 × 11 cm.)
Maur A113
Staatsgalerie Stuttgart: Schlemmer Family Estate Deposit
Ill. p. 12

111. FAMILY
[Familie]
1922
Pen and ink on light brown paper
19¼ × 12½ in. (48.7 × 31.6 cm.)
Grohmann-Schlemmer ZT190
Staatsgalerie Stuttgart: Collection Karin and U. Jaïna Schlemmer Deposit
Ill. p. 232

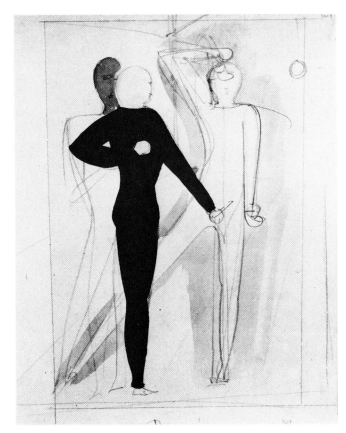

Cat. no. 148.

229

Studies for the Figural Cabinet.
(Cat. nos. 112–114).

112. FIGURAL CABINET
[Das figurale Kabinett]
(1922)
Pen and ink on transparent paper
11¼ × 16⅞ in. (28.7 × 43 cm.)
S537
Oskar Schlemmer Theater Estate, Collection UJS
Ill. p. 136

113. FIGURAL CABINET
[Das figurale Kabinett]
(1922)
Watercolor, pencil, pen and ink on paper
12¼ × 17¾ in. (30.9 × 45.1 cm.)
Maur A97
The Museum of Modern Art, New York: The Joan and
Lester Avnet Collection (162.78)
Ill. p. 135

114. FIGURAL CABINET, VERSION II
[Das figurale Kabinett, II. Fassung]
(1922)
Gouache, collage, and photo-montage on black glossy
paper, mounted on gray board
14¼ × 21 in. (36.2 × 53.2 cm.)
Maur A98
Oskar Schlemmer Theater Estate, Collection UJS
Ill. p. 135

115. FIGURE WITH ATTRIBUTES
[Figur mit Attributen]
(ca. 1922)
Pencil, pen and tinted ink, and watercolor on tissue paper,
mounted on white board
11⅞ × 9⅛ in. (30.3 × 23.1 cm.)
Maur A111
Staatsgalerie Stuttgart: Schlemmer Family Estate Deposit
Ill. p. 230

116. FIGURINE
[Figurine]
(ca. 1922)
Pen and tinted ink over pencil, watercolor, silver and gold-
bronze on tissue paper, serrated at left, mounted on white
board
11³⁄₁₆ × 8¾ in. (28.4 × 22.2 cm.)
Maur A112
Oskar Schlemmer Theater Estate, Collection UJS
Ill. p. 230

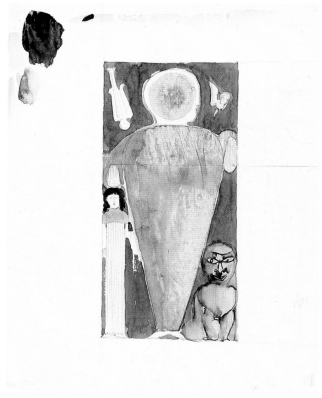

Cat. no. 115.

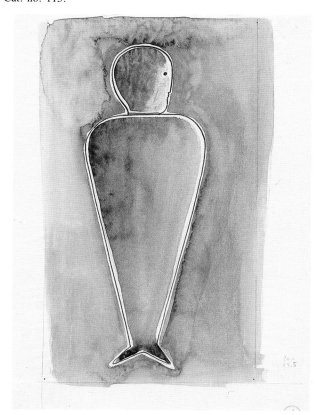

Cat. no. 116.

117. FEMALE BUST, DESIGN FOR A WOOD
SCULPTURE
[Weibliche Büste, Entwurf für eine Holzplastik]
(1922–1923)
Pencil and brown watercolor on thin whitish paper,
serrated at left
11⅛ × 8¼ in. (28.2 × 21.1 cm.)
Maur A116
Family Estate of Oskar Schlemmer
Ill. p. 231

118. IVO, DESIGN FOR A SCULPTURE
[Ivo, Entwurf für eine Plastik]
(ca. 1922–1923)
Pencil, pen and violet ink, and watercolor on white tissue
paper, serrated at left
11⅛ × 8¾ in. (28.4 × 22.2 cm.)
Maur A115
Private Collection, Stuttgart
Ill. p. 108

Cat. no. 158.

119. ABSTRACT HEAD: WORKING DRAWING FOR A
WIRE SCULPTURE
[Abstrakter Kopf, Werkzeichnung für eine Drahtplastik]
(1923)
Pencil, and red, blue, and black ink on white paper
22⅜ × 16⅝ in. (56.9 × 42.2 cm.)
Grohmann-Schlemmer ZT210
Staatsgalerie Stuttgart (DKM, Gr.443)
Ill. p. 113

120. ABSTRACT TORSO
[Abstrakte Halbfigur]
1923
Pen and brush in red, blue, and black ink on whitish
transparent paper
20¼ × 12⅝ in. (51.5 × 32 cm.)
Grohmann-Schlemmer ZT207
Staatsgalerie Stuttgart: Collection Karin and U. Jaïna
Schlemmer Deposit
Ill. p. 110

121. COMPANY AT TABLE II
[Tischgesellschaft II]
(1923)
Watercolor over pencil on gray-white paper
16¾ × 18⅜ in. (42.7 × 46.8 cm.)
Maur A133
Staatsgalerie Stuttgart (C24/9)
Ill. p. 214

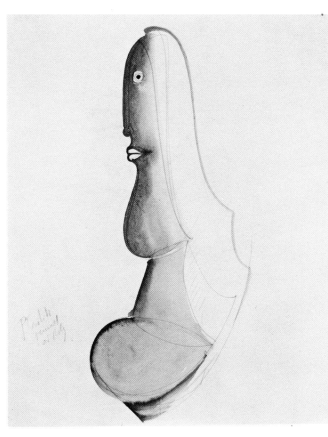

Cat. no. 117.

Cat. no. 111.

124. FIGURINE FACING RIGHT WITH GEOMETRIC
FORMS
[Figurine nach rechts mit geometrischen Formen]
1923
Gouache on handmade paper, mounted on Japan paper
22⅛ × 16⅛ in. (56.2 × 42.1 cm.)
Maur A129
Private Collection, Frankfurt
Ill. p. 28

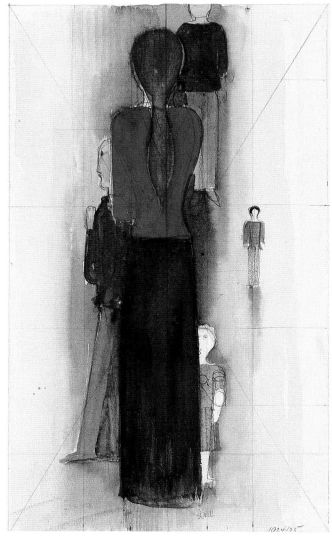

Cat. no. 123.

122. DIVIDED FIGURE FACING LEFT AND PROFILE
HEAD
[Geteilte Figur nach links und Kopfprofil]
1923
Gouache over pencil on handmade paper, mounted on
board
23⅛ × 12⅝ in. (58.7 × 32 cm.)
Maur A127
Staatsgalerie Stuttgart: Schlemmer Family Estate Deposit
Ill. p. 28

123. FAMILY
[Familie]
(ca. 1923)
Watercolor over pencil on heavy watercolor paper
12 × 7 in. (30.4 × 17.9 cm.)
Maur A134
Staatsgalerie Stuttgart (C46/54)
Ill. p. 232

Cat. no. 127.

125. FRIEZE OF HEADS, MURAL STUDY
[Köpfe-Fries, Wandbildstudie]
(1923)
Pencil, watercolor, and pen and tinted ink on white transparent paper
12 × 9⁷⁄₁₆ in. (30.5 × 24 cm.)
Maur A119
Bauhaus-Archiv, Berlin
Ill. p. 240

126. HEAD IN BRONZE WITH FIGURAL MOTIFS
[Kopf in Bronze mit Figuralmotiven]
1923
Pencil, pen and blue and red ink, watercolor, and silver and gold-bronze on whitish Japan paper, mounted on white paper and board
16¼ × 11½ in. (41.3 × 29.2 cm.)
Maur A125
Family Estate of Oskar Schlemmer
Ill. p. 233

127. HOUSE WITH SEVEN FIGURES
[Haus mit sieben Figuren]
(1923)
Pencil and watercolor on whitish paper
16¾ × 22 in. (42.5 × 56 cm.)
Maur A135
Family Estate of Oskar Schlemmer
Ill. p. 233

128. MASTER PLAN OF MURAL PAINTING INSIDE THE WORKSHOP BUILDING OF THE WEIMAR BAUHAUS, GROUND PLAN AND PERSPECTIVE
[Gesamtplan der Wandgestaltung im Werkstattgebäude des Staatlichen Bauhauses Weimar, Grundriss und Perspektive]
(1923)
Pencil and watercolor on paper, mounted on board
16⅞ × 21⅝ in. (42.9 × 55 cm.)
Maur A123
Staatsgalerie Stuttgart: Schlemmer Family Estate Deposit
Ill. p. 102

129. THREE MURAL STUDIES FOR THE WORKSHOP BUILDING OF THE WEIMAR BAUHAUS
[Drei Wandbildstudien]
(1923–1928)
Three collage studies, in pencil, ink, watercolor, poster paint, gold- and silver-bronze on brownish paper, mounted on whitish board
15⅞ × 21⅝ in. (40.3 × 55 cm.)
Maur A124
Family Estate of Oskar Schlemmer
Ill. p. 102

130. PARACELSUS
[Paracelsus]
(1923)
Pencil on brownish transparent paper
13⅛ × 9¾ in. (33.4 × 24.7 cm.)
S298
Staatsgalerie Stuttgart (C64/1369)
Ill. p. 234

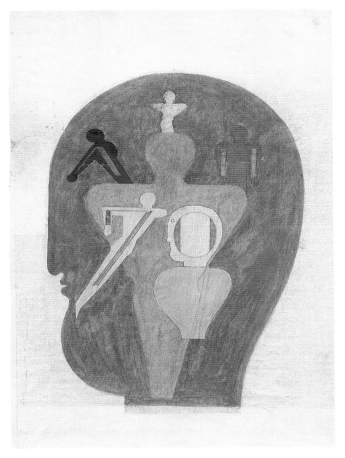

Cat. no. 126.

233

Cat. no. 130.

Cat. no. 131.

131. PIERROT AND TWO FIGURES
[Pierrot und zwei Figuren]
(ca. 1923)
Watercolor and ink over pencil on Japan paper
9¹/₁₆ × 11¹³/₁₆ in. (23 × 30 cm.)
Maur A144
Bauhaus-Archiv, Berlin (24)
Ill. p. 234

132. TORSO WITH ACCENTUATED BLACK LINES
[Halbfigur mit schwarz betonten Linien]
(1923)
Pencil and pen and brush and ink on brownish parchment
paper
21¾ × 15⅞ in. (55.4 × 40.2 cm.)
Grohmann-Schlemmer ZT182
Staatsgalerie Stuttgart: Collection Karin and U. Jaïna
Schlemmer Deposit
Ill. p. 109

133. EGOCENTRIC SPACE-DELINEATION
[Egozentrische Raumlineatur]
(1924)
Pen and ink on whitish paper
8⅛ × 10⅝ in. (20.8 × 27 cm.)
Grohmann-Schlemmer ZT231
Staatsgalerie Stuttgart: Schlemmer Family Estate Deposit
Ill. p. 137

134. MAN THE DANCER (HUMAN EMOTIONS) I
[Tänzermensch (Menschliche Empfindungen) I]
(1924)
Pen and ink on light parchment paper
9⅜ × 6⅞ in. (23.8 × 17.4 cm.)
Grohmann-Schlemmer ZT237
Staatsgalerie Stuttgart: Schlemmer Family Estate Deposit
Ill. p. 235

**135. MAN THE DANCER (HUMAN EMOTIONS) I:
PERFORMER AND SPECTATOR II**
[Tänzermensch (Menschliche Empfindungen) I:
Schauspieler und Zuschauer II]
(ca. 1924)
Pen and ink, with collage elements, on paper
8⅝ × 11⅜ in. (22 × 29 cm.)
Grohmann-Schlemmer ZT232
Bauhaus-Archiv, Berlin: Schlemmer Family Estate Deposit
Ill. p. 14

136. MAN THE DANCER (HUMAN EMOTIONS) II
[Tänzermensch (Menschliche Empfindungen) II]
(1924)
Pen and ink on gray-white paper, corrected in places with
poster paint, mounted on board
8⅞ × 6⅝ in. (22.4 × 16.7 cm.)
Grohmann-Schlemmer ZT235
Staatsgalerie Stuttgart: Schlemmer Family Estate Deposit
Ill. p. 235

Cat. no. 134.

Cat. no. 136.

137. PROFILE WITH DOTTED LINES
[Profil mit pointillierten Linien]
1924
Pen and ink on gray-brown parchment paper
21¾ × 15 in. (55.4 × 38.1 cm.)
Grohmann-Schlemmer ZT228
Staatsgalerie Stuttgart: Schlemmer Family Estate Deposit
Ill. p. 110

138. STANDING FIGURE AND TWO PROFILE HEADS
IN RECTANGULAR FIELDS
[Stehende und zwei Profilköpfe in Rechteckfeldern]
(ca. 1924)
Watercolor over pencil on white tissue paper, mounted on
heavy paper
10½ × 8⅝ in. (27.3 × 21.9 cm.)
Maur A160
Staatsgalerie Stuttgart (C51/352)
Ill. p. 243

139. FOUR FIGURES IN STEREO-PERSPECTIVE
[Vier Figuren in Raumperspektive]
(ca. 1924–1925)
Watercolor, highlighted with chalk, over pencil on white
tissue paper, mounted on paper
10½ × 8⅝ in. (27.3 × 21.9 cm.)
Maur A199
Staatsgalerie Stuttgart (C51/354)
Ill. p. 84

140. THE PASSERBY
[Vorübergehender]
(ca. 1924–1925)
Pencil and watercolor on transparent paper, mounted on
white board
9⅜ × 8½ in. (23.9 × 21.7 cm.)
Maur A166
Staatsgalerie Stuttgart: Collection Karin and U. Jaïna
Schlemmer Deposit
Ill. p. 55

235

Cat. no. 145.

141. TWO STANDING FIGURES AND A FIGURE ON A NARROW STAIRCASE
[Zwei Stehende und Figur auf schmaler Treppe]
(ca. 1924–1925)
Watercolor over pencil on white tissue paper, mounted on heavy paper
10¾ × 8⅝ in. (27.2 × 21.9 cm.)
Maur A198
Staatsgalerie Stuttgart (C46/51)
Ill. p. 84

142. COMPANY AT TABLE WITH CONTEMPLATIVE FIGURE
[Tischgesellschaft mit Sinnendem]
(1925)
Watercolor and pen and black ink on white transparent paper, mounted on paper
8⅝ × 10¾ in. (21.9 × 27.4 cm.)
Maur A212
Staatsgalerie Stuttgart (C51/356)
Ill. p. 236

Cat. no. 142.

Cat. no. 144.

143. CONTEMPLATIVE FIGURE I
[Sinnender I]
(1925)
Watercolor over pencil on tissue paper, mounted on
yellowish paper
10¾ × 8⅝ in. (27.4 × 21.9 cm.)
Maur A213
Staatsgalerie Stuttgart: Schlemmer Family Estate Deposit
Ill. p. 59

144. FIGURE BOTH IN FRONT OF AND BEHIND THE
WINDOW
[Figur vor und hinter dem Fenster]
(1925)
Pencil and watercolor on white tissue paper, mounted on
paper
10¾ × 8¹¹⁄₁₆ in. (27.4 × 22 cm.)
Maur A215
Family Estate of Oskar Schlemmer
Ill. p. 236

145. LARGE HEAD WITH FIVE FIGURES
[Grosser Kopf mit fünf Figuren]
(1925)

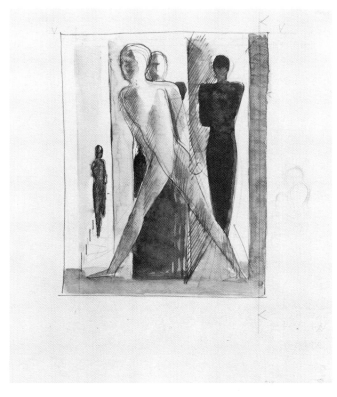

Cat. no. 147.

Watercolor over pencil on white tissue paper, mounted on
heavy white paper
8⅝ × 10¾ in. (21.9 × 27.2 cm.)
Maur A220
Staatsgalerie Stuttgart: Collection Karin and U. Jaïna
Schlemmer Deposit
Ill. p. 236

146. STANDING FIGURES AND FIGURE STRIDING
PAST IN INTERIOR
[Stehende und Voruberschreitender in Interieur]
(ca. 1925)
Pencil and watercolor on white tissue paper, mounted on
white board
10¾ × 8⅝ in. (27.3 × 21.9 cm.)
Maur A227
Staatsgalerie Stuttgart: Schlemmer Family Estate Deposit
Ill. p. 237

147. STRIDING FIGURE AND THREE FIGURES IN
ARCHITECTURE
[Schreitender und drei Figuren in Architektur]
(ca. 1925)
Pencil, pen and black ink, and watercolor on white trans-
parent paper, mounted on white board
10⅞ × 8⅝ in. (27.5 × 21.9 cm.)
Maur A228
Staatsgalerie Stuttgart: Schlemmer Family Estate Deposit
Ill. p. 237

Cat. no. 146.

237

Cat. no. 152.

148. THREE DANCERS
[Drei Tänzer]
(ca. 1925)
Pencil and watercolor on yellowish transparent paper,
mounted on white board
9⅜ × 7 in. (23.8 × 17.8 cm.)
Maur A224
Staatsgalerie Stuttgart: Schlemmer Family Estate Deposit
Ill. p. 229

149. THREE HEADS
[Drei Köpfe]
(1925)
Watercolor over pencil on white tissue paper, mounted on
heavy paper
10¾ × 8⅝ in. (27.4 × 21.9 cm.)
Maur A187
Staatsgalerie Stuttgart (C51/357)
Ill. p. 238

150. TRIPTYCH III
[Dreiteilung III]
(1925)
Pencil and watercolor on white tissue paper, mounted on
board
10½ × 8⅞ in. (27.4 × 22.5 cm.)
Maur A195
Staatsgalerie Stuttgart: Schlemmer Family Estate Deposit
Ill. p. 60

151. TRIPTYCH V
[Dreiteilung V]
1925
Pencil and watercolor on white tissue paper, mounted on
brown board
9¼ × 5½ in. (23.4 × 14 cm.)
Maur A197
Staatsgalerie Stuttgart: Schlemmer Family Estate Deposit
Ill. p. 60

**152. WOMAN'S HEAD AND MALE NUDE IN
VERTICAL STRIPES**
[Frauenkopf und männlicher Akt in Vertikalstreifen]
(1925)
Pencil, pen and black ink, and watercolor on thin white
paper, mounted on heavy white paper
6½ × 5½ in. (16.5 × 14 cm.)
Maur A190
Staatsgalerie Stuttgart: Schlemmer Family Estate Deposit
Ill. p. 238

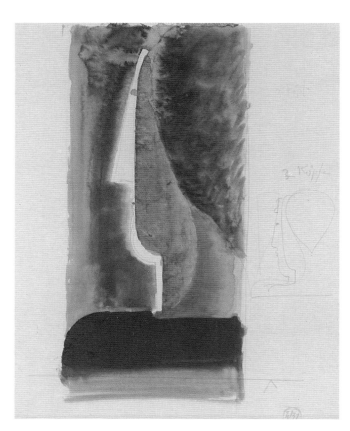

Cat. no. 149.

153. WOMEN AT TABLE III
[Frauen am Tisch III]
(1925)
Pencil, watercolor, and pen and black ink on brownish
graph paper, mounted on board
8⅛ × 10⅝ in. (20.5 × 27 cm.)
Maur A203
Staatsgalerie Stuttgart: Schlemmer Family Estate Deposit
Ill. p. 239

154. EXAMPLES OF COSTUME FORMS
[Darstellung von Kostümbildungen]
(ca. 1926)
Watercolor over pencil on chamois-colored paper, mounted
on board
17¼ × 22⅞ in. (43.7 × 58.1 cm.)
Maur A249
Oskar Schlemmer Theater Estate, Collection UJS
Ill. p. 178

155. FIGURE TYPES AND COAT COSTUME TYPES
[Typenfiguren und Mantelkostümtypen]
(ca. 1926)
Pen and watercolor over pencil on chamois-colored
watercolor paper, mounted on board
18¼ × 24⅛ in. (46.3 × 61.2 cm.)
Maur A248
Oskar Schlemmer Theater Estate, Collection UJS
Ill. p. 178

Cat. no. 153.

156. MASK VARIATIONS
[Masken-Variationen]
(ca. 1926)
Watercolor over pencil on chamois-colored watercolor
paper, mounted on paper
18¹⁄₁₆ × 24⅛ in. (45.9 × 61.3 cm.)
Maur A250
Oskar Schlemmer Theater Estate, Collection UJS
Ill. p. 178

157. DESIGN FOR A PANTOMIME AT THE STAGE OF
THE BAUHAUS
[Entwurf für eine Pantomine der Bauhausbühne]
(1927)
Pencil, watercolor, gouache, and ink on white paper,
mounted on black paper
14³⁄₁₆ × 21⁵⁄₁₆ in. (36 × 54.1 cm.)
Maur A256
Oskar Schlemmer Theater Estate, Collection UJS
Ill. p. 200

158. HEAD FACING LEFT
[Kopf nach links]
(1927)
Pencil on paper
14⅜ × 10¾ in. (36.4 × 27.3 cm.)
Grohmann-Schlemmer ZB147
Staatsgalerie Stuttgart (C1951/385)
Ill. p. 231

Cat. no. 78.

159. STILT-RUNNER
[Stelzenläufer]
(1927)
Watercolor over pencil on chamois-colored watercolor
paper
17⅞ × 23⅞ in. (45.3 × 60.7 cm.)
Maur A255
Oskar Schlemmer Theater Estate, Collection UJS
Ill. p. 126

160. LOUNGE WITH SEVEN FIGURES
[Ruheraum mit sieben Figuren]
(ca. 1927–1928)
Pencil and watercolor on white linen-textured notepaper,
mounted on heavy paper
8⅝ × 11 in. (22 × 27.8 cm.)
Maur A297
Staatsgalerie Stuttgart: Schlemmer Family Estate Deposit
Ill. p. 240

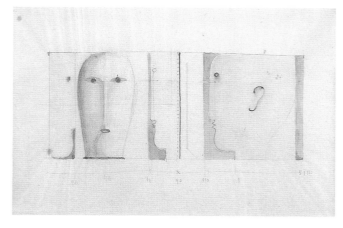

Cat. no. 125.

161. LOUNGE WITH SIX FIGURES
[Ruheraum mit sechs Figuren]
(ca. 1927–1928)
Pencil and watercolor on thin white linen-textured
notepaper, mounted on white board
8⅝ × 11 in. (22 × 27.8 cm.)
Maur A296
Staatsgalerie Stuttgart: Collection Karin and U. Jaïna
Schlemmer Deposit
Ill. p. 240

Cat. no. 160.

Drawings from the Dessau Bauhaus
Instructional Series, Man. [Der Mensch]. (ca. 1928).
(Cat. nos. 162–167).

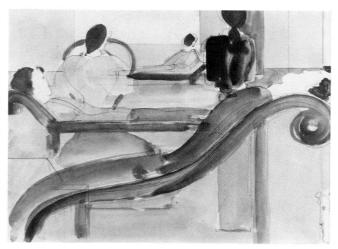

Cat. no. 161.

162. SIMPLE HEAD CONSTRUCTION (FACING LEFT)
[Einfachste Kopfkonstruktion]
Pencil on paper
11¹³⁄₁₆ × 8¼ in. (30 × 21 cm.)
Bauhaus-Archiv, Berlin: Schlemmer Family Estate Deposit
Ill. p. 241

163. SIMPLE HEAD CONSTRUCTION (FRONTAL
VIEW)
[Einfachste Kopfkonstruktion]
Pencil, colored pencil, and ink on paper
11¹³⁄₁₆ × 8¼ in. (30 × 21 cm.)
Bauhaus-Archiv, Berlin: Schlemmer Family Estate Deposit
Ill. p. 241

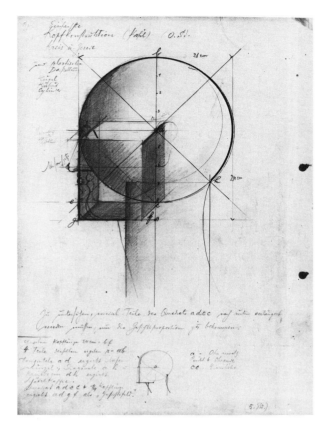

Cat. no. 162.

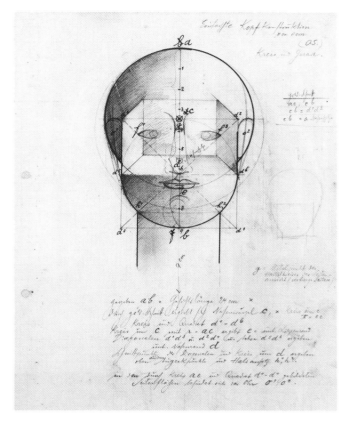

Cat. no. 163.

**164. DANCE TRANSCRIPTION STUDIES: VIABILITY
AND RADIUS OF ACTION OF RECTILINEAR AND
CURVILINEAR FIGURES**
[Tanzschrift-Studien: Lebens- und Aktionsfähigkeit
geradliniger und gebogener Figuren]
Pencil on paper
Double page, $11^{13}/_{16} \times 16^{1}/_{2}$ in. (30 × 42 cm.)
S684/1–2
Bauhaus-Archiv, Berlin: Schlemmer Family Estate Deposit
Ill. p. 242

165. HEAD TYPE
[Kopf-Typus]
Ink and pencil on paper
$11^{13}/_{16} \times 8^{1}/_{4}$ in. (30 × 21 cm.)
Bauhaus-Archiv, Berlin: Schlemmer Family Estate Deposit
Ill. p. 242

166. MAN IN THE SPHERE OF IDEAS
[Der Mensch im Ideenkreis]
Pen and ink, pencil, and colored pencil on paper, mounted
on board
$20^{7}/_{8} \times 16^{1}/_{8}$ in. (53 × 41 cm.)
Maur K2
Bauhaus-Archiv, Berlin: Schlemmer Family Estate Deposit
Ill. p. 15

167. MAN IN THE SPHERE OF IDEAS
[Der Mensch im Ideenkreis]
Pen and sprayed black ink, opaque white paint, and red
pencil on heavy gray-white paper, mounted on board
$29^{3}/_{8} \times 19^{1}/_{4}$ in. (74.5 × 48.9 cm.)
S676
Family Estate of Oskar Schlemmer
Ill. p. 15

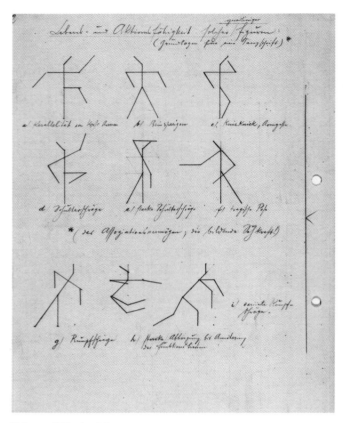

Cat. no. 164, sheet 1.

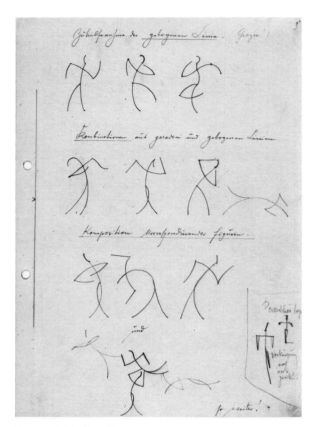

Cat. no. 164, sheet 2.

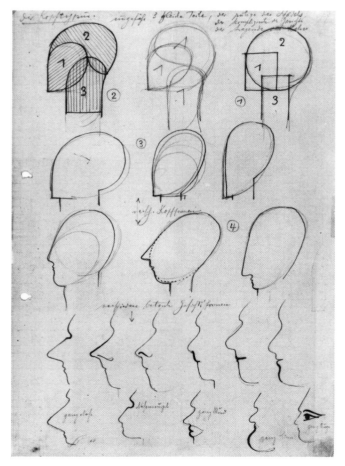

Cat. no. 165.

168. CONCENTRIC GROUP OF YOUTHS
[Konzentrische Jünglingsgruppe]
(1928)
Watercolor, gouache, and ink over pencil on whitish paper
21⅛ × 14⅝ in. (53.5 × 37.3 cm.)
Maur A375
Ulmer Museum (1968/2516)
Ill. p. 243

**169. DESIGN FOR "THE NUTCRACKER," PER-
FORMED 7 NOVEMBER 1928, DRESDEN:
STAGE SET FOR THE ANNUAL FAIR**
[Bühnenbild zum Jahrmarkt]
(1928)
Watercolor over pencil on paper
10¼ × 7¾ in. (26 × 19.7 cm.)
Maur A327
Private Collection, Karin Schlemmer
Ill. p. 254

Cat. no. 138.

170. DESIGNS FOR "SCARECROWS" [Vogelscheuchen],
a pantomime with words, premiered 14 November 1928,
Hagen, with sets and costumes by Oskar Schlemmer
Oskar Schlemmer Theater Estate, Collection UJS

170-a. STAGE SET WITH THE SIX SCARECROWS
[Bühnenbild mit den sechs Vogelscheuchen]
1928
Pen and ink on whitish paper, touched with poster paint,
on white board
12⅞ × 19⅝ in. (32.6 × 49.8 cm.)
S655
Ill. p. 244

**170-b. THE MADMAN, A FIGURINE FROM
"SCARECROWS"**
[Der Irre, Figurine zu "Vogelscheuchen"]
(1928)
Pencil and pen and ink on whitish paper, mounted on
board
18½ × 12¼ in. (47 × 31 cm.)
S656
Ill. p. 244

Cat. no. 168.

Cat. no. 170-a.

Cat. no. 170-b.

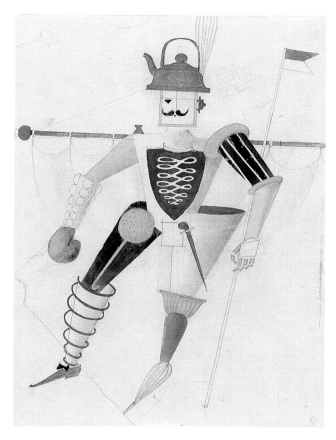

Cat. no. 170-c.

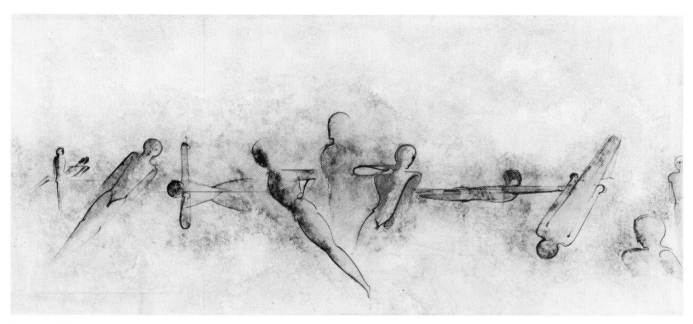

Cat. no. 171.

170-c. THE KNIGHT, A FIGURINE FROM
"SCARECROWS"
[Der Ritter, Figurine zu "Vogelscheuchen"]
(1928)
Pencil, watercolor, gold- and silver-bronze on whitish
paper, mounted on board
20 × 15⅛ in. (50.9 × 38.3 cm.)
Maur A331
Ill. p. 244

171. DESIGN FOR A FRIEZE
[Entwurf zu einem Wandfries]
(1928)
Pencil, bronze chalk, and silver-bronze on yellowish paper,
mounted on board
9⁷⁄₁₆ × 21¼ in. (24 × 54 cm.)
Maur A332
Bauhaus-Archiv, Berlin (1523)
Ill. p. 245

172. FIGURES IN STAR FORM
[Figuren in Sternform]
(1928)
Pencil on glossy white notepaper
8⅞ × 5¾ in. (22.5 × 14.5 cm.)
Grohmann-Schlemmer ZB244
Staatsgalerie Stuttgart: Schlemmer Family Estate Deposit
Ill. p. 245

Cat. no. 172.

Cat. no. 175.

175. HEAD IN RHYTHMIC CURVES
[Kopf in rhythmischen Kurven]
1928
Blue and black ink and watercolor, head squared with
pencil, on whitish paper
9¹/₁₆ × 7½ in. (23 × 19 cm.)
Maur A307
Collection of Leonard and Evelyn Lauder, New York
Ill. p. 246

176. TORSO FROM THE SIDE, BROWN HEAD
[Halbfigur von der Seite, Brauner Kopf]
(1928)
Pen and sprayed black and brown ink over pencil on white
paper
22⅛ × 16¾ in. (56.2 × 42.5 cm.)
Maur A315
Family Estate of Oskar Schlemmer
Ill. p. 246

173. FOLKWANG GROUP I: INSTRUCTION
[Unterricht, Folkwang-Gruppe I]
(1928)
Watercolor and tempera on whitish paper
18⅝ × 12⅝ in. (47.4 × 32.1 cm.)
Maur A335
Staatsgalerie Stuttgart (C53/506)
Ill. p. 63

**174. FOLKWANG GROUP IV: GROUP WITH FIGURES
ASCENDING STAIRCASE**
[Gruppe mit Treppensteigenden, Folkwang-Gruppe IV]
(1928)
Tempera on watercolor paper, mounted on board
20¹⁵/₁₆ × 13⅜ in. (53.2 × 34 cm.)
Maur A338
Staatsgalerie Stuttgart (C53/508)
Ill. p. 63

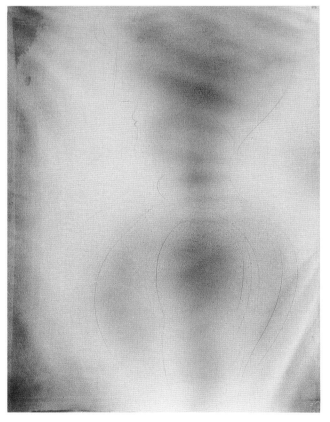

Cat. no. 176.

177. COSTUME DESIGNS FOR "THE FOX" ("LE RENARD") [Reinecke Fuchs] (a burlesque story after a Russian folk march, with music and libretto by Igor Stravinsky; premiered in Breslau, 11 December 1929, with choreography by Valerie Godard and Oskar Schlemmer) Oskar Schlemmer Theater Estate, Collection UJS

177-a. STUDY FOR THE ROOSTER
[Entwurf zum Hahn]
(1929)
Pencil and watercolor on the printed instruction form, "Der Mensch"
19⅝ × 25⅝ in. (50 × 65.1 cm.)
Maur A394a
Ill. p. 30

177-b. STUDY FOR THE TOMCAT AND THE FOX
[Entwurf zum Kater und Fuchs]
(1929)
Pencil and watercolor on the printed instruction form, "Der Mensch"
19⅝ × 17⅝ in. (50 × 44.8 cm.)
Maur A394b
Ill. p. 30

178. STAGE DESIGNS FOR "THE NIGHTINGALE" ("LE CHANT DE ROSSIGNOL") [Die Nachtigall] (a fairy tale in three acts by Hans Christian Andersen, set to music by Igor Stravinsky, premiered in Paris, 1914; second staging, Mannheim, 5 May 1923; Breslau, 11 December 1929) Oskar Schlemmer Theater Estate, Collection UJS

178-a. SCENERY WITH MOON
[Bühnenbild mit Mond]
(1929)
Gouache and collage on colored, treated paper, on heavy black paper
18⅛ × 24⅝ in. (46.1 × 62.5 cm.)
Maur A384
Ill. p. 247

178-b. THE EMPEROR OF CHINA'S THRONE ROOM
[Thronsaal des Kaisers von China]
(1929)
Collage of various colored papers and white colored pencil on black paper
17⅜ × 23¾ in. (44.2 × 60.5 cm.)
Maur A385
Ill. p. 247

178-c. THE EMPEROR OF CHINA'S BEDROOM WITH GHOSTS
[Schlafzimmer des Kaisers mit Geistern]
(1929)
Gouache, white crayon, and collaged silver paper on heavy black paper
10⅞ × 18⅝ in. (27.6 × 47.3 cm.)
Maur A386
Ill. p. 247

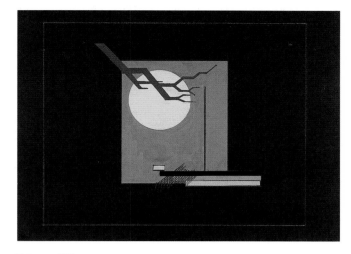

Cat. no. 178-a.

Cat. no. 178-b.

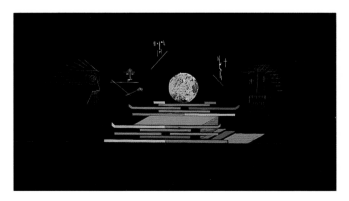

Cat. no. 178-c.

179. FOLKWANG CYCLE II: ECHELON OF THREE
YOUTHS WITH OUTSTRETCHED ARMS
[II Folkwang-Zyklus: Drei gestaffelte Jünglingsfiguren mit
ausgestreckten Armen]
(1929–1930)
Pastel over charcoal on yellowish transparent paper
Approx. 88⅝ × 59 in. (225 × 150 cm.)
Maur K16
Staatsgalerie Stuttgart (C53/510g)
Ill. p. 66

180. FOLKWANG CYCLE II: FLOATING AND
STRETCHING YOUTH IN A CIRCULAR FORM
[II Folkwang-Zyklus: Schwebende und gestreckte
Jünglingsfigur in Kreisform]
(1929–1930)
Pastel over charcoal on yellowish transparent paper
91⅛ × 60⅞ in. (231.5 × 154.5 cm.)
Maur K18
Staatsgalerie Stuttgart (C53/510c)
Ill. p. 66

181. FOLKWANG CYCLE II: STEPPED GROUP OF
FOUR WITH ANGULAR ARM GESTURES
[II Folkwang-Zyklus: Getreppte Vierergruppe mit
rechtwinkligen Armgesten]
(1929–1930)
Pastel over charcoal on yellowish transparent paper.
90 × 60⅝ in. (228.5 × 154 cm.)
Maur K11
Staatsgalerie Stuttgart (C53/510d)
Ill. p. 66

182. MASTER PLAN FOR THE HOUSE OF DR. RABE
[Gesamtplan für Haus Dr. Rabe]
(1930)
Pencil and colored pencil on heavy, gray-white paper
22¼ × 26¼ in. (56.4 × 66.5 cm.)
Maur K36
Family Estate of Oskar Schlemmer
Ill. p. 116

183. SEATED ''HOMO'' WITH BACK-VIEW FIGURE
ON ITS HAND
[Sitzender ''Homo'' mit Rückenfigur auf der Hand]
(1930)
Charcoal and colored chalk on light brown board, in two
adjoined parts; squared with pencil; contours outlined with
a perforating wheel
121⅝ × 89⅜ in. (309 × 227 cm.)
Maur K37
Staatsgalerie Stuttgart (C67/1521)
Ill. p. 115

184. DARK FIGURE WITH WHITE SHEET OF PAPER
[Dunkle Figur mit weissem Blatt]
(1931)
Watercolor and poster paint over pencil sketch, features
shaded in pencil, on thin white paper mounted on paper
10⅞ × 8⅝ in. (27.5 × 22 cm.)
Maur A406
Staatsgalerie Stuttgart (C51/361)
Ill. p. 17

185. DESIGNS FOR THE MURAL PAINTINGS OF THE
MUSEUM FOLKWANG ESSEN
[Entwürfe zu den Wandbildern im Museum Folkwang in
Essen]
(1931)
Staatsgalerie Stuttgart (C53/512a-b-c)

185-a. Pen and ink and colored pencil on graph paper
9¼ × 5¾ in. (23.4 × 14.7 cm.)
Grohmann-Schlemmer ZF52(a)
Ill. p. 249

185-b. Pen and ink and colored pencil on graph paper
9⅛ × 6⅜ in. (23.3 × 16.1 cm.)
Grohmann-Schlemmer ZF52(b)
Ill. p. 249

185-c. Colored pencil and pencil on graph paper
9⅛ × 6½ in. (23.3 × 16.5 cm.)
Grohmann-Schlemmer ZF52(c)
Ill. p. 249

186. FEMALE NUDE STRETCHING UPWARD
[Emporgereckter weiblicher Akt]
(1931)
Pen and brush in blue and brown inks and wash on white
linen-textured notepaper, mounted on paper
10⅞ × 3⁷⁄₁₆ in. (27.8 × 8.7 cm.)
Maur A442
Staatsgalerie Stuttgart (C51/362)
Ill. p. 90

187. FIGURE BENDING BACKWARD IN SYSTEM OF
COORDINATES
[Sich Zurückbeugender im Achsenkreuz]
(1931)
Pen and ink on glossy white paper
11¼ × 8⅝ in. (28.5 × 22 cm.)
Grohmann-Schlemmer ZT264
Kunstmuseum Düsseldorf Graph. Sammlung: Schlemmer
Family Estate Deposit
Ill. p. 87

Cat. no. 185-a.

Cat. no. 185-b.

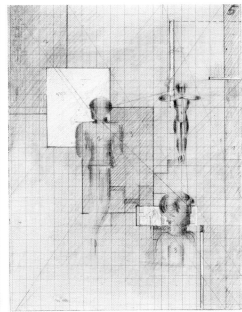

Cat. no. 185-c.

188. GROUP OF FIGURES
[Figurengruppe]
(1931)
Pen and brown ink on light, faded yellow, linen-textured
notepaper
11 × 8⅝ in. (27.8 × 22 cm.)
Grohmann-Schlemmer ZT254
Staatsgalerie Stuttgart: Schlemmer Family Estate Deposit
Ill. p. 87

189. GROUPS TOWARD EACH OTHER
[Gruppen gegeneinander]
(1931)
Pen and black-brown ink on yellowish, linen-textured
notepaper
11 × 8⅝ in. (27.8 × 22 cm.)
Grohmann-Schlemmer ZT250
Staatsgalerie Stuttgart: Collection Karin and U. Jaïna
Schlemmer Deposit
Ill. p. 249

190. SCENE WITH NUDE AT BANISTER
[Szene mit Akt am Geländer]
(1931)
Pen and brush in blue ink wash on white linen-textured
notepaper
11 × 8⅝ in. (27.9 × 21.9 cm.)
Maur A443
Staatsgalerie Stuttgart: Schlemmer Family Estate Deposit
Ill. p. 91

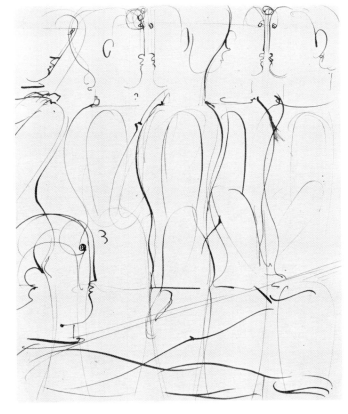

Cat. no. 189.

191. TWO FIGURES IN MOTION
[Zwei Schwingende]
(1931)
Pen and ink on glossy whitish notepaper
11¼ × 8⅝ in. (28.5 × 22 cm.)
Grohmann-Schlemmer ZT274
Staatsgalerie Stuttgart (C1948/139)
Ill. p. 87

Transfer Drawings
(Studies for Paintings, 1931–1932).
(Cat. nos. 192–198).

192. BANISTER SCENE
[Geländerszene]
(1931)
Charcoal and blue chalk on transparent paper
40¼ × 27¾ in. (102.4 × 70.5 cm.)
Maur K40
Family Estate of Oskar Schlemmer
Ill. p. 89

193. BLUE GROUP OF WOMEN
[Blaue Frauengruppe]
1931
Charcoal and red chalk on transparent paper
61¼ × 47¼ in. (155.7 × 120 cm.)
Maur K45
Family Estate of Oskar Schlemmer
Ill. p. 89

194. GROUP AT THE BANISTER
[Gruppe am Geländer]
(1931)
Charcoal and brown chalk on transparent paper
36⅜ × 24½ in. (92.5 × 62.2 cm.)
Maur K46
Family Estate of Oskar Schlemmer
Ill. p. 88

195. SCENE AT THE BANISTER
[Szene am Geländer]
(1931)
Charcoal on transparent paper
40½ × 25⅞ in. (103 × 65.7 cm.)
Maur K47
Family Estate of Oskar Schlemmer
Ill. p. 88

196. NUDE AT SPIRAL BANISTER, MEN'S STEPS
[Akte an geschwungenem Geländer, Männertreppe]
(1931)
Charcoal, red and blue chalk, and pencil on transparent paper
61¾ × 38 in. (156.7 × 96.5 cm.)
Maur K49
Family Estate of Oskar Schlemmer
Ill. p. 88

197. THREE FACING SHADOWS
[Drei vor Schatten]
1932
Charcoal and red chalk on transparent paper
31¼ × 23¾ in. (79.5 × 60.2 cm.)
Maur K51
Staatsgalerie Stuttgart: Schlemmer Family Estate Deposit
Ill. p. 89

198. BAUHAUS STAIRWAY
[Bauhaustreppe]
1932
Charcoal on transparent paper
63 × 43⁵⁄₁₆ (160 × 110 cm.)
Maur K52
Bauhaus-Archiv, Berlin
Ill. p. 88

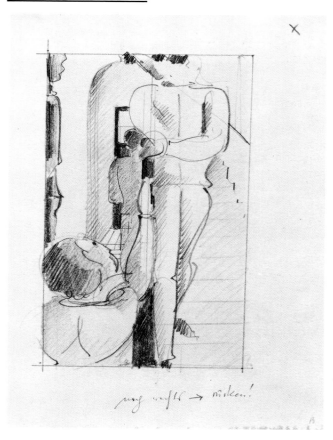

Cat. no. 199.

Cat. no. 200.

199. STAIRWAY SCENE
[Treppenszene]
(1931–1932)
Pencil on thin, slightly yellowed paper
11⅝ × 8¼ in. (29.5 × 20.9 cm.)
Grohmann-Schlemmer ZB336
Staatsgalerie Stuttgart: Schlemmer Family Estate Deposit
Ill. p. 250

200. APART
[Auseinander]
(1932)
Watercolor over pencil on light, yellowish paper, mounted on board
13⅝ × 21¼ in. (34.7 × 54 cm.)
Maur A487
Staatsgalerie Stuttgart: Schlemmer Family Estate Deposit
Ill. p. 251

201. GIRL'S HEAD IN VERTICAL STRIPES
[Mädchenkopf in Verticalstreifen]
(1932)

Watercolor over pencil on thin white paper, mounted on paper
11 × 8⅝ in. (28 × 21.9 cm.)
Maur A480
Staatsgalerie Stuttgart (C51/360)
Ill. p. 91

202. PROFILE IN DIAGONALS
[Profil in Diagonalen]
1932
Watercolor over pencil on white paper
16⅜ × 21⅛ in. (41.5 × 53.7 cm.)
Maur A488
Staatsgalerie Stuttgart: Collection Karin and U. Jaïna Schlemmer Deposit
Ill. p. 91

203. SEATED FIGURE, IN COLORED STRIPES IN FRONT OF CHECKERED BACKGROUND
[Sitzender, farbig gestreift vor kariertem Grund]
1932
Watercolor over pencil on white paper, mounted on board
22 × 16½ in. (55.8 × 42 cm.)
Maur A499
Staatsgalerie Stuttgart: Schlemmer Family Estate Deposit
Ill. p. 76

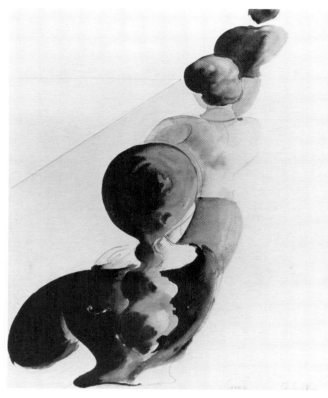

Cat. no. 205.

204. THEME: CONFRONTATION
[Thema: Gegeneinander]
(1932)
Pencil on thin whitish paper
11⅝ × 8¼ in. (29.5 × 20.9 cm.)
Grohmann-Schlemmer ZB267
Staatsgalerie Stuttgart: Schlemmer Family Estate Deposit
Ill. p. 92

205. THREE WOMEN FROM THE BACK,
DIAGONALLY ECHELONED
[Drei Frauen von rückwärts, diagonal gestaffelt]
1932
Watercolor over pencil on white linen-textured notepaper
10⅞ × 8⅝ in. (27.7 × 21.9 cm.)
Maur A475
Collection of the Heirs of Emil Frey
Ill. p. 252

206. DESIGNS SUBMITTED IN THE COMPETITION
FOR THE DECORATION OF THE CONGRESS HALL IN
THE DEUTSCHES MUSEUM, MUNICH
[für den Wettbewerb zur Ausgestaltung des Kongress-Saals
im Deutsches Museum München]
(1934).

206-a. WALL SECTION IN SCALE OF 1:5
[Wandausschnitt Massstab 1:5]
Colored pencil and chalk on beige board, in two adjoined parts
36⅛ × 71⅜ in. (91.7 × 181.3 cm.)
Maur K60
Family Estate of Oskar Schlemmer
Ill. p. 33

206-b. ENLARGED DETAIL FROM THE LENGTHWISE
WALL
[Detailvergrösserung aus der Längswand]
Pastel on beige board, squared in red pencil
50¾ × 78 in. (129 × 198.1 cm.)
Maur K61
Family Estate of Oskar Schlemmer
Ill. p. 33

206-c. GIRL'S HEAD FACING LEFT, WITH HER
HAND ON THE SHOULDER OF ANOTHER FIGURE
[Mädchenkopf nach links mit Hand auf der Schulter einer
anderen Figur]
Pastel on board
18⅞ × 10 in. (47.9 × 25.5 cm.)
Maur K63
Staatsgalerie Stuttgart (C67/1510)
Ill. p. 35

206-d. HEAD LOOKING UP
[Aufblickender Kopf]
Pastel on brownish paper
14¾ × 11⅝ in. (37.5 × 29.5 cm.)
Maur K66
Family Estate of Oskar Schlemmer
Ill. p. 36

207. CONVERSATION
[Unterhaltung]
1935
Pen and ink on paper
9⅞ × 12⅞ in. (25 × 32.7 cm.)
Grohmann-Schlemmer ZT343
Staatsgalerie Stuttgart: Collection Karin and U. Jaïna
Schlemmer Deposit
Ill. p. 253

Cat. no. 207.

208. HEADS ON TOP OF EACH OTHER
[Köpfe übereinander]
1935
Pen and colored inks and oilstick on heavy paper
25¾ × 13⅝ in. (65.3 × 34.7 cm.)
Maur K84
Staatsgalerie Stuttgart: Schlemmer Family Estate Deposit
Ill. p. 92

209. FOUR GIRLS' HEADS IN ECHELON
[Vier gestaffelte Mädchenköpfe]
(1936)
Oilstick on heavy paper
25⅝ × 19⅝ in. (65.2 × 50 cm.)
Maur K99
Staatsgalerie Stuttgart (C67/1514)
Ill. p. 93

210. FOUR IN FRONT OF SHADOW
[Vier vor Schatten]
1936
Pen and colored ink on yellowed parchment paper
8½ × 5⅛ in. (21.5 × 13 cm.)
Grohmann-Schlemmer ZT381
Staatsgalerie Stuttgart: Schlemmer Family Estate Deposit
Ill. p. 253

211. WOOL AND WEAVING: TWO GIRLS WITH RED THREAD
[Wolle und Weben, Zwei Mädchen mit rotem Faden]
(1936)
Oilstick on heavy paper
25¾ × 19¾ in. (65.3 × 50.2 cm.)
Maur K89
Staatsgalerie Stuttgart (C67/1516)
Ill. p. 93

Cat. no. 210.

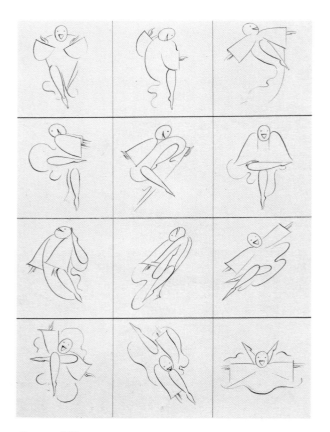

Cat. no. 212-a.

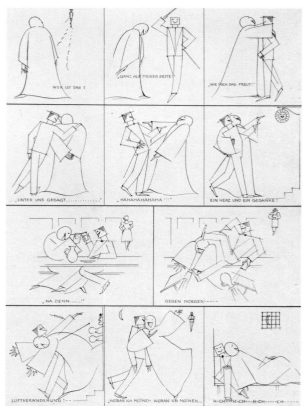

Cat. no. 212-b.

212. DRAWINGS FROM THE SERIES, MISTER EY
(cartoons featuring the one-man clown act, ''Mr. Ey,''
invented by Schlemmer)
(1937)
Family Estate of Oskar Schlemmer

212-a. MR. EY DANCES
[Mr. Ey tanzt]
Pen and brush and ink on board
26¹¹⁄₁₆ × 18⁷⁄₈ in. (67.8 × 48 cm.)
S609
Ill. p. 254

212-b. WHO IS THAT?
[Wer ist Das?]
Pen and black ink over pencil on board
26¹¹⁄₁₆ × 18⁷⁄₈ in. (67.8 × 48 cm.)
Ill. p. 254

Cat. no. 169.

Monotypes

213. TILTED HEAD I
[Schräger Kopf I]
(1941)
Monotype in oil color on printing paper
7⅛ × 4¹⁄₁₆ in. (18 × 10.3 cm.)
Maur G585/1
Family Estate of Oskar Schlemmer
Ill. p. 80

214. TWO SHADOWY FORMS (IN JAPANESE STYLE)
[Zwei schemenhafte Gestalten (Japanisch)]
(1941)
Monotype in oil color on printing paper
7⅛ × 4¹⁄₁₆ in. (18 × 10.3 cm.)
Maur G590
Family Estate of Oskar Schlemmer
Ill. p. 255

Cat. no. 214.

Prints

215. TORSO FACING RIGHT
[Halbfigur (nach rechts)]
(1918–1919)
Lithograph on gray-green paper
19¾ × 12½ in. (50.3 × 32.4 cm.)
Grohmann-Schlemmer GL2
Staatsgalerie Stuttgart (A50111)
Ill. p. 256

216. THREE PROFILES, THE MIDDLE ONE VERTICAL
[Drei Profile, das mittlere senkrecht]
(1920)
Lithograph executed with spray technique in violet on whitish paper
18 × 11⅝ in. (45.8 × 29.5 cm.)
Grohmann-Schlemmer GL14
Staatsgalerie Stuttgart
Ill. p. 86

217. THREE ASCENDING PROFILES, BETWEEN THE VERTICAL AND THE DIAGONAL
[Drei senkrechte Profile, zwischen der Senkrechten und der Diagonalen]
1920
Lithograph executed with spray technique in red-brown, on whitish paper
18 × 11½ in. (45.7 × 29.2 cm.)
Grohmann-Schlemmer GL13
Staatsgalerie Stuttgart
Ill. p. 86

218. THREE PROFILES IN VERTICAL LINES, ONE TURNED TO THE RIGHT
[Drei Profile in Senkrechten, eines nacht rechts]
(1920)
Lithograph executed with spray technique in gray-black on whitish paper
18¼ × 11¾ in. (46.4 × 29.7 cm.)
Grohmann-Schlemmer GL17
Staatsgalerie Stuttgart
Ill. p. 86

219. DANCER
[Tänzerin]
1923
Lithograph on white China paper
24¼ × 17⅛ in. (61.5 × 43.5 cm.)
Grohmann-Schlemmer GL9
Staatsgalerie Stuttgart (A66/4343)
Ill. p. 85

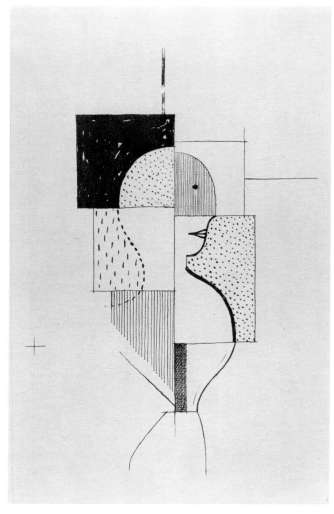

Cat. no. 215.

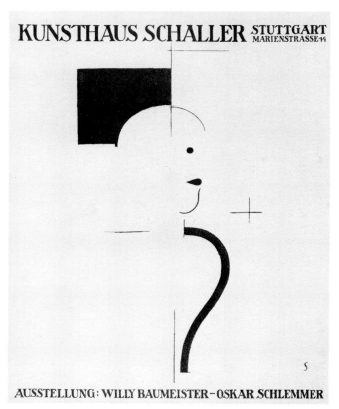

Cat. no. 220.

Posters and Graphic Designs

220. POSTER: FIGURE FACING RIGHT
(KUNSTHAUS SCHALLER)
[Figur nach rechts, Plakat]
(1918)
Lithograph on yellowish paper
25⅝ × 20⅛ in. (65 × 51 cm.)
S516
Staatsgalerie Stuttgart
Ill. p. 256

221. COVER FOR "UTOPIA"
[Umschlag für "Utopia"]
(1921)
Watercolor and poster paint, silver- and gold-bronze over
outline drawing in pen and ink, on parchment paper
12⅞ × 9⅞ in. (32.8 × 24.9 cm.)
Maur A94
Staatsgalerie Stuttgart: Oskar Schlemmer Archiv
Ill. p. 257

222. BAUHAUS LOGO
[Bauhaus-Signet]
(1922)
Lithograph in green on brownish paper
9⅞ × 11⅞ in. (25.2 × 30.1 cm.)
S520
Bauhaus-Archiv, Berlin
Ill. p. 197

223. POSTER FOR THE TRIADIC BALLET
(LEIBNIZ-AKADEMIE)
[Plakat zum Triadischen Ballett]
(1924)
Lithograph, colored with tempera, mounted on board
31⅞ × 22 in. (81 × 56 cm.)
Maur A149a
Oskar Schlemmer Theater Estate, Collection UJS
Ill. p. 175

224. COVER DESIGN FOR ''THE OPERA''
[Die Oper, Umschlagbild]
(1929)
Lithograph in gray and red on brownish paper
9¼ × 10⅛ in. (23.5 × 25.7 cm.)
S532
Oskar Schlemmer Theater Estate, Collection UJS
Ill. p. 257

Cat. no. 224.

Cat. no. 221.

Due to circumstances beyond the Museum's control, the following objects were not included in the Baltimore Museum exhibition or circulation: cat. nos. 9, 21, 23, 24, 26, 33, 35, 39, 47, 51, 52, 74, 77, 95, 99, 102, 122, 130, 134, 141, 147, 151, 160, 166, 169, 188. Unfortunately, these deletions were made after the book was in press, which precluded corrections to the catalogue's checklist and captions.

Illustrated Works Not in Exhibition

The following are detailed citations for Schlemmer works of art illustrated in the texts but not included in the exhibition.

Maur Essay

FIVE FIGURES IN A ROOM (CLASSICAL STYLE)
[Fünf Figuren im Raum, Römisches]
1925
Oil on canvas
38³⁄₁₆ × 24⅜ in. (97 × 62 cm.)
Maur G137
Kunstmuseum Basel: Öffentliche Kunstsammlung (1752)
Ill. p. 38

THE GESTURE (DANCER)
[Die Geste, Tänzerin]
(1922)
Oil and tempera on canvas
78¾ × 51³⁄₁₆ in. (200 × 130 cm.)
Maur G118
Neue Pinakothek, Munich: Bayerische
Staatsgemäldesammlungen (13421)
Ill. p. 50

COMPANY AT TABLE
[Tischgesellschaft]
1923
Oil and enamel on canvas
25³⁄₁₆ × 39⅞ in. (64 × 101.4 cm.)
Maur G124
Private Collection
Ill. p. 54

WOMEN AT TABLE
[Frauen am Tisch]
1923
Oil on canvas
28¾ × 24 in. (73 × 61 cm.)
Maur G125
Kunstsammlung Nordrhein-Westfalen, Düsseldorf (1007)
Ill. p. 55

IDEALISTIC ENCOUNTER
[Idealistische Begegnung]
1928
Oil and pencil on canvas
36⁷⁄₁₆ × 23¹³⁄₁₆ in. (90 × 60.5 cm.)
Maur G147
Collection of Rolf and Margit Weinberg, Zurich
Ill. p. 61

GROUP OF FOURTEEN IN IMAGINARY
ARCHITECTURE
[Vierzehnergruppe in imaginärer Architektur]
1930
Oil and tempera, partially sprayed, on canvas
36 × 47⁷⁄₁₆ in. (91.5 × 120.5 cm.)
Maur G198
Museum Ludwig, Cologne (2985)
Ill. p. 68

GROUP AT BANISTER
[Gruppe am Geländer]
1931
Oil on canvas
36⅜ × 23¹³⁄₁₆ in. (92.5 × 60.5 cm.)
Maur G250
Kunstsammlung Nordrhein-Westfalen, Düsseldorf (1038)
Ill. p. 72

STAIRWAY SCENE
[Treppenszene]
1932
Oil on muslin, mounted on plywood
47⅝ × 22¹⁄₁₆ in. (121 × 56 cm.)
Maur G264
Hamburger Kunsthalle (2910)
Ill. p. 73

SEATED FIGURE AT TABLE (SEEN FROM BEHIND)
[Rücklings-Sitzender am Tisch]
(1936)
Oil on oiled paper, mounted on board
29⅝ × 23⁵⁄₁₆ in. (75.3 × 59.3 cm.)
Maur G345
Museum Folkwang Essen (G237)
Ill. p. 79

ORNAMENTAL SCULPTURE ON DIVIDED FRAME
[Ornamentale Plastik auf geteiltem Rahmen]
1919/1923
Painted wood
37⁷⁄₁₆ × 26¾ × 1¹¹⁄₁₆ in. (90 × 68 × 4.2 cm.)
Maur P1
Kunstsammlung Nordrhein-Westfalen, Düsseldorf (200)
Ill. p. 94

RELIEF JG (WITH PAINTED MOUNT I)
[Relief JG (mit farbiger Fassung I)]
(1919/1921)
Painted plaster, in original frame
27¾ × 15³⁄₁₆ in. (70.5 × 38.5 cm.), without frame
Maur P11
Nationalgalerie, Staatliche Museen, Berlin,
German Democratic Republic (BII22)
Ill. p. 99

RELIEF JG (WITH PAINTED MOUNT II)
[Relief JG (mit farbiger Fassung II)]
(1919/1921)
Painted wood
26⁹⁄₁₆ × 12¹¹⁄₁₆ in. (67.5 × 32.2 cm.)
Maur P12
Kunstmuseum Düsseldorf (5580)
Ill. p. 99

ABSTRACT FIGURE (FREE STANDING SCULPTURE G)
[Abstrakte Figur (Freiplastik G)]
(1921/1923)
Plaster, with metal shaft
42⅛ in. (107 cm.) high
Maur P13
Staatsgalerie Stuttgart: Schlemmer Family Estate Deposit
(PL185)
Ill. p. 106

MYTHICAL FIGURE
[Mythische Figur]
(1923)
India ink and collage made of colored papers, sprayed in
places, mounted on heavy board
29½ × 68⅛ in. (75 × 173 cm.)
Maur G126
Staatsgalerie Stuttgart (3216)
Ill. p. 111

SELF-PORTRAIT WITH RAISED HAND
[Selbstbildnis mit erhobener Hand]
(1931–1932)
Watercolor on paper
21¼ × 15⁹⁄₁₆ in. (54 × 39.5 cm.)
Maur A463
Collection of Peter Kamm, Zug, Switzerland
Ill. p. 118

Troy Essay

FIGURE AND SPACE-DELINEATION
[Figur und Raumlineatur]
1924
Pen and ink on white paper
8⅝ × 11 in. (22 × 28 cm.)
Grohmann-Schlemmer ZT229
Staatsgalerie Stuttgart: Schlemmer Family Estate Deposit
Ill. p. 137

THE MARIONETTE
[Die Gliederpuppe]
1924
Pen and ink, corrected in places with opaque white paint,
on gray-white paper
8¹³⁄₁₆ × 4⁹⁄₁₆ in. (22.4 × 11.6 cm.)
Grohmann-Schlemmer ZT234a
Staatsgalerie Stuttgart: Schlemmer Family Estate Deposit
Ill. p. 138

THE SYMBOL IN MAN (DEMATERIALIZATION)
[Die Zeichen im Menschen (Entmaterialisierung)]
(1924)
Pen and ink, corrected in places with opaque white paint,
on gray-white paper
8¹³⁄₁₆ × 5⅜ in. (22.4 × 13.8 cm.)
Grohmann-Schlemmer ZT234b
Staatsgalerie Stuttgart: Schlemmer Family Estate Deposit
Ill. p. 138

Chronology

SEATED MALE NUDE
[Sitzender Mann]
(1906)
Pencil on paper
11⅞ × 10¹⁵⁄₁₆ in. (30.2 × 27.8 cm.)
Grohmann-Schlemmer ZB1c
Family Estate of Oskar Schlemmer
Ill. p. 195

CURTAIN FOR ''THE TRIADIC BALLET''
[Vorhang zum ''Triadischen Ballett'']
(1922)
Cotton sateen, in three panels, with appliqué
149⅝ × 133⅞ in. (380 × 342 cm.)
S565
Oskar Schlemmer Theater Estate, Collection UJS
Ill. p. 197

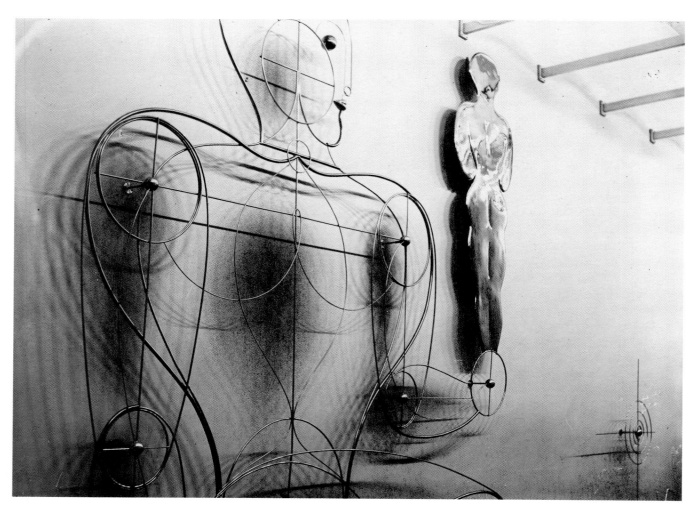

"Homo Wire Figure," detail of installation at the house of Dr. Rabe, 1931.

The following entries comprise a selected bibliography, drawn primarily from those sources cited by authors in the present volume. Entries are cited alphabetically by author and, in those instances of multiple author entries, by chronology. While the literature on Schlemmer is extensive, it is primarily in German and, often, in specialized publications. The following sources will be most useful for a general reader interested in Schlemmer and the period. For more definitive bibliography and exhibition history, readers should consult Karin von Maur, *Oskar Schlemmer: Monographie*, vol. 1 (Munich: Prestel-Verlag, 1979), pp. 367–393; and for post-1978 bibliographic references, *Oskar Schlemmer*, exhibition catalogue, Jahrhunderthalle Hoechst, Frankfurt-Hoechst, 1984.

Umbro Apollonio, ed. *Futurist Manifestos*. Translated by Robert Brain et al. The Documents of 20th-Century Art. New York: Viking Press, 1973.

Ned A. Bowman. "Bauhaus Influences on an Evolving Theatre Architecture: Some Developmental Stages." *Theatre Survey* 6, no. 2 (November 1965), pp. 116–135.

André Breton. "D'une décalcomanie sans objet préconçu." *Minotaure* 3, no. 8 (June 1936), pp. 18–24.

Craig Bromberg. " 'Bauhaus Dances' at Ethnic Folk Arts Center." *Art in America* 71, no. 2 (February 1983), p. 137.

Gerhard Bry. *Wages in Germany 1871–1945*. Princeton: Princeton University Press, 1960.

Joan Campbell. *The German Werkbund: The Politics of Reform in the Applied Arts*. Princeton: Princeton University Press, 1978.

Roger Chickering. *We Men Who Feel Most German: A Cultural Study of the Pan-German League 1886–1914*. Boston, London, and Sydney: George Allen & Unwin, 1984.

Edward Gordon Craig. "The Actor and the Über-Marionette." *The Mask* 1, no. 2 (April 1908), pp. 3–15.

Gordon A. Craig. *The Politics of the Prussian Army 1640–1945*. New York: Oxford University Press, 1964.

Istvan Deak. *Germany's Left-Wing Intellectuals: The Political History of the Weltbühne and its Circle*. Berkeley: University of California Press, 1968.

Konrad Düssel. "Neue Kunst im Kunstgebäude II." *Stuttgarter Neues Tagblatt*, 20 November 1919.

Kasimir Edschmid. *Frühe Manifeste*. Hamburg: C. Wegner, 1957.

C. Einstein and P. Westheim, eds. *Europa-Almanach*. Potsdam: G. Kiepenheuer Verlag, 1925.

Peter Gay. *Weimar Culture: The Outsider as Insider*. New York: Harper and Row, 1968.

Sidney Geist. *Brancusi: A Study of the Sculpture*. New York: Grossman, 1968.

Will Grohmann. *Oskar Schlemmer: Zeichnungen und Graphik, Oeuvrekatalog*. Stuttgart: Verlag Gerd Hatje, 1965.

Helmut Günther. "Vom dämonischen zum triadischen Ballett: Neues Material über Oskar Schlemmer." *Stuttgarter Zeitung*, 6 July 1963.

Werner Haftmann. *Malerei im zwanzigsten Jahrhundert: Eine Bildenzyklopädie*. 2 vols. Munich: Prestel Verlag, 1965.

Roger Held. "Endless Innovations: The Theories and Scenic Designs of Frederick Kiesler." Ph.D. dissertation, Bowling Green University, 1977.

Wulf Herzogenrath. *Oskar Schlemmer: Die Wandgestaltung der neuen Architektur*. Munich: Prestel Verlag, 1973.

Hans Hildebrandt. *Oskar Schlemmer*. Munich: Prestel Verlag, 1952.

Bertold Hinz. *Art in the Third Reich*. Translated by Robert and Rita Kimber. New York: Pantheon Books, 1979.

Thomas P. Hughes. *Networks of Power: Electrification in Western Society, 1880–1930*. Baltimore: Johns Hopkins University Press, 1983.

Hans L. C. Jaffé, ed. *De Stijl*. Translated by R. R. Symonds et al. 1967. Reprint. London: Thames and Hudson, 1970.

Wassily Kandinsky and Franz Marc, eds. *Der Blaue Reiter*. Munich: R. Piper, 1912.

Wassily Kandinsky. *Über das Geistige in der Kunst*. 1912 (actually 1911). Reprint. Edited by Max Bill. Bern-Bümpliz: Benteli-Verlag, 1952.

Wassily Kandinsky. *Concerning the Spiritual in Art and Painting in Particular*. Translated by Michael Sadleir et al. The Documents of Modern Art, no. 5. 1947. Reprint. New York: George Wittenborn, 1972.

Donald A. Karshan, ed. *Archipenko: An International Visionary*. Washington, D.C.: Smithsonian Institution, 1969.

Justin Kerner. *Klecksographien von Justinus Kerner, mit Illustrationen nach den Vorlagen des Verfassers*. Stuttgart, Leipzig, Berlin, Vienna, 1890.

Friedrich Kiesler. *International Ausstellung neuer Theatertechnik*. 1924. Reprint. Vienna: Konzerthaus, 1975.

Friedrich Kiesler. "Debacle of the Modern Theatre." *The Little Review* 11, no. 2 (Winter 1926), pp. 61–72.

Michael Kirby. *Futurist Performance*. New York: E. P. Dutton, 1971.

Anna Kisselgoff. "The Bauhaus Works Were Prophetic." *The New York Times*, 29 January 1984, section 2, p. 14.

Paul Klee. *Das bildnerische Denken*. Edited by Jörg Spiller. Basel and Stuttgart: B. Schwabe, 1956.

Heinrich von Kleist. "Essay on the Puppet Theater." Translated by Eugene Jolas. *The Partisan Review* 14, no. 1 (January–February 1947), pp. 67–72.

Max Klinger. *Malerei und Zeichnung*. Leipzig: Insel-Verlag, 1907.

Donald Kuspit. "Oskar Schlemmer's Bauhaus Dances." *Artforum* 21, no. 8 (April 1983), pp. 70–71.

Walter Laqueur. *Weimar: A Cultural History 1918–1933*. New York: G. P. Putnam's Sons, 1974.

Fernand Léger. "Concours chorégraphique international au théâtre des Champs-Elysées. Juillet 1932." *Cahiers d'art* 7 (1932), p. 288.

El Lissitzky. "The Electrical-Mechanical Spectacle." Translated by Standish D. Lawder. *Form* 3 (15 December 1966), p. 12.

Sophie Lissitsky-Kuppers. *El Lissitzky: Life, Letters, Texts*. Translated by Helene Aldwinckle. London: Thames and Hudson, 1968.

Karin von Maur. *Oskar Schlemmer: Sculpture*. Translated by Anne Engel. New York: Abrams, 1972.

Karin von Maur. *Oskar Schlemmer und die Stuttgarter Avantgarde 1919*. Stuttgart: Staatliche Akademie der bildenden Künste Stuttgart, Institut für Buchgestaltung, 1975.

Karin von Maur. *Oskar Schlemmer* (exhibition catalogue). Staatsgalerie Stuttgart, 1977.

Karin von Maur. *Oskar Schlemmer: Monographie und Oeuvrekatalog der Gemälde, Aquarelle, Pastelle und Plastiken*. 2 vols. Munich: Prestel-Verlag, 1979.

Annabelle Henkin Melzer. *Latest Rage the Big Drum: Dada and Surrealist Performance*. Studies in Fine Arts: The Avant-Garde, no. 7. Ann Arbor: UMI Research Press, 1980.

Eric Michaud. *Théâtre au Bauhaus (1919–1929)*. Lausanne: La Cité, L'Age d'Homme, 1978.

László Moholy-Nagy. *Von Material zu Architektur*. Munich: Langen Verlag, 1929.

Friedrich Nietzsche. *Nietzsches Werke*. 11 vols. Edited by E. Foerster-Nietzsche and P. Gast. Leipzig: C. G. Naumann, 1906.

Henry Pachter. *Weimar Etudes*. New York: Columbia University Press, 1982.

Peter Paret. *The Berlin Secession: Modernism and Its Enemies in Imperial Germany*. Cambridge, Massachusetts and London: Harvard University Press, 1980.

Koppel Pinson. *Modern Germany: Its History and Civilization*. 1954. Reprint. New York: MacMillan Company, 1966.

Clark V. Poling. *Kandinsky: Russian and Bauhaus Years, 1915–1933* (exhibition catalogue). New York: Solomon R. Guggenheim Museum, 1983.

Harold L. Poor. *Kurt Tucholsky and the Ordeal of Germany, 1914–1935*. New York: Charles Scribner's Sons, 1968.

Hans Richter. *Dada: Art and Anti-Art*. New York and Toronto: McGraw-Hill Book Company, 1965.

Rainer Maria Rilke. *Briefe*. 2 vols. Edited by Rilke Archives, Weimar. Wiesbaden: Insel-Verlag, 1950.

Gerhard Ritter. *The Sword and the Scepter: The Problem of Militarism in Germany*. Translated by Heinz Norden. 4 vols. 1955. Reprint. Vol. 2.

Jean-Jacques Roubine. *Théâtre et mise en scène 1880–1980*. Paris: Presses Universitaires de France, Litteratures Modernes, 1980.

Xanti Schawinsky. "From the Bauhaus to Black Mountain." *The Drama Review* 15, no. 3a (Summer 1971), pp. 31–44.

Dirk Scheper. *Oskar Schlemmer: Das Triadische Ballett*. Berlin: Akademie der Künste, 1977.

Friedrich Schiller. *Schillers sämmtliche Werke*. 12 vols. Stuttgart and Tübingen: J. G. Cotta, 1838.

Oskar Schlemmer. "Gestaltungsprinzipien bei der malerisch-plastischen Ausgestaltung des Werkstattgebäudes des Staatlichen Bauhauses." *Das Kunstblatt* 7, no. 11–12 (November–December 1923), pp. 340–343.

Oskar Schlemmer. "Piscator und das moderne Theater." *Das neue Frankfurt* 2, no. 2 (February 1928), pp. 22–26.

Oskar Schlemmer. *Théâtre et abstraction (L'Espace du Bauhaus)*. Translated and edited by Eric Michaud. Lausanne: La Cité, L'Age d'Homme, 1978.

Oskar Schlemmer, László Moholy-Nagy, and Farkas Molnár. *The Theater of the Bauhaus*. Translated by Arthur S. Wensinger. Edited by Walter Gropius. 1961. Reprint. Middletown, Connecticut: Wesleyan University Press, 1979.

Tut Schlemmer, ed. *Oskar Schlemmer: Briefe und Tagebücher*. Munich: Albert Langen-Georg Müller Verlag GmbH., 1958.

Tut Schlemmer, ed. *The Letters and Diaries of Oskar Schlemmer*. Translated by Krishna Winston. Middletown, Connecticut: Wesleyan University Press, 1972.

Paul Ferdinand Schmidt. *Saarbrücker Zeitung*, 20 August 1920.

Fritz Schneider. ''Herbstschau Neuer Kunst.'' *Süddeutsche Zeitung*, 14 November 1919.

Gary D. Stark. *Entrepreneurs of Ideology: Neoconservative Publishers in Germany, 1890–1933*. Chapel Hill: University of North Carolina Press, 1981.

Fritz Stern. *The Politics of Cultural Despair: A Study in the Rise of the Germanic Ideology*. Berkeley: University of California Press, 1961.

Nancy J. Troy. ''Figures of the Dance in De Stijl.'' *The Art Bulletin* 66, no. 4 (December 1984), pp. 645–656.

Peter Vergo. *Art in Vienna 1898–1918: Klimt, Kokoschka, Schiele and their contemporaries*. Ithaca, New York: Cornell University Press, Phaidon, 1975.

Shulamit Volkov. *The Rise of Popular Antimodernism in Germany*. Princeton: Princeton University Press, 1978.

Robert G. L. Waite. *Vanguard of Nazism: The Free Corps Movement in Postwar Germany 1918–1923*. 1952. Reprint. New York: W. W. Norton & Company, 1969.

Frank Whitford. *Bauhaus*. London: Thames and Hudson, 1984.

John Willett. *Art and Politics in the Weimar Period: The New Sobriety, 1917–1933*. New York: Pantheon Books, 1978.

John Willett. *The Weimar Years: A Culture Cut Short*. New York: Abbeville Press, 1984.

Hans M. Wingler. *The Bauhaus: Weimar, Dessau, Berlin, Chicago*. Translated by Wolfgang Jabs and Basil Gilbert. 1969. Reprint. Cambridge, Massachusetts: MIT Press, 1981.

Der schöne Mensch in der Neuen Kunst (exhibition catalogue). Städtische Ausstellungsgebäude, Darmstadt, 1929.

Oskar Schlemmer (exhibition catalogue), Jahrhunderthalle Hoechst, Frankfurt-Hoechst, 1984.

In addition to the above, two recently-published exhibition catalogues of monographic scope include significant material on Schlemmer:

Otto Meyer-Amden, Begegnungen mit Oskar Schlemmer, Willi Baumeister, und anderen Künstlern, exhibition catalogue, Kunstmuseum Bern, 1985.

Christoph Joachimides, Norman Rosenthal, and Wieland Schmied, eds., *German Art in the Twentieth Century*, exhibition catalogue, Royal Academy, London (Prestel Verlag/Weidenfeld and Nicholson), 1985.

OSKAR SCHLEMMER

printed in an edition of 4000 copies.
Typography in Times Roman text with Gill Sans titling
set by Monotype Composition Company, Baltimore.
Color separations by Prolith International, Laurel, Maryland.
Text paper is Warren's Lustro offset enamel, 100 pound;
cover paper is Warren's Lusterkote twelve point;
end papers are Simpson Teton 80 pound text, Indigo.
Printing by Schneidereith and Sons, Baltimore.
Design by Alex and Caroline Castro, Baltimore.
© 1986 The Baltimore Museum of Art

LIBRARY OF CONGRESS CATALOGING-IN-PUBLICATION DATA

Schlemmer, Oskar, 1888–1943.
  Oskar Schlemmer: the Baltimore Museum of Art.

  Exhibition catalog.
  Bibliography: p.
  1. Schlemmer, Oskar, 1888–1943—Exhibitions.
2. Schlemmer, Oskar, 1888–1943—Criticism and
interpretation. I. Lehman, Arnold L. II. Richardson,
Brenda. III. Title.
N6888.S358A4   1986   709′.2′4   85-28647
ISBN 0-912298-60-X

Cover: *Divided Figure*. (1915–1918). [Cat. no. 11].

Pages 2–3: The "Masked Chorus" from *Choral Pantomine*, a stage
production conceived and directed by Oskar Schlemmer at the Theater Workshop, Dessau Bauhaus, 1928. Photograph by Ruth Hollos or
Erich Consemüller.

Page 4: *Self-Portrait with Mask and Wire Disk*. (1931). Photograph
by Oskar Schlemmer.

Pages 18–19: Oskar Schlemmer Studio, Stuttgart, 1919.

Pages 124–125: *Light Play*, with dancer Werner Siedhoff, a stage
production conceived and directed by Oskar Schlemmer at the Theater Workshop, Dessau Bauhaus, 1926. Photograph by Ruth Hollos or
Erich Consemüller.

Pages 192–193: *Curtain Design* (Study for "The Triadic Ballet").
1919. Watercolor. 11⅜ × 17¼ in. Oskar Schlemmer Theater Estate,
Collection UJS. [Cat. no. 87].